Spectres of Fascism

Spectres of Fascism

Historical, Theoretical and International Perspectives

Edited by
Samir Gandesha

First published 2020 by Pluto Press
345 Archway Road, London N6 5AA

www.plutobooks.com

Copyright © Samir Gandesha 2020

British Library Cataloguing in Publication Data
A catalogue record for this book is available from the British Library

ISBN   978 0 7453 4063 0   Hardback
ISBN   978 0 7453 4064 7   Paperback
ISBN   978 1 7868 0598 0   PDF eBook
ISBN   978 1 7868 0600 0   Kindle eBook
ISBN   978 1 7868 0599 7   EPUB eBook

This book is printed on paper suitable for recycling and made from fully managed and sustained forest sources. Logging, pulping and manufacturing processes are expected to conform to the environmental standards of the country of origin.

Typeset by Riverside Publishing Solutions, Salisbury, England

Simultaneously printed in the United Kingdom and United States of America

I dedicate this book to my father, Suresh Narbheram Gandesha, who taught me a great deal about standing up to the scourge of fascism, which he first encountered in colonial East Africa, with dignity and humanity.

Contents

PART III   THE CONTEMPORARY HORIZON

Figures

Acknowledgements

This book is the result of a year-long free school entitled "Spectres of Fascism" hosted by the Institute for the Humanities at Simon Fraser University (SFU) between February and November, 2017, which I organized as Director of SFU's Institute for the Humanities, with my SFU colleague Stephen Collis, a Steering Committee member and Acting Director of the Institute during the 2018–19 academic year. The free school can be situated within programming that stretches back several years and specifically addresses the increasingly authoritarian cast of politics globally and in Canada in particular. In Canada such an authoritarian turn was closely linked to Stephen Harper's project of transforming Canada into an "emerging energy superpower." Broadly speaking, the Institute has focused its attention on the resulting criminalization of dissent in this respect, in particular through the use of strategic lawsuits to limit public participation (SLAPPs) and the Anti-Terrorism Act that was passed in 2015 and was designed specifically to target opposition, particularly from Indigenous communities, to pipeline projects. We also hosted a large conference with participation by academics, intellectuals, Indigenous communities and lawyers entitled "The State of Extraction: Corporate Imperatives, Public Knowledge and Global Alternatives" in March 2015.

Generously hosted by Unit/Pitt Artist Run Space and Selector Records, the format of the free school was typically a lecture followed by discussion addressing the return of fascism in historical and theoretical terms and in the contemporary period, followed by music specifically curated for each individual lecture or panel, with refreshments and food on offer. In some cases, the discussions took the form of panels. Speakers were largely drawn from universities and other institutions in Vancouver's Lower Mainland although there were also visiting speakers who participated, and this volume includes chapters that were solicited, having had no connection whatever to the free school. The free school was bisected by a conference, "Spectacle of Fascism," devoted to the 50th anniversary of the publication of both Guy Debord's *The Society of the Spectacle* and Raoul Vaneigem's *The Revolution of Everyday Life*. The papers presented there were published in an issue of the Institute's online journal *Contours*.

The idea of the free school was to create an intellectually vibrant yet social and convivial atmosphere, as a concrete measure to help combat the growing anti-intellectualism and increasingly isolating conditions of our neo-liberal times that seem to be palpably contributing to the rise of authoritarianism and neofascist organizations. In this, we felt that we were properly discharging the academic mandate of the Institute, which is to "address the fundamental questions of our age by way of the humanities tradition broadly understood."

I would like to thank the following individuals and institutions for their help and support at various stages of this project: John Abromeit, Ian Angus, Chin Bannerjee, Rosemary Bechler, Ajay Bhardwaj, the contributors to this volume, Stephen Collis, Tania Ehret, Kit Fortune, Harjap Grewal, Sanem Güvenç-Salgırlı, Robert Hackett, Johan Hartle, Daniel Musekamp, Cristina Serverius, Gurpreet Singh, Harriet Olivette Wills, Morgan Young, Jerry Zaslove, the Institute for the Humanities (SFU), The Rabble.ca, SANSAD (South Asian Network for Secularism and Democracy), and the Vancity Office for Community Engagement (SFU) under the canny and eminently capable leadership of Am Johal. A considerable debt of gratitude is owed to the Institute's Program Assistant, Huyen Pham, who is the irreplaceable engine room of the Institute, and to Maxwell Kristen who did an excellent job of copy-editing the manuscript and helped with various other facets of manuscript preparation. I would also like to thank Brady Cranfield, Kay Higgins and Jamie Ward for the warmth, generosity, good humour and above all solidarity with which they hosted the free school at both Unit/Pitt Projects and at the sadly now-defunct Selector Records – yet another casualty of the mounting Vancouver real estate crisis. Jamie did an expert job of curating music specifically for each evening's lecture. I would also like, finally, to extend a heartfelt thanks to Dr. Jennifer Simons and the Simons Foundation, without whose initial bequest to SFU the Institute would never have been founded and for financial and moral support of the Institute on an ongoing basis, particularly during my tenure as Director these past ten years. Finally, I would like to thank my wife, Rachia, and my two children Milan and Ruby, for putting up with me and my many absences throughout this and other Institute-related projects.

My thanks as well to Brekhna Aftab, Melanie Patrick, David Shulman, Neda Tehrani and Robert Webb at Pluto Press and Paul Beaney at Riverside Publishing Solutions for their excellent editorial assistance and support.

1

Introduction[1]

Samir Gandesha

The electoral successes and growing public profile of a number of author-itarian political parties and movements throughout Europe, particularly in Italy, Poland and Hungary, the success of the Leave side in the Brexit referendum of 23 June 2016, and the election of Donald J. Trump as the 45th President of the United States of America on 8 November 2016, have contributed to a renewed interest in the concept of fascism.[2] Parties such as, for example, the National Rally Party in France led by Marine Le Pen have been understood to represent a form of "post-fascism," which is to say a form of far-right politics inspired by twentieth-century fascism that, nevertheless, has largely come to accept the rules of liberal democracy, although the threat remains that they could turn back into neofascist parties and therefore someday seek to mobilize violently against liberal democracy.[3] Critics have suggested that what we confront today is a form of "late fascism" based on the displacement of the utopian elements of what Ernst Bloch called non-synchronous temporalities, organized by twentieth-century fascisms, by the fantasy of complete synchronicity in an eternalized neo-liberal present.[4] Commentators have also charted the logic of "fascist creep" which is to say the convergence of left- and right-wing ideas in notions of National Bolshevism, National Anarchism, the French Nouvelle Droite as well as Aleksandr Dugin's "fourth polit-ical theory" beyond liberalism, fascism and socialism.[5] Critics have also sought to understand Islamism as a form of fascism that, in turn, has influenced the contemporary far-right.[6]

Rather than witnessing the return of fascism, then, as many others have suggested,[7] what we see is the spectre or, rather, "*spectres* of fascism" in the plural today. The word "spectre"[8] suggests the figure of the phantom, both as *Geist* (spirit) and *Gespenst* (ghost) that, in turn, suggests the uncanny (*das Unheimliche*) or the unhomely which, as Freud reminds us, is itself in part signified by the word homely or familiar (*das Heimliche*).[9] In his recently published lecture to the Austrian Socialist Students' Union at the University of Vienna on 6 April 1967, Theodor W. Adorno speaks of the fascism's "own ghostly shape" (*eigenegespenstische Gestalt*).[10] The ghost of fascism, we might say, is quickly becoming the spirit of our times. We speak of *spectres* because it is not simply in the original domicile of fascism, which is to say Europe, that we see the return of fascism to public life but rather it has become a truly global phenomenon. In India, Turkey, Brazil, Egypt and the Philippines, we see the return of elements of fascist politics, though not the fully fledged counter-revolutionary fascist mass movement as had emerged in Europe in the 1920s and 1930s.

Twenty-first-century fascism is also uncanny precisely because, as already suggested, it transcends the seemingly original birthplace of fascism; its *real* point of origin was, as Aimé Césaire had pointed out already in 1950, Europe's colonies. These were the original laboratories for Italian and German forms of fascism.[11] The uncanny is strangely familiar because, for Freud, it suggests that which, having undergone repression, returns later as something discordantly strange, barely recognizable; the barbaric side of civilization. Fascism is uncanny insofar as it is a phenomenon that seems to belong to a distant age in a previous century yet has been all too close at hand in the first two decades of the present one. It entails, then, a socioeconomic, social-psychological and political condition in which previous historical traumas were not worked through or, if they were, then only in a partial and one-sided way. "I consider the survival of National Socialism *within* democracy to be potentially more menacing," as Adorno put it in a key lecture in the post-war Bundesrepublik, "than the survival of fascist tendencies *against* democracy."[12]

Fascism haunts us still because liberal democracy was and remains constitutionally unable to address the fundamental contradiction bequeathed to it by the bourgeois revolution in which it was born. This is the basic contradiction between a democratic polity and a liberal economy, constituting the subject as inherently divided between universal *citoyen* and particularistic *homo economicus*.[13] Fascism would always continue to figure as a ghostly presence within this order, occasionally taking material form. As Slavoj Žižek extrapolates from Walter Benjamin's "Theories of German Fascism," and his "On the Concept of History," "every rise of fascism bears witness to a failed revolution."[14] Benjamin was thinking of the German Revolution about a decade earlier.

We might, however, suggest that the roots of fascism lie in the serial failure to bring to completion the bourgeois revolution, the most important episode of which – after the Haitian Revolution (1791–1804) led by Toussaint L'Ouverture[15] – was the debacle of 1848. "The tradition of all dead generations weighs like a nightmare on the brains of the living,"[16] as Marx wrote, commenting on this event. Other failures, no doubt brought about by capital's not inconsiderable political and military efforts, were the dissolution of the Paris Commune in 1871, the ossification of the Russian Revolution after the death of Lenin, if not earlier with the crushing of Kronstadt, and the destruction of the Bavarian Council Republic in 1918.

Finally, one could add to this list the revolutionary moment of 1968, the main battles of which were fought out by national-liberation and revolutionary movements in the Global South – and this, in part, would help explain the global dimensions of the authoritarian resurgence there today. The failed Revolution of 1848 was an especially consequential event for Europe, particularly the German principalities, as this was the precise moment at which nationalism veered from a republican to an increasingly authoritarian direction, as personified in the particular trajectories of erstwhile proverbial veterans of the barricades in the so-called Vormärz period: Richard Wagner and Bruno Bauer.[17] The end of this cycle of revolutionary activity in France at this time produced the Bonapartism that would in many ways anticipate twentieth-century fascism. It would be seen as a transitional way-station between parliamentarism and fascism.[18]

HISTORY OF THE PRESENT

Today, the uncanny return of fascism can be situated between two key events: the Al-Qaeda attacks of 11 September 2001, and the financial crisis of 2007–8.[19] The first event, tragic though it was, became the justification for a full-blown neoconservative foreign policy of aggressive and direct (as opposed to by proxy) regime change. This had already been envisaged by the Project for the New American Century (PNAC) think tank that had been co-founded by William Kristol and Robert Kagan in 1997 and remained active until 2006. Including such neoconservative luminaries as Elliott Abrams, William J. Bennett, Jeb Bush, Dick Cheney, Francis Fukuyama, Norman Podhoretz, Donald Rumsfeld and Paul Wolfowitz, the PNAC sought to identify "challenges and opportunities" for the United States in the twenty-first century. It sought increases in military spending, the strengthening of ties with "democratic allies" in confronting its enemies, the promotion of political and economic "freedom" abroad and the assertion of the "unique role in preserving and extending an international order friendly to our security, our prosperity and our principles."[20]

In the attacks of 11 September 2001, it found *both* such challenges and opportunities, as the then National Security Advisor to the Bush Administration, Condoleezza Rice, put it in a much publicized speech at the Paul H. Nitze School of Advanced International Studies at Johns Hopkins University:

> ... If the collapse of the Soviet Union and 9/11 bookend a major shift in international politics, then this is a period not just of grave danger, but of enormous opportunity. Before the clay is dry again, America and our friends and our allies must move decisively to take advantage of these new opportunities. This is, then, a period akin to 1945 to 1947, when American leadership expanded the number of free and democratic states – Japan and Germany among the great powers – to create a new balance of power that favored freedom.[21]

Rice and the Bush administration, having hardly waited for the clay to dry, took cunning advantage of such an "opportunity." By the time of Rice's speech, the United States had already toppled the Taliban in Afghanistan, weakened Al-Qaeda, and was training its sights on the regime of Saddam Hussein in Iraq under the false claim that it possessed Weapons of Mass Destruction (WMD) – and would commence the invasion of that country less than a year after Rice's Johns Hopkins speech. The policy of regime change tacitly articulated by Rice contributed massively not only to the rise of terrorist organizations such as ISIS in Iraq but also, consequently, a crisis of displaced persons not seen since World War II, if ever. According to the UNHCR, there are some 70 million displaced persons globally.[22] The stateless produced by these policies constituted, according to Hannah Arendt, "a new type of human being, the kind that are put in concentration camps by their foes and in internment camps by their friends."[23] This in turn authorized, as Agamben has shown, the exercise of sovereignty in a new form of biopower via the reduction of the human being as "bare life" to the status of *homo sacer*, the subject that legitimately could be put to death.[24]

If neoconservativism produced a crisis of displaced persons of unimaginable proportions, then 40 years of neoliberal policies of deregulation and privatization, accelerated in crucial ways by the "extreme centre"

(Bill Clinton and Tony Blair), created a social order in which crisis was no longer managed (as had been the case 1945–75) but had simply become normalized. This ranged from Black Monday, 19 October 1987, through the so-called Asian Flu of 1998 sparked by untrammelled currency speculation in south-east Asian economies, to a near meltdown of the global financial order provoked by the proliferation of subprime mortgages and collateralized debt obligations, by virtue of which high-risk investments were camouflaged amidst apparently low-risk vehicles in 2007–8.[25] The extreme centre, according to Tariq Ali, "is the political system that has grown up under neoliberalism. It has existed in the States for at least a century and a half, where you have two political parties with different clientele but funded by the same source, and basically carrying out the same policies."[26] The paradoxical neoconservative tactic of "humanitarian intervention" in the interest of regime change was coupled with the neoliberal remaking of the state via accumulation by dispossession, privatization, deregulation and upward (and *outward*) redistribution of wealth in Iraq.[27] If the collapse of the Soviet Union and 9/11 form one set of bookends, then 9/11 and the financial meltdown of 2007–8 form another set establishing the unique conjuncture within which the spectre of fascism haunts the present.

But what precisely do we mean when we speak of "fascism," and does the term properly apply to the contemporary period? Distant historical antecedents can be found at the origins of the Western tradition of political thought, notably Plato's *Republic* which, intimating his own aristocratic bias, depicts the degeneration of democracy into tyranny by way of the emergence of the demagogue capable of manipulating and harnessing the disaffections of those citizens constitutionally unable to control their baser impulses.[28] Antecedents can also be located in the rise of the era of the Caesars in Rome, who wielded near-dictatorial power in part by buying off the masses with elaborate spectacles in the Coliseum: Augustus, Tiberius, Caligula, Claudius and Nero with Julius Caesar's crossing of the Rubicon on 10 January 49 BCE and the subsequent establishment of himself as Emperor. From this is derived the concept of Caesarism.[29] Yet too much focus on these antecedents would be misleading insofar as fascism is a distinctively modern phenomenon. The bourgeois "freedom movements," as Max Horkheimer has shown, from the sixteenth century themselves contained elements that would later form part and parcel of the fascist ideology of social psychology of the twentieth century.[30] But perhaps the nearest anticipation of twentieth-century fascism was the phenomenon of Bonapartism. In the aftermath of the revolutions that swept through Europe, and on the backdrop of particularly militant workers' uprisings during the June days of 1848, Louis Bonaparte with the support of the *Lumpenproletariat* and the peasantry and appealing in turn to the examples of the Roman Republic and Empire, managed to seize power under the aegis of the "Party of Order" (see Chapter 11). In the eyes of Marx, in a very literal way this constituted a counter-revolution.[31]

TWENTY-FIRST CENTURY FASCISM:
BRINGING COLONIALISM BACK HOME

Historically, the emergence of fascism seemed to contradict Marx and Engels' historical prognosis. In *The Communist Manifesto*, published on the eve of the revolutions of 1848, the authors argue that the contradiction between the forces of production, that is, the development of the industrial form of capitalism, and the communications and transportation infrastructure that it necessitated, would hasten the conflict between an ever-shrinking bourgeoisie and a growing, unified and politically conscious proletariat, which, like Dr. Frankenstein's creation, was to be the bourgeoisie's "grave-digger." Later, in the 1859 "Preface to the Contribution to the Critique of Political Economy," Marx elaborates on this "fundamental contradiction" of capitalist society:

> At a certain stage of development, the material productive forces of society come into conflict with the existing relations of production or – this merely expresses the same thing in legal terms – with the property relations within the framework of which they have operated hitherto. From forms of development of the productive forces these relations turn into their fetters. Then begins an era of social revolution. The changes in the economic foundation lead sooner or later to the transformation of the whole immense superstructure.[32]

Yet, in the early twentieth century this contradiction between the productive forces and relations of production, far from leading to "social revolution," led to the opposite: *counter-revolution*. Perhaps one could say that while Marx and Engels were good at forecasting revolution they were not as good at understanding the potentials for political counter-revolution, which is, of course, paradoxical inasmuch as they were driven into exile by it themselves. The material productive forces of society, technology in particular, were incorporated into a radically masculinist, anti-modern and militaristic vision of society emphasizing hierarchy and a social Darwinist understanding of the struggle amongst races for survival and domination. As Walter Benjamin put it in "Theories of German Fascism," "Deeply imbued with its own depravity, technology gave shape to the apocalyptic face of nature and reduced nature to silence – even though this technology had the power to give nature its voice."[33] The roots of this "reactionary modernism"[34] can be found in the account of the crisis of the inter-war German capitalism, and its role in creating the conditions for the rise of Nazism can be found in *Economy and Class Structure of German Fascism* by Alfred Sohn-Rethel. In this text, Sohn-Rethel shows the way in which the contradiction between the forces and relations of production were in a sense "solved" through imperialist policies forwarded towards central Europe by German industrial capital.[35] Of course, such a solution was to be rather short-lived.

An influential account of fascism is that it constitutes an ultra-nationalist, revolutionary response to the existential crisis of meaning that emerges within a social and historical crisis of modern, secular societies. Such a crisis is perceived as a crisis of the health of the race or nation.[36] While this account does well to highlight the existential nature of the crisis, it fails to understand it properly within a class analysis situated within a larger understanding of the socioeconomic crisis of capitalism.[37] In contrast, the classical Marxian account of fascism, as alluded to above, is that fascism represents the bourgeoisie's response to a militant working class and its institutions that threaten to bring about a fundamental social transformation of property relations (revolution) against the backdrop of a socioeconomic and political crisis of capitalism within an international order characterized by mounting and intensifying inter-imperialist rivalries. The classical Marxian approach, for the most part, is, however, unable to properly come to terms with the existential and psychological dimensions of the crisis, namely the problem of insecurity, although it is implicit in its understanding of the social base of fascism as the petite bourgeoisie or the middle class.

This is the contribution made by Western Marxism, in particular Georg Lukács and the Frankfurt School, to understanding the subjective dimensions of the crisis that made the working class susceptible to the siren song of fascism. A key mediator, it must be emphasized, was imperialism which was motivated by the dynamics of capital accumulation but was justified by way of a form of ultra-nationalism and the positing of Europe's "civilizing mission." By displacing class via national identities, the bourgeoisie is able to gain the support of the lower petite bourgeoisie and the *Lumpenproletariat*, or those classes whose social precarity renders them particularly insecure and susceptible to xenophobia and extreme forms of nationalism within the context of an imperialist project. As Sohn-Rethel had shown, and as was confirmed by a number of Marxist theorists in the first decades of the twentieth century, capitalism seeks to address its fundamental crises of overaccumulation as well as the tensions between the accelerating technological development (forces of production) and the relations of production by seeking out non-capitalist or undercapitalized societies as the basis of renewed profit or surplus value extraction.[38]

The colonial aspects of fascism become clear in Mussolini's assertion of Italian power over Abyssinia under the aegis of building a new Rome, and in Hitler's project for a thousand-year Reich constructed in the east and the expulsion and liquidation of the Jews and the enslavement of the Slavic peoples living there. In particular, the experience of African colonization and the colonial imaginary of the westward expansion of the US republic in the nineteenth century played a key role as models for the Nazi project to secure *Lebensraum* for the German *Volk*.[39] The colonial imaginary was also central to Mussolini's vision of fascism, itself nurtured on the militaristic fantasies of the Futurists (see Chapter 3 for a more nuanced view in this volume). The Italian bombing of Abyssinia was central to the aesthetics of fascism – understood as an exemplary case of the "the aestheticizing of politics"[40] – the spectacle of war, violence and domination. Moreover, Hitler's ignominious vision was fuelled by both the genocides of the Herero and Nama peoples in addition to the aforementioned stories of conquest of the Western US frontier. At the same time, modernism was also able to throw critical light on the growing authoritarianism in inter-war Europe and imperialism as in, inter alia, Franz Kakfa's short story "In the Penal Colony."

Building on Arendt's Luxemburgian analysis of the connection between imperialism and Nazism and Foucault's understanding of biopower, Enzo Traverso has argued that fascism represented the application of colonial techniques of violence that had hitherto been applied with little comment to European colonies now to Europe itself. As suggested above, in this sense fascism is uncanny or unhomely. In fascism, Europe (and North America) confronts its own strangely familiar colonial image.

This deep connection between imperialism and fascism was already recognized, however, in 1950 by Aimé Césaire in his *Discourse on Colonialism*, in which he condemns the hypocrisy of certain self-righteous forms of European anti-fascism:

> ... before they were its victims, they were its accomplices; that they tolerated Nazism before it was inflicted on them, that they absolved it, shut their eyes to it, legitimized it, because, until then, it has been applied only to non-European peoples; that they have cultivated that Nazism, that they are responsible for it, and that before engulfing the whole edifice of Western, Christian civilization in its reddened waters, it oozes, seeps and trickles from every crack.[41]

FOSSIL COUNTER-REVOLUTION

"The incessant excavation of the earth in peacetime was already a type of trench war."[42]

Max Horkheimer

It is against this understanding of fascism that we must pose the question of whether we are truly witnessing fascism's return. In a recent editorial of the *New Left Review* after the US mid-term elections, sociologist Dylan Riley notes the surfeit of invocations of fascism across the political spectrum. Yet, on the basis of four axes – geopolitical dynamics, economic crisis, the relation between class and nation, and the character of political parties and civil societies – he carefully and quite persuasively lays out the case *against* considering a figure like Donald J. Trump to be a fascist.[43] While compelling, Riley's brief is, ultimately, unconvincing because he fails to take seriously the undermining of the institutions of liberal democracy, against a backdrop of the chronic (rather than acute) socio-economic crisis, in the name of collective identities which one witnesses not simply in the United States with the advent of the Trump presidency but globally. And, as we shall suggest, herein lies the core of *contemporary fascism*.

Focusing on the US case, Holocaust historian Christopher R. Browning argues that there are several *continuities* and one significant *discontinuity* with the Weimar period. Then, as with the present, the United States was becoming increasingly isolationist. Then, as with the present, we saw an undermining of the institutions of liberal democracy; the part of President

Paul von Hindenburg, who momentously agreed to appoint Hitler as Chancellor in 1933, today is played by Mitch McConnell. "Like Hitler's conservative allies," Browning argues, "McConnell and the Republicans have prided themselves on the early returns in their investment in Trump."[44] A key *discontinuity*, according to Browning, between Weimar and the current period involves the unlikelihood of witnessing the rise of an organized, disciplined mass-based fascist movement today. He foresees, rather, an incremental and subtler "suffocation of democracy," that is, the rise of what he calls "illiberal democracy" insofar as authoritarian leaders and movements typically make exclusionary-populist appeals to the "demos" or the "people" on the basis of which they seek to subvert the rule of law and constitutionality.

In the main, Browning's analysis is cogent, particularly the argument that fascism today poses the threat of "illiberal democracy."[45] And if we look at the rise of other authoritarian regimes across the globe (from the United States and Canada to Poland and Hungary) we see the undermining of checks and balances on the executive branch of the state – the locus of sovereignty (Schmitt) – in particular by the judiciary and the press, as well as political dissent per se. This is precisely the manner in which democracy is threatened according to Adorno: not from without but from *within*.

What remains absent, perhaps unsurprisingly, from Browning's liberal account, is an explanation of the social conditions that led to the rise of fascism in the 1930s and how those conditions might be paralleled by those we are witnessing today. Any convincing account of the spectre of the 1930s must link it not only to a determinate *political crisis* of democratic institutions such as in Germany the mendacity and duplicity of the political elites and their betrayal, but also the distinctive *socioeconomic* crisis not just of the 1930s but also the earlier period of the infamous German inflation of 1924–5. "If you don't want to talk about capitalism," as Max Horkheimer famously put it, "then you'd better keep quiet about fascism."[46]

In this respect, Samir Amin's recent discussion of fascism is more helpful (although Schmidt contests it in Chapter 2 of this volume). Amin contends that "Fascism is a particular political response to the challenges with which the management of capitalist society may be confronted in specific circumstances." He goes on to suggest that it is comprised of two features. The first is that, underlying its diatribes against "capitalism" or "plutocracies," fascism represents a distinctive response to capitalist crises. Amin argues that the second feature of fascism is that this particular response is a "*categorical* rejection of 'democracy'" (emphasis added). Amin argues:

> Fascism always replaces the general principles on which the theories and practices of modern democracies are based – recognition of a diversity of opinions, recourse to electoral procedures to determine a majority, guarantee of the rights of the minority, etc. – with the opposed values of submission to the requirements of collective discipline and the authority of the supreme leader and his main agents.[47]

Yet, perhaps, with Browning, Amin's otherwise apposite formulation should be modified to read that fascism embodies an attack not on democracy – a rather more protean concept – but instead on *liberal democracy*. Because it understands fascism as a response to socioeconomic crises, it is a much stronger formulation than Browning's. Amin's definition of fascism constitutes the crucial framework within which to situate the truly *global* re-emergence of fascism today.

If in the 1930s, the specific contradictions resulting from the accelerated development of the productive forces under the aegis of industrial capital constituted a colonizing logic, today such a logic is impelled by the ever-more abstract *irrational rationality* of finance. The use of finance, as Vijay Prashad has shown, was key to neocolonialism in the post-independence period within the developing world.[48] The IMF's strategy of structural adjustment in the 1980s and 1990s played a key part in forcibly liberalizing societies in which the state played an important role in the provision of services and a modicum of wealth redistribution, etc. But financialization also contributes to ontological insecurity and anxiety.

Today, finance has displaced industrial capital and exercises its power not just directly, that is, by military means, but increasingly by means of the politics of debt.[49] As Césaire remarks in noting the transition from colonialism to neocolonialism in the immediate post-war period: "'*Aid to the disinherited countries*,' says Truman. 'The time of the old colonialism has passed.' That's also Truman. Which means that American high finance considers that the time has come to raid every colony in the world. So, dear friends, here you have to be careful!"[50] The key point here is that, like twentieth-century fascism, contemporary authoritarianism also entails the self-colonization of Europe itself, as we see in the case of post-referendum Greece. The "violence of financial capital"[51] in Europe is also evident in Emmanuel Macron's use of brutally heavy-handed policing tactics against the *gilets jaunes*, who have protested against austerity, among other things, in the Place de la République. Here we might point to the role of security services as harbingers of fascism insofar as they are often complicit with the far-right and directly target the left.[52]

Financial capital, though indirectly in the form of investments in futures markets, is closely tied to extractivism (see Chapter 14).[53] If we look specifically at oil, we can discern how it led the development of the global economy, as the post-war "relationship between the American state and US oil companies … already epitomized 'globalization.'"[54] The unity of the global market with the circulation of fossil fuels was further cemented by the linking of oil to the US dollar, and the US dollar to the global financial system.[55]

Such an intertwined system is not without its weaknesses and dangers, and the current "carbon bubble" is "the result of an over-valuation of oil, coal and gas reserves held by fossil fuel companies … At least two-thirds of these reserves will have to remain underground if the world is to meet existing internationally agreed targets to avoid the threshold for 'dangerous' climate change. If the agreements hold, these reserves will be in effect unburnable and so worthless – leading to massive market losses."[56] The new far-right could be said to represent a new fossil counter-revolution underwritten by the Koch Brothers.[57] Thus the financial mechanisms of the global market are so tied to resource extraction that failure in one sector will inevitably lead to failure in the other. This is sometimes described as "locked-in" climate change, and highlights the way in which the current struggle for alternatives is as much a struggle over spaces as it is a struggle over times; that is, the contradiction between the market's inherent "short-termism" and the "long-termism" of the environmental and climate consequences of market-driven fossil fuel production.

This brings us back to Césaire's reflection on the deep connection between colonialism and fascism. Just as surplus labour time is extracted by capital from an increasingly internationalized, racialized and precarious workforce, so too are resources forcibly extracted from the earth via renewed forms of primitive accumulation. These disproportionately affect societies located in the Global South and Indigenous communities across the globe.[58] The accelerated development of capitalism in the twenty-first century – especially in the area of fossil fuels and resource extraction – has taken this fractured metabolic process to and beyond its sustainable limit, depleting non-renewable resources at an alarming rate, damaging the environmental and social fabrics of communities, contributing greatly to anthropogenic climate change, and reducing biodiversity to the point at which scientists are speaking of an unfolding planetary mass extinction.[59]

Extractive states place unbearable pressure on the extant fault lines of formal democratic institutions and processes. As the UN special rapporteur on extreme poverty and human rights, Philip Alston, has suggested, "… democracy and the rule of law, as well as a wide range of civil and political rights are every bit at risk."[60] As Timothy Mitchell notes, "countries that depend upon petroleum resources for a large part of their earnings from exports tend to be less democratic"; indeed, "existing forms of democratic government appear incapable of taking the precautions needed to protect the long-term future of the planet" because "economic calculation" occupies "the space of democratic debate."[61] Such developments point to the very real possibility of the constitution of what has been called a "climate leviathan" or a form of authoritarian planetary sovereignty.

While Amin draws attention to the explicitly anti-liberal-democratic "values of the submission to the requirements of collective discipline and the authority of the supreme leader and his main agents," he fails to provide an adequate account of how this is possible. "The masses have a right to changed property relations; fascism seeks to give them *expression* in keeping these relations unchanged,"[62] as Walter Benjamin argued. As his Frankfurt colleagues would show, this expression also had a profoundly social-psychological component: the insecurity generated by fear, anxiety and frustration of the masses in a period of economic turbulence and insecurity was actively and consciously desublimated by fascist movements and turned against *civilization* itself. Franz L. Neumann argues that authoritarian politics entails the transformation of *real* into *neurotic* anxiety.[63]

The spectre of fascism is due not simply to economic insecurity nor to cultural anxieties or the loss of privilege. It is actively produced by the authoritarian populist translation of economic insecurities into cultural anxieties against the backdrop of the prospect of ecological collapse. As Neumann states, "The intensification of anxiety into persecutory anxiety is successful when a group (class, religion, race) is threatened by loss of status, without understanding the process which leads to its degradation."

It has led to the transformation of the social "stranger" (Simmel) into a political "enemy" (Schmitt) in the absence of political parties and movements that could offer genuine alternatives to the neoliberal dispensation of deepening and crushing inequality and austerity.[64] The continuity between twentieth- and twenty-first-century fascisms, in part, is to be located here.[65]

Financialization is only putatively challenged by authoritarian political discourses grounded in the charismatic appeal to authenticity: discourse that transforms the people into a mass (see Chapters 2 and 8 of this volume).[66] A global order, dominated by the ever-more abstract and accelerated operations of finance capital leading to ever-more pronounced forms of anxiety and insecurity, produces an "ontological need," a need for a connection to authentic Being, which is expressed in the form of homogenous collective identities.[67]

To summarize the discussion so far, contemporary fascism can be regarded as a militantly anti-liberal-democratic way of addressing the nature of the crisis of capitalist social relations. Collective identities and cultural traditions are re-invented and mobilized in such a way as to confront and undermine formal democratic institutions and rule of law, by way of an appeal to patriarchal, supposedly "authentic" collective identities (see Chapters 7 and 13) that were themselves nurtured and sustained by a social Darwinist vision of an unforgiving struggle for existence among competing races and individuals. Such a mobilization tends to reinforce new colonial forms of primitive accumulation or accumulation by dispossession via redoubled colonialism based on the "financialization of life," central to which is intensified financial investment in resource extraction.[68] The precise manner, however, in which this logic plays depends on the diachronic or historical circumstances of a given society as well as its synchronic, which is to say structural, location within global capitalism as a whole. Amin's framework is particularly helpful insofar as what we confront today is a truly globalized rise of the spectre of fascism from the US parts of Latin America, Brazil in particular, to Europe through Turkey and Egypt to India.

THE "FUTURE" IN THE ERA OF ITS
PLANNED OBSOLESCENCE

In contrast, though, to Mussolini's attempt to build a "New Rome" or Hitler's thousand-year Reich, which above all centred on a distinctive temporal politics, a politics oriented to colonizing not just space but time, that is, the *future*, today the "spectre of fascism" responds to the ecological limits of capitalism within which the future itself – within existing property relations – becomes increasingly unimaginable.[69]

The spectre of fascism returns, then, as a response to a particular financial and ecological crisis of capitalism. If twentieth-century fascism, in part, offered a solution to the economic slump via an acceleration of the extraction of absolute and relative surplus-value extraction by smashing independent trade unions and other working-class institutions, today fascism centres on a deepening of resource extraction on the very precipice of massive deskilling of labour, and widespread automation and employment of robotics, machine learning and artificial intelligence, to wit: the prospective obsolescence of humanity itself. Such a logic entails what Achille Mbembe calls the "becoming Black of the world," the creation of "abandoned subjects":

> There are no more workers as such. There are only laboring nomads. If yesterday's drama of the subject was exploitation by capital, the tragedy of the multitude today is that they are unable to be exploited at all. They are abandoned subjects, relegated to the role of a "superfluous humanity."[70]

If we take as our definition the classic account of fascism as that reactionary mass movement comprised of an alliance between industrial capital and the petite bourgeoisie against the working class and its political organizations in the context of imperialist rivalries and capitalist crises of overproduction, then it is far from clear that what we face today can in any straightforward way be described as "fascism" in this sense. Today, after the defeat of organized labour, there is precious little resistance to dead labour's extraction of surplus value from living labour. This drives growing colonization, militarism, jingoism and, ultimately, war against peoples – Indigenous peoples in particular (see Chapter 12) especially in North America, India and Brazil – and the very planet itself. Far from having to confront the revolutionary force of organized labour today, at least not in Europe and North America (Brazil and India evince different logics), today fascism emerges from the phenomenon of accelerated global migration flows resulting from the economic, social and political violence (new forms of primitive accumulation) attendant upon globalization and global climate change. It also responds to the increasing ontological *insecurity* of citizens of these states, whose fear in an age of massive, irreversible climate change is increasingly mobilized against pariah peoples.[71] Such mobilization is based on the recognition that, under the late form of neoliberalism, the line between citizen and migrant, parvenu and pariah, in other words, "genuine" and "super-fluous" humanity is coming to be increasingly blurred.

Yet, if Benjamin's "failed revolution" can be understood not simply in the singular but rather as *several* failed attempts at completing, realizing and transcending the bourgeois revolutions of 1789/1848, then the task of the left surely must be to consider its future in light of its own melan-choly past. What does this mean? In the context of fascisms that under-mine liberal democracy from within, on the backdrop of a combination of the ongoing crisis tendencies of the financialized neoliberal order and the looming threat of ecological collapse that we are now experiencing, rather than a resigned dismissal of liberal democracy, the left must make significant efforts to distinguish itself from the far-right's attack on these institutions. To engage in such a dismissal would be to violate the condi-tions of what Christian Lenhardt, following Walter Benjamin, called "anamnestic solidarity"[72] with previous generations who struggled to shape these institutions, imperfect though they may be, in a more genu-inely democratic and egalitarian direction. The right engages in what we could call an *abstract* negation, a simple *cancellation*, of the institu-tions of liberal democracy in the name of "natural" hierarchies of various sorts. In order to avoid "fascist creep" and offer a genuine alternative, the left must take up a genuinely dialectical politics of *determinate* negation, which is to say, it must simultaneously cancel *and* preserve aspects of the very liberal democracy targeted by the far-right on the horizon of a refashioned universalism. It must struggle to defend and preserve civil rights and to expand and deepen *social rights* while criti-quing and limiting bourgeois *property rights*. While cancelling the separ-ation between the political and economic spheres – the very separation between "liberalism" (negative freedom) and "democracy" (equality), which means also urgently rethinking and reconfiguring the vital rela-tionship between economic *production* and social reproduction – the left must insist upon a thorough-going democratization of society.[73] Along with such democratization, the left must insist, as well, on the tradition of "autonomous individualism" for which, in the words of Fanonian political philosopher Ato Sekyi-Otu, "the assertion of individuality is virtually an intrinsic value, and never more valuable than in social orders and historical conditions in which it is extinguished or suppressed, discounted or misdirected: racist culture, the colonial regime, fascism."[74]

This means fighting energetically to maintain and deepen rights and freedoms, especially of association, speech and expression, due process, etc. that are profoundly threatened today around the globe and will only continue to be so under the gathering dark clouds of global climate change. Only thus would it be possible to redeem the promise of the free and autonomous life – one that also necessitates a non-dominating relationship with external nature – that inheres within the revolutionary horizon of the modern era.

The essays assembled here are thoroughly interdisciplinary and draw upon the specialized disciplines of art history, communications, philosophy, political economy, political science, psychoanalysis and sociology. In this, the book could be said to take its inspiration from the Institute for Social Research, founded in 1923, with the aim of understanding the transformations in the nature of capitalism in Europe and resulting changes at all levels of society including and especially the production of subjectivity. The book is divided into three sections: History, Theory, and The Contemporary Horizon. The first section builds on the Introduction to provide the historical context to enable us to make sense of the return of fascism in the twenty-first century. Ingo Schmidt provides a thorough overview of Marxist debates in understanding fascism and in the practical struggles against it in Germany in the 1920s and 1930s. Jaleh Mansoor brushes received art history against the grain to disclose the hitherto overlooked political ambivalence, largely due to the influence of Walter Benjamin, of Italian Futurism. Alec Balasescu examines the strange similarities between the excessive "aesthetics salvation" of totalitarian regimes such as that of the Ceauşescu regime in his native Romania and Donald J. Trump's Versailles pretentions, which could be understood as an architectural will to autarky. Tamir Bar-On sets forth a comparative assessment of the French Nouvelle Droite led by Alain de Benoist that began to become influential in the 1980s and the newly constituted "alt-right," claiming that while there are family resemblances between the two, they must be understood as ideologically quite distinct.

The next section, "Theory," provides a constellation of conceptual approaches to fascism. Am Johal provides an examination of a fascist thinker with whom the left has flirted now for several decades, Carl Schmitt, and poses the question of whether he could be of use today (if he ever really was!). In an important re-assessment of the soon to be rereleased two volumes of Klaus Theweleit's *Male Fantasies*, Laura Marks expresses certain reservations about its essentialist implications for understanding contemporary far-right discourse and calls for a more historically specific account, in which one's relationship to others need not be one of mastery, but of "self-loss, openness, or curiosity." Gary Genosko shows how, in developing a notion of "micro-fascism," by understanding it in a decentred way, Piérre-Felix Guattari grasps the process by which the energy of mass desire is directed towards self-destruction. Having studied Donald J. Trump since the 1980s, Guattari is uniquely placed not only to understand the multiple resonances of Trump but also the way in which these contain both "reactionary forces and their proto-revolutionary enemies." In a rather different way, in my chapter, I provide a reading of Adorno's crucial summation of his work on the social psychology of authoritarianism, arguing that Adorno's understanding of the agitator provides profound insight into the strange appeal of Donald Trump's authoritarian populist rhetoric today. Also in a psycho-analytical vein deeply informed by the "Lacanian left," Hilda Fernandez-Alvarez argues that a crisis in the Master signifier leads to a reversion to predominance of imaginary mechanisms such as identitarian politics. Much hinges upon the way in which left and right articulate the relation between the Master signifier and universality: while the right re-institutes the Master signifier as a false universal of race or the ethnos, the left is attentive (or should be) to the traumatic residues that exceed any given claim to universality. Like Marks, Fernandez-Alvarez lays claim to the feminine logic of the "not-all" beyond the will to mastery.

In the final section we look at the rise of fascism as a global and transnational phenomenon. Vladimir Safatle argues that we can understand the election of Bolsonaro as a kind of "pre-emptive counter-revolution" that responded to the accumulation of popular demands that constituting the revolutionary conjuncture of 2013. In a remarkably situated way, drawing on the concept of "Red intersectionality" and echoing Aimé Césaire, Patricia Barkaskas suggests that what the left ought not to forget, amidst a certain hyperbolic concern with the return of fascism to Western liberal democracies, is that the genocidal nature of settler colonialism always already enforced a form of horrific domination of Indigenous peoples and as such could be regarded as one of fascism's original laboratories. The colonial imaginary of fascism is reinforced by Joan Braune in her intellectual and political profile of Steve Bannon – *Breitbart* editor, former Trump advisor and instigator of a new "Fascist International" or "the Movement," for whom Jean Raspail's novel *The Camp of the Saints* is core inspiration. Through its depiction of a Europe overrun by denizens of the Global South, the novel presents a vision of the coming Kali Yuga or period of decline that precedes a moment of rebirth within which the old hierarchies are violently re-asserted. Ajay and Vijay Gudavarthy claim that in India what one witnesses is not so much fascism as an authoritarian regime with fascist characteristics. They explain its appeal by unearthing the particular and contradictory dynamics of neoliberal capitalism in the complex fabric of Indian society. Finally, Johan F. Hartle argues that the rise of fascism can, in part, be attributed to the fact that so much of left politics, at least within the spheres of art practices and art activism, today hinges upon an aestheticized politics of representation and inclusion within the liberal confines of formal equality – yet such a normative horizon is in fact part of the problem insofar as it occludes the relation of power and domination which are the necessary conditions for the rise of fascism in the first place.

NOTES

Unless otherwise stated, URLs were last accessed on 15 September 2019.

1. I would like to express my gratitude to John Abromeit, Ian Angus, Joseph Baines, Johan F. Hartle, Am Johal, Harry-Helmut Loewen, Hilda Fernandez-Alvarez, Anders Malm, Jaleh Mansoor, Jeremy Rayner, Ingo Schmidt, Willow Verkerk and Harriet Olivette Wills for their helpful comments on earlier drafts of this text. Any errors of fact and or interpretation are mine alone. Earlier drafts were presented at Historical Materialism London (Nov 2018) and Athens (May 2019) as well as at Johan F. Hartle's Seminar at the Staat-liche Hochschule für Gestaltung Karlsruhe and King's College London (Feb 2019). I thank Magnus Ryner and Julia Nicholls for the kind invitation and help with logistics at Kings. A slightly different version of this Introduction entitled "The Spectre of the 1930s" is forthcoming in Jeremy Rayner, Susan Falls, George Souvlis, and Taylor Nelms, eds., *Back to the 30s? Recurring Crises of Capitalism, Liberalism and Democracy* (Palgrave MacMillan).
2. See, for example, recent contributions: Madeleine Albright, *Fascism: A Warning* (New York: Harper, 2018), Jason Stanley, *How Fascism Works: The Politics of Us and Them* (New York: Random House, 2018) and Timothy Snyder, *On Tyranny: Twenty Lessons from the Twentieth Century* (New York: Tim Duggan Books, 2017).
3. Enzo Traverso, *The New Faces of Fascism* (London: Verso, 2019).
4. Alberto Toscano, "Notes on Late Fascism," *Historical Materialism* (blog), 2 April 2017, www.historicalmaterialism.org/blog/notes-late-fascism.

5. Alexander Reid Ross, *Against the Fascist Creep* (Chico, CA: AK Press, 2017).

6. Hamed Abdel-Samad, *Islamic Fascism* (New York: Prometheus Books, 2016).

7. See Dylan Riley, "Editorial: What is Trump?" *New Left Review*, No. 114 (November–December 2018): 5–31.

8. See Jacques Derrida, *Spectres of Marx: The State of the Debt, the Work of Mourning and the New International*, trans. Peggy Kamuf (London: Routledge, 1993).

9. Sigmund Freud, "The 'Uncanny,'" in James Strachey, ed., *The Standard Edition of the Complete Psychological Works of Sigmund Freud* (London: Hogarth Press, 1955), 17:217–56.

10. Theodor W. Adorno, *Aspekte des neuen Rechtsradikalismus* (Frankfurt am Main: Suhrkamp, 2019), 34.

11. Aimé Césaire, *Discourse on Colonialism*, trans. Joan Pinkham (New York: Monthly Review Press, 1972). See also Hannah Arendt, *Origins of Totalitarianism* (New York: Harcourt, 1976) and Enzo Traverso, *The Origins of Nazi Violence* (New York: The New Press, 2003).

12. T.W. Adorno, "The Meaning of Working Through the Past," in *Critical Models: Interventions and Catchwords*, trans. Henry W. Pickford (New York: Columbia University Press, 1998), 90.

13. Karl Marx, "On the Jewish Question," in *Karl Marx and Frederick Engels: Collected Works* (New York: International Publishers, 1975), 3: 146–74.

14. Slavoj Žižek, "The Palestinian Question: The Couple Symptom / Fetish Islamo-Fascism, Christo-Fascism, Zionism – Mieux Vaut Un Désastre Qu'un Désêtre," lacan.com, accessed 16 August 2019, www.lacan.com/essays/?page_id=261.

15. See the classic account by C.L.R. James, *The Black Jacobins: Toussaint L'Ouverture and the San Domingo Revolution* (New York: Vintage, 1989); as well as the more recent work by Susan Buck-Morss, *Hegel, Haiti, and Universal History* (Pittsburgh, PA: University of Pittsburgh Press, 2009).

16. Karl Marx, "The Eighteen Brumaire of Louis Napoleon," in *Karl Marx and Frederick Engels: Collected Works* (London: Lawrence and Wishart, 2010), 11:103.

17. On the former, see Juliet Koss, *Modernism After Wagner* (Minneapolis, MN: University of Minnesota Press, 2010); and on the latter, see Doug Moggach, *The Philosophy and Politics of Bruno Bauer* (Cambridge: Cambridge University Press, 2003).

18. Leon Trotsky, "Bonapartism and Fascism (1934)," marxists.org, accessed 11 August 2019, www.marxists.org/archive/trotsky/germany/1934/340715.htm.

19. Vladimir Safatle and Samir Gandesha, "The Brazilian Matrix: Between Fascism and Neoliberalism – Vladimir Safatle and Samir Gandesha in Conversation," *Krisis* (forthcoming).

20. "PNAC Statement of Principles," accessed 2 August 2019, www.rrojasdatabank.info/pfpc/PNAC—statement%20of%20principles.pdf.

21. Condoleezza Rice, "Remarks by National Security Advisor Condoleezza Rice on Terrorism and Foreign Policy," The White House, 29 April 2002,

georgewbush-whitehouse.archives.gov/news/releases/2002/04/20020429-9.html.

22. As of June 2019, the UNHCR estimates 70 million displaced persons globally. Adrian Edwards, "Global Forced Displacement Tops 70 Million," UNHCR, 19 June 2019, www.unhcr.org/news/stories/2019/6/5d08b6614/global-forced-displacement-tops-70-million.html.

23. Hannah Arendt, "We Refugees," in Jerome Kohn and Ron H. Feldman, eds., *The Jewish Writings* (New York: Schocken Book, 2007), 265.

24. Giorgio Agamben, *Homo Sacer: Sovereign Power and Bare Life*, trans. Daniel Heller-Roazen (Palo Alto, CA: Stanford University Press, 1998).

25. See Adam Tooze, *Crashed: How a Decade of Financial Crises Changed the World* (New York: Penguin, 2019).

26. "Interview with Tariq Ali: Renationalise the Railways. Cut Military Spending. Argue With Whoever Says it Can't be Done," *Guardian*, 20 February 2015, www.theguardian.com/politics/2015/feb/20/tariq-ali-interview-renationalise-the-railways.

27. See Wendy Brown's excellent account in *Undoing the Demos: Neoliberalism's Stealth Revolution* (Cambridge, MA: Zone Books, 2015), 115–50.

28. Plato, *Republic*, trans. Paul Shorey in *The Collected Dialogues of Plato* (Princeton, NJ: Princeton University Press, 1961), 555b–76b.

29. See the work of Antonio Gramsci as well as Franz L. Neumann, "Anxiety and Politics," *Triple C: Journal for a Global Sustainable Information Society* 15, No. 2 (2017), doi.org/10.31269/triplec.v15i2.901.

30. See Max Horkheimer, "Egoism and the Freedom Movement: On the Anthropology of the Bourgeois Era," *Telos* 1982, No. 54 (December 1983): 10–60, and also John Abromeit, *Max Horkheimer and the Foundations of the Frankfurt School* (Cambridge: Cambridge University Press, 2013), 248–300.

31. Samir Gandesha, "Three Logics of the Aesthetic in Marx," in Samir Gandesha and Johan F. Hartle, eds., *Aesthetic Marx* (London: Bloomsbury, 2017), 16. See also David Harvey's excellent book on Second Empire Paris, *Paris: Capital of Modernity* (London and New York: Routledge, 2005) which demonstrates how the attacks on workers continued unabated in the 1850s and 1860s by Napoleon III. Second Empire Paris was also the most important model for Benjamin's theorization of authoritarian "modernization" with highly regressive social consequences.

32. Karl Marx, "Preface to the Contribution to the Critique of Political Economy," in *Marx and Engels: Collected Works* (New York: International Publishers, 1987), 29:263.

33. Walter Benjamin, "Theories of German Fascism," in *Selected Writings*, Volume 2, Part 1, *1927–1930* (Cambridge, MA: Belknap Press of Harvard University Press, 1999), 319.

34. Jeffrey Herf, *Reactionary Modernism: Technology, Culture, and Politics in Weimar and the Third Reich* (Cambridge: Cambridge University Press, 1984).

35. Alfred Sohn-Rethel, *Economy and Class Structure of German Fascism*, trans. Martin Sohn-Rethel (London: Free Association Books, 1987).

36. See Roger Griffin, *The Nature of Fascism* (London: Routledge, 1993).

37. See William I. Robinson, "Can Twenty-First Century Fascism Resolve the Crisis of Global Capitalism?," *Marxist Sociology* (blog), 24 April 2019, marxistsociology.org/2019/04/can-twenty-first-century-fascism-resolve-the-crisis-of-global-capitalism/.

38. See Richard B. Day and Daniel Gaido, *Discovering Imperialism: Social Democracy to World War I* (London: Haymarket Books, 2012).

39. See Richard Evans, *The Third Reich in History and Memory* (Oxford: Oxford University Press, 2015), 355–89; Dunbar-Ortiz, *An Indigenous People's History of the United States* (Boston, MA: Beacon Press, 2015); Bradley Naranch and Geoff Eley, eds., *German Colonialism in a Global Age* (Durham, NC: Duke University Press, 2015).

40. Walter Benjamin, "The Work of Art in the Age of its Technological Reproducibility: Second Version," in Howard Eiland and Michael W. Jennings, eds., *Walter Benjamin: Selected Writings*, trans. Edmund Jephcott, Howard Eiland and Others (Cambridge, MA: Harvard University Press, 2002), 3:122.

41. *Discourse on Colonialism*, 3.

42. Max Horkheimer, "The Jews and Europe," in Stephen Eric Bronner and Douglas Kellner, eds., *Critical Theory and Society: A Reader* (New York: Routledge, 1989), 91.

43. Riley, "What is Trump?"

44. Christopher R. Browning, "The Suffocation of Democracy," *New York Review of Books*, 25 October 2018, www.nybooks.com/articles/2018/10/25/suffocation-of-democracy/.

45. It is an analysis confirmed by Richard J. Evans, who notes the enabling role of the courts in the rise of National Socialism; see his *Third Reich*: 87–117. Here the contemporary parallels with the recent "judicial coup" in Brazil are uncanny. See Perry Anderson, "Bolsonaro's Brazil," *London Review of Books* 41, No. 3 (February 2019), www.lrb.co.uk/v41/n03/perry-anderson/bolsonaros-brazil.

46. Max Horkheimer, "The Jews and Europe," in Stephen Eric Bronner and Douglas Kellner, eds., *Critical Theory and Society: A Reader* (New York: Routledge, 1989), 77–194.

47. Samir Amin, "The Return of Fascism Within Contemporary Capitalism," *Monthly Review*, 1 September 2014, monthlyreview.org/2014/09/01/the-return-of-fascism-in-contemporary-capitalism/.

48. Vijay Prashad, *The Darker Nations: A People's History of the Third World* (New York: The New Press, 2008), 224–44.

49. Maurizio Lazzarato, *Governing by Debt*, trans. Joashua David Gordan (New York: Semiotext(e), 2014).

50. Césaire, *Discourse on Colonialism*, 23.

51. Christian Marazzi, *The Violence of Finance Capital* (New York: Semiotext(e), 2010).

52. See, for example, the case of Germany in which the very agencies responsible for protecting the constitution are those who most endanger it by sins of omission: Katrin Bennhold, "A Political Murder and Far-

Right Terrorism: Germany's New Hateful Reality," *New York Times*, 7 July 2019, www.nytimes.com/2019/07/07/world/europe/germany-murder-far-right-neo-nazi-luebcke.html.

53. The next few paragraphs are drawn from Samir Gandesha and Stephen Collis, "State of Extraction: A Conference Primer" (unpublished manuscript).

54. Leo Panitch and Sam Gindin, *The Making of Global Capitalism: The Political Economy of the American Empire* (London: Verso, 2013), 103.

55. Timothy Mitchell, *Carbon Democracy: Political Power in the Age of Oil* (London: Verso, 2011), 30.

56. Damian Carrington, "Carbon Bubble Will Plunge the World into Another Financial Crisis," *Guardian*, 19 April 2013, www.theguardian.com/environment/2013/apr/19/carbon-bubble-financial-crash-crisis.

57. I owe this formulation to Ingo Schmidt.

58. Glen Coulthard and Voices Rising, "For Our Nations to Love Capitalism Must Die," *Unsettling America* (blog), 5 November 2013, unsettlingamerica. wordpress.com/2013/11/05/for-our-nations-to-live-capitalism-must-die/.

59. This is what John Bellamy Foster has called, following Marx, the "global metabolic rift," which refers to the "overall break in the human relation to nature arising from an alienated system of capital accumulation without end." John Bellamy Foster, Brett Clark and Richard York, *The Ecological Rift: Capitalism's War on the Earth* (New York: Monthly Review Press, 2010), 18.

For an alternative attempt to theorize the relation between capitalism and nature, see Jason Moore, *Capitalism in the Web of Life: Ecology and the Accumulation of Capital* (London: Verso, 2015).

60. Damian Carrington, "'Climate Apartheid': UN Expert Says Human Rights May Not Survive," *Guardian*, 25 June 2019, www.theguardian.com/environment/2019/jun/25/climate-apartheid-united-nations-expert-says-human-rights-may-not-survive-crisis.

61. Mitchell, *Carbon Democracy*, 1, 11.

62. Walter Benjamin, "The Work of Art," 121.

63. Neumann, "Anxiety and Politics."

64. Samir Gandesha, "The Political Semiosis of Populism," *The Semiotic Review of Books* 13, No. 3 (2003): 1–7.

65. See John Abromeit, "Frankfurt School Critical Theory and the Persistence of Right-Wing Populism in the United States," in Jeremiah Morelock, ed., *Critical Theory and Authoritarian Populism* (London: University of Westminster Press, 2018), 3–28.

66. T.W. Adorno, "Freudian Theory and the Pattern of Fascist Propaganda," in Andrew Arato and Eike Gebhardt, eds., *Essential Frankfurt School Reader* (New York: Continuum, 1982), 118–37. See Chapter 8 of this volume for a reading of this important essay.

67. Adorno, *Negative Dialectics*, trans. E.B. Ashton (New York: Continuum, 2007), 61–96.

68. Costas Lapavitsas, *Profiting Without Producing: How Finance Exploits Us All* (London: Verso, 2013).

69. See Geoff Mann and Joel Wainwright, *Climate Leviathan* (London: Verso, 2018) in which the authors argue that what seems likely in the face of catastrophic climate change, in the absence of a bottom-up anti-capitalist movement, is a planetary form of sovereignty, "Climate Leviathan," or populist forms of "Climate Behemoth" addressing the climate catastrophe from the narrow and ultimately self-defeating ambit of the nation-state.

70. Achille Mbembe, *Critique of Black Reason* (Durham, NC: Duke University Press, 2017), 3.

71. Tomasz Konicz, "Zu Effizient für Diese Welt," *Analyze &Kritik*, No. 642 (16 October 2018), www.akweb.de/ak_s/ak642/17.htm. Also see Jordan von Manalastas, "Walls on a Drowning World," *Aestheticide*, 29 April 2019, aestheticide.com/2019/04/28/walls-on-a-drowning-world/.

72. Christian Lenhardt, "Anamnestic Solidarity: The Proletariat and its *Manes*," *Telos*, No. 25 (21 September 1975): 133–54.

73. See Tithi Bhattacharya, ed., *Social Reproduction Theory: Remapping Class, Recentering Oppression* (London: Pluto Press, 2017).

74. Ato Sekyi-Otu, *Left Universalism, Africacentric Essays* (New York: Routledge, 2019), 171.

PART I

History

2

The "Hope of the Hopeless": Contemporary Lessons from Marxist Struggles Against Hitler and Mussolini

Ingo Schmidt

In the hallways of the ages, on the road to history,

What we do now will always be with us.

It's a chance to give new meaning to every move we make,

In the caverns, in the caves, where we come from.

Instead of cursing the darkness,

Light a candle for where we're going,

There's something ahead, worth looking for.

Light a candle in the darkness,

So others might see ahead …

Neil Young[1]

Back in the 1990s, the liberal centre enjoyed unprecedented power and legitimacy. With the bursting of the New Economy bubble, the war on terror, and a world economic crisis later, the same centre seems to be challenged by a populist upsurge.[2] Some authors on the left see populism as an overly vague catch-all term that lumps together new political formations on the right and the left but glosses over the links between capitalist crises and the emergence of such new formations.[3] However, this doesn't mean that labelling new formations on the right as *fascist* makes things much clearer. To the contrary, fascism has a long history as a curse word, devoid of content across the political spectrum. As an analytical term, liberals and conservatives have often equated fascism with communism, much like today's liberals who throw left- and right-wing populists into the same basket. In both cases, liberals and conservatives present capitalism, which they equate with liberal democracy, as the alternative. On the left, Horkheimer's dictum that "whoever is not willing to talk about capitalism should also keep quiet about fascism" may actually be the only point of agreement.[4]

Beyond that, the new right is being labelled as everything from "proto-fascist" to "post-fascist."[5] Underlying definitions can be as generic as Amin's claim that fascism is about managing capitalism in an authoritarian manner.[6] This would include nineteenth-century monarchies in Germany and Russia as much as a plethora of twentieth-century military dictatorships. Amin doesn't include any of them in his discussion of the historical origins of contemporary fascism and doesn't make clear what exactly distinguishes formations he calls fascist from other forms of authoritarian rule. And so, we come full circle. To avoid the vagueness of the concept of fascism, other authors on the left prefer to use another vague label: populism.[7] Distinguishing between left- and right-wing populisms may make things somewhat clearer, but it would be far-fetched to call either of them well defined.[8]

It would be easy to establish an a priori checklist and then go out and see whether it matches observable realities.[9] This is what many liberal and conservative theoreticians of totalitarianism have done and, sure enough, they did find analogies between historical fascism and communism. But they never looked for the socioeconomic conditions that might have produced the political phenomena on their checklist. The question of whether fascist and communist political regimes operate on the same economic basis or whether different economic systems could produce similar, if not identical, political regimes wasn't even asked. The political purpose of equating fascism and communism and separating them from capitalism and its liberal superstructures was hidden behind a priori definitions. In this respect, Amin and Foster just reiterate, and rightly so, the standard left critique of liberal and conservative theories of totalitarianism. Yet, as shown, this neither implies that all political movements on the right are necessarily fascist nor does it mean that the concepts of fascism or, for that matter, populism, are anywhere near clarity.

Lack of clarity is often the result of scholarly sloppiness or political intentions taking precedence over scientific rigour. But it can also point to a situation in which reality changes faster than theoretical and empirical work can capture. In this regard, contradictory and vague terms such as "proto-fascism," "post-fascism" or "right-wing populism" may simply reflect the emergence and transformations of political formations that are still very much in flux. And that is the point of departure for the following attempt to catch at least a glimpse of the origins and possible transformations of today's new right. To this end, I will introduce Marxist theories of fascism in their historical context and compare that context with the conditions under which today's new right is developing. The rationale behind the focus on Marxism is twofold: Marxist socialism was the fascists' declared enemy in the 1920s and 1930s and socialists sought to develop anti-fascist struggles on the basis of Marxist theories.

In a similar vein, the following analysis seeks to understand the new right of today in a way that could help to build left alternatives to it. It will reveal parallels between historical fascism and the new right, namely that both developed in the aftermath of deep economic crises and attract their mass support from segments of the working and middle classes. But the analysis will also highlight significant differences. The economic crises to which historical fascism responded was part of a larger crisis caused by rivalries between national capitals firmly tied to colonial powers. No such rivalries exist today. Contemporary capitalism dominates states in such a way that they sustain a global regime of capital mobility. Under neoliberal globalization, great power struggles over colonial empires and zones of influence have become baseless. If there is a threat to global capitalism, it comes from right-wing, and sometimes left-wing, movements that promise protections against the downgrading that the popular classes suffered under the reign of global capital. By contrast, historical fascism was a response to the socialist challenge that became possible during the crises of colonial capitalism. No such challenge exists today. The new right attracts the discontents of neoliberal globalization and will continue to do so until socialist alternatives emerge, possibly out of the struggles against the new right.

CAPITAL, STATES AND CRISES

It was beyond dispute amongst Marxists during the 1920s and 1930s that the social dislocations and misery brought about by World War I and the economic crises in its aftermath were a breeding ground for fascism in Europe. The only controversial question was whether or not capitalism could get back on track. Drawing on Lenin's argument that the complete division of the world among the great powers depleted capitalism's potential for market expansion,[10] some communist Marxists argued that things got even worse for market-seeking capitalists when the emergence of the

Soviet Union actually *diminished* the world market.[11] Others derived the diagnosis of a general or terminal crisis of capitalism from the argument that it was the factors Marx had identified as temporary offsets to the fall of the profit rate which had been depleted.[12] This diagnosis was shared by dissident communists like Trotsky and Thalheimer but disputed by the Menshevik economist Kondratieff and by Hilferding, chief theoretician of the German Social Democrats. Kondratieff argued that the post-World War I crisis was part of a long downswing that would eventually pave the way for another long boom.[13] Hilferding went even further, arguing that the fusion between industries and banks into a highly concentrated finance capital allowed company executives to relocate funds between different sectors of the economy in such a way that major crises could be avoided.[14] Under the reign of the Hohenzollern Empire, finance capital fused its power with the vested interests of large landowners and the military into a project of protectionism and imperialist expansion. However, the political representation of the working class in the Weimar Republic, Hilferding argued, could serve as a countervailing power to capital and steer the economy from imperialist adventures into a prosperous future.[15]

From this angle, the post-World War I crisis was not part of a general crisis of capitalism, but just a hangover from the war. These ideas might have had some currency during the short period of economic and political stabilization during the mid-1920s, but once the Great Depression rendered them illusory, Hilferding and most other Social Democrats with him turned back to the orthodox view that crises are an unpreventable part of the capitalist game. Instead of mobilizing support for the fiscal stimulus ideas from unions and some state functionaries, Social Democrats who did not see any chance for a socialist transition, which, according to Second International orthodoxy, would have been the only way to overcome crises, supported bourgeois coalition governments and their austerity policies in parliament. Efforts to keep the Nazis out of government by tolerating any bourgeois coalition backfired, because social democracy's affiliation with the austerity policies of these governments cost them so dearly at the ballot box that they lost their vetoing minority. However, the increasing difficulty of forming governments without the Nazis wasn't the only reason that ruling elites eventually supported a coalition under Hitler's chancellorship. Communist gains in the two elections before Hitler became chancellor were far from signalling a return of the revolutionary upheavals that had flared up between

1918 and 1923, but were enough to convince the ruling elites that it was time to take pre-emptive measures (see Chapter 11).

With the onset of the Great Depression, communists found their thesis of a general crisis of capitalism confirmed and expected impoverished proletarian masses to rally behind their revolutionary banners. But these masses were far from forming a revolutionary force. A united front with the Social Democrats, for which dissident currents on both wings of the workers' movement were calling, might have been strong enough to stop Hitler's rise to power but lacked any programmatic basis. While the Social Democrats defended a dying Weimar Republic, the Communists dreamt of a Soviet Germany. The Keynesian policies that might have helped to solve the immediate problems of mass unemployment and poverty were beyond the horizon of both, even though there was no shortage of respective proposals in Germany as in other countries.[16] It was left to Hitler to pick up such proposals to build the Nazi war machine that, in the short run, did create employment and, in the long run, aimed at paying for the war through the super-exploitation of populations in occupied territories.[17]

Less concerned with economic policies than with state structures, some Marxists tried to understand what kind of regime it was that the Nazis had established. Neumann called it "totalitarian monopoly capitalism" but argued that the regime was riven by internal conflicts and hence much less stable than it appeared.[18] Pollock, on the other hand, considered the Nazi regime as a new economic order that transcended capitalist cycles of crises.[19] Economically, it was just another variety of "state capitalism" to him.[20] In other words, the possibility of an organized *democratic* capitalism, that Hilferding wanted the Weimar Republic to be, became reality as an organized *terrorist* capitalism under the Nazis. Kalecki realized that a terrorist regime didn't need an industrial reserve army of labour to keep wages within the bounds deemed acceptable by capitalists.[21]

These authors were writing at a time when nineteenth-century liberal states, almost exclusively concerned with the protection of private property rights, collided with emerging twentieth-century interventionist states that would add political rules to the capitalist game and funnel large sums of money through their accounts to keep capital accumulation on track. Inevitably, in such times of fast changes and collisions, the concepts they used were provisional, marked by old certainties that no longer made sense and speculation about a future still hard to grasp.

Nevertheless, they were on to something that was unfolding in Germany and other European countries. Tragically though, it was only after the Nazis had consolidated their terror regime that democratic capitalism came to terms with Keynesian interventionism.[22] And even that coming to terms happened, as in Sweden, only on the periphery of the capitalist centres or, as in the United States, was heavily influenced by the Nazi challenge. After all, New Deal policies focused on micro-economic regulations in ways akin to Hilferding's plans for an organized capitalism, but weren't able to pull the economy out of recession. This didn't happen until the turn to "military Keynesianism" that prepared the United States' entry to World War II.

After World War II, some kind of balance between welfare states and warfare economies was reached, while imperialist rivalries gave way to the formation of a collective imperialism under US leadership.[23] In this new imperialism, the United States ran a vast military-industrial complex that guaranteed, along with the US dollar as international reserve currency and technological leadership, its dominant position. The Cold War helped to keep labour under control as any activist stepping beyond the corporatist borders of the Keynesian state was considered an outside enemy. Under these conditions, most, but not all, layers of Western working classes could be integrated, helping to stabilize the long post-war boom as aspiring consumers. However, after years of high employment and under increasing pressures to work faster to compensate capitalists for the rising real wages they had to pay, some workers did step outside the business unionists' rulebook. A series of wildcat strikes, accompanied by new social movements protesting the exclusion of women, ethnic minorities and immigrants from the Keynesian deal, raised Kalecki's spectre of a profit squeeze under democratic capitalism. This happened at a time when the World War II adversaries, Germany and Japan, flooded world markets with mass-produced goods and the US economy felt increasingly burdened with the costs of sustaining collective imperialism.[24]

Interestingly, capitalist and middle-class responses to this left upsurge of the 1960s and 1970s were very different from those in the 1920s and 1930s. The latter produced historical fascism as an attempt to restore the pre-World War I order – which combined liberalism for the propertied classes with authoritarianism for the popular masses – but supplemented it with a popular basis and pushed the development of the forces of production beyond the level that had been reached under colonial capitalism. Yet the ideological integration around "imagined communities" of superior peoples did not achieve the material gains that fascist movements had promised.[25] The tension between popular classes' expectations and the capitalist dictatorship need to keep such expectations under control was one of the key reasons for the infighting in the fascist "Behemoth."[26] The other was conflicts about timing, strategy and financing of the war effort. Unprecedented propaganda machines notwithstanding, the main lever of fascist rule vis-à-vis domestic popular classes and external adversaries was brute force.

Capitalist responses to the "long 1960s" upsurge,[27] at least in the capitalist centres, saw violence restricted to an ultima ratio and installed finance as the key lever to roll back insurgent movements and the institutional bastions of labour in the Keynesian welfare state. There were neofascist responses also, but the dominant factions of capital had no interest in using them as storm troopers like Italian and German capitalists had done in the 1920s and 1930s. They could rely on a blend of authoritarian and market populist propaganda that was effectively dispersed by the media-corporate complex.[28] And whereas Hilferding had witnessed a *merger* of industry and banks,[29] finance from the 1980s onwards acquired a *dominant* position. To meet the profit benchmarks established by private banking, central banks, ministries of finance and global governance institutions, welfare states had to cut back some provisions and privatize others. At the same time, production processes were restructured in a way that systematically bypassed "unreasonable" legal standards and union representation. However, fiscal and financial crises that helped to open new markets in the peripheries and public sectors of the centres from the 1980s to the 1990s have turned inwards since the bursting of the New Economy bubble in 2001. Since then, even low-paying jobs and reduced social benefits have become increasingly insecure. Growing inequalities are being loaded on top of even faster-growing insecurities. In the face of these developments, market populism has now lost its currency and created a severe legitimation crisis.[30] Yet unlike in the aftermath of World War I or during the "long 60s," there is no left challenge to capitalist rule that would induce capitalists to seek fascist support to ward off such a challenge.

CLASS RELATIONS

Responding to the rise of Italian fascism in the early 1920s, Zetkin defined fascism as "concentrated expression of the general offensive undertaken by the world bourgeoisie against the proletariat"; she characterized it as "a punishment of the proletariat for failing to carry on the revolution begun in Russia" and argued that it is sustained "not by a narrow caste but by broad social layers, large masses that reach even into the prole-tariat."[31] As could be expected from any good communist, she put the failure to carry on the revolution at social democracy's doorstep, a charge that Comintern leaders soon escalated to the much further-reaching charge that social democrats really are "social fascists." The so charged, it should be noted, returned the favour by calling communists "red painted fascists." These mutual charges are not only another example of the inflationary use of the word fascism, which makes it difficult to use it as a scholarly concept, but, more importantly, they also give a hint at the poisonous atmosphere between social democrats and communists that left little room for the dissidents in each camp to work towards a united front against fascism.

These dissidents took seriously Zetkin's argument that fascism differed from other forms of authoritarian rule in having a popular mass basis, but tended to downplay working-class support and focused very much on old and new middle classes. Drawing on Marx's *18th Brumaire*, Thalheimer, a leading figure of the Communist Party opposition in Germany, and Trotsky argued that war, crises and revolutionary upheavals had created a precarious balance between workers and capitalists.[32] In this situation, the middle classes, economically impoverished and socially dislocated just as much as the working classes, supported Mussolini and Hitler like French peasants supported Louis Bonaparte after the defeat of the 1848 revolution. To maintain their social position, capitalists would leave political power to the fascists, which, as Bauer, one of the leaders of the Austrian Social Democrats, pointed out, meant not only the terrorist suppression of communist insurgencies, but also the rollback of the social reforms that workers had won even though the further-reaching goals of those insurgencies had not been reached.[33] Mussolini and Hitler came to power *after* revolutionary movements had been defeated; in this sense they don't represent, contrary to Zetkin's claims, the "general *offensive* undertaken by the world bourgeoisie against the proletariat" but the *consolidation* of the counter-revolution.[34]

Bauer, Thalheimer, Trotsky and some others were certainly right in pointing at the fact that fascism was more than an instrument in the hands of capital, and also in stressing the contradictions between fascist mass organizations and business elites. However, they glossed over what was for socialists the inconvenient truth that mass support came not only from the middle classes, but also from the working classes. Workers were less likely than middle-class folks to follow Mussolini or Hitler, but the very fact that some of them did, along with individuals from all other classes, indicated that the fascist promise to dissolve class society and struggle in an ethnically purified nation found an echo amongst the socially dislocated who were eager to play their assigned roles within the national community. Taking the cross-class support for fascists into account would have required a change in political strategy. The united front that communist and social democratic dissidents fought for during the Great Depression was very much modelled after the general strike against the Kapp Putsch in 1920. That strike was called by the social-democratic-leaning Union Federation and, after some hesitation, also supported by the Communists. The putsch was carried out by right-wing militias but couldn't rely on support from mass organizations comparable to the Nazi party and their storm troopers a decade later.

The need to build an anti-fascist front beyond the ranks of the workers' movement was recognized only belatedly by the Comintern that, like the Social Democrats, had steadfastly opposed calls for a united front until the Nazis came to power. However, the turn to the Popular Front announced by the Comintern at its 1935 congress didn't delve very much into the question of why many of the individuals from different class backgrounds that were now called to unite in anti-fascist action had supported fascists in the first place. Dimitroff, who announced the turn to the Popular Front, reiterated the long-held Comintern definition of fascism as "the open terrorist dictatorship of the most reactionary, most chauvinistic and most imperialist elements of finance capital."[35] In a way, this is a truism. But it glosses over the fact that this dictatorship came into power with the help of many who did not belong to the most reactionary, most chauvinistic and most imperialist elements of finance capital, but who supported these elements anyway. In this respect, Dimitroff neglected the reasons why the alliance between fascists and finance capital had support from the popular classes, like Bauer, Thalheimer and Trotsky had done. The latter had registered the *fact* of middle-class support for fascism, but didn't look into individuals' motives for it. Dimitroff saw fascist supporters largely as victims of Nazi propaganda and as those misguided by the Social Democrats. He even pointed at some mistakes that the Communists made before turning to the Popular Front, but didn't ask why Nazi propaganda resonated so strongly and whether this would also have been the case if there had been a united workers' front before Hitler was appointed chancellor.

In terms of mass support, similarities between historical fascism and today's new right seem striking. However, the underlying class relations and therefore, one would think, the reasons for this support are completely different. Theories of fascism that were developed in the tracks of Marx's *18th Brumaire* argued that the middle classes, unable to pursue their class interests on their own terms, were helplessly squeezed between the two main classes of capitalism, the proletariat and the bourgeoisie.[36] Whether this was true back then is open for debate, but it certainly isn't true today. As a class *in* itself, the working class today is much bigger, within the capitalist centres and even more so on a global scale,[37] but as a class *for* itself, and hence as a social force with a determining impact on capitalist development, it exists only in small pockets at best.[38]

Fascist regimes in the 1930s had promised their followers a prosperous future. In actuality, they established a reign of terror over the popular classes and eventually sent them off to die in unwinnable wars. Democratic capitalism, after World War II, institutionalized the countervailing powers of the working class and although it preserved capitalists' right to manage, it did offer popular classes unprecedented material gains during the long post-World War II boom. Yet, when militant movements overstepped the limits of "reasonable" demands and the end of the boom cut into profits, capitalists turned to unmaking the then existing working classes to roll back their bargaining power. For the most part, this unmaking occurred within the institutional framework of the Keynesian state, but the triad of labour-saving technologies, reorganization and relocation drained the bargaining power once enshrined in these institutions. At the same time, the new social movements that might have formed a united front with workers' movements, and thereby helped the latter to get over their own limitations, saw their radical wings clipped and their mainstream bodies co-opted into some kind of progressive neoliberalism. All of this left individuals who were discontented with neoliberal capitalism with the choice of either taking their concerns to a seemingly outdated and toothless labour movement or to the friendly front organizations of neoliberalism, where any possibly profit-impeding idea was filtered out. At least, this was the choice until the new right showed a third way between old labour and new identity politics: a way leading into a fancied order of clearly demarcated nation-states where world market competition no longer existed and people were not expected to constantly re-invent themselves in a competitive fashion.[39]

Today's new right does have some support from big capitalists, but certainly not, unlike during the inter-war period in Italy and Germany, from the dominant factions of national bourgeoisies, let alone those segments of big capital that have turned themselves into a transnational capitalist class. The dominant factions of capital are far from seeking an alliance with the new right and its mass-support basis to consolidate counter-revolutionary victories. The counter-reform that they initiated from the 1980s onwards has been so successful that no revolutionary, or even mildly reformist, challenge from the left exists today. In the absence of challenges from the left, the discontent produced by neoliberal counter-reform is expressed in xenophobic and protectionist terms. Xenophobia is just a nuisance for progressive neoliberalism, though a viable threat to many who are targeted as enemies of a "chosen people." However, protectionism could be a challenge to the neoliberal globaliz-ation on which the power and profits of the dominant factions of capital rely. Accordingly, rather than seeking an alliance with the new right, these factions seek refuge in governments of appointed experts, rather than elected politicians. Needless to say, the injection of even more technocracy into democratic institutions perfectly plays into the hands of the new right that presents itself as the authentic representation of the people vis-à-vis disconnected and arrogant elites.

SOCIAL PSYCHOLOGY

The Nazis promised everything to everybody. Workers were looking forward to jobs and generous pay cheques, peasants awaited good prices for their crops, storekeepers prepared for rising sales, and capitalists couldn't wait to restore crisis-shattered profits. All it took to make this dream come true: support the Führer in his relentless efforts to cleanse the German people of Jewish decadence in all its manifestations, from stock market speculation to social democratic defence of democracy and communist agitation for a Bolshevik revolution. And the burden of the Versailles Treaty, another Jewish conspiracy against the Germans, needed to be thrown off.

Anti-fascists of different stripes, whatever else they disagreed on, denounced Nazi demagogy and tried to explain that the Nazis wouldn't be able to make good on all of their promises. Most anti-fascists also argued that Nazi ties to finance capital, however conflicted these ties may have been, implied that profits and war, the Nazi's dearest passions, would be on the top of their agenda. Some anti-fascists felt that rational arguments had no chance against Nazi demagogy. A few went even further and suggested that this demagogy was not only silencing reason, which implied that the latter would prevail if the former could be turned off, but that it was *demagogy itself* that made the Nazis so appealing. For example, Reich took as his point of departure the argument that,

A cleavage [had developed] between the economic basis, which developed to the Left, and the ideology of broad layers of society, which developed to the Right. This cleavage was overlooked; consequently, no one gave a thought to asking how broad masses living in utter poverty could become nationalistic. Explanations such as "chauvinism," "psychosis," "the consequences of Versailles," are not of much use, for they do not enable us to cope with the tendency of a distressed middle class to become radicalized by the right; such explanations do not really comprehend the processes at work in this tendency.[40]

Reich, though breaking new theoretical ground by trying to apply Freudian psychoanalysis to the analysis of social phenomena, focused as much on the middle classes as on the theories of fascism drawing on Marx's *18th Brumaire*. His main argument was that socialization through families, schools and churches produces sexual repression that, in turn, breeds sadism. The Nazis, with their vicious propaganda, invited individuals to either act out their sadism or enjoy themselves watching others doing it. The "enemies" against which Nazi violence was directed were defined in racial terms, allegedly representing a threat to "racial purity" that the Aryans had to ward off to gain the strength needed to build the Third Reich. Crucially, Reich established a connection between sexual repression and the openness to Nazi racism, in general, and anti-semitism, in particular.

In a similar fashion, Fromm identified an authoritarian personality attracted to Nazi demagogy and violence. But, whereas Reich found the sources of sexual repression that shaped the social character of his contemporaries within institutions, Fromm traced the roots of authoritarian personalities back to the dawn of capitalism. Liberation from serfdom and guild laws, Fromm argued, produced economic insecurities, anxieties and alienation.[41] This was the basis for the authoritarian personality desperately seeking stability in a seemingly chaotic world – even if this meant surrendering one's freedom to new masters. Among all their other promises, fascists in Italy and Germany also pledged to the creation of a corporate state that would assign a secure role to everyone. The hope for social stability might have been as least as important in attracting support as the prospect of economic advancement.

It should be noted that the generation that constituted historical fascism's mass basis was socialized in families, schools and churches at a time when these institutions, by and large, carried forward pre-capitalist values. These values offered little orientation in the face of the diffusion of the capitalist mode of production in general, and particularly not during times when the then existing capitalism and remnants of the old feudal order had collapsed. The dissolution of the pre-capitalist order and the complementary rise of capitalist insecurities, at least for the popular classes, may have been producing authoritarian personalities with repressed sexualities for a long time, but these people didn't come out to join counter-revolutionary mass movements before capitalism, more precisely nineteenth-century colonial capitalism, and being drowned in war, economic crises and revolution.

The promise to restore order helped the Nazis to channel mass desperation and sadism into a counter-revolutionary movement. This gave their project a decidedly *conservative* character. At the same time, though, their response to the challenge from the left led them to the co-optation and perversion of left ideas, hence the label "national *socialists*." The claim to be progressive in some sort of socialist way was dropped once the Nazis were in power, but the totalitarian state that they created pushed forward the destruction of pre-capitalist institutions that, however repressive they had been, had offered some protection against capitalist insecurities. In this regard, the Nazi project carried *capitalist modernity* forward. Families, schools and churches didn't disappear – the family was actually hailed by the Nazis – but they no longer represented feudal values and were fully subjugated to the Nazi regime instead.[42]

The "de-feudalization" of families, schools and churches, carried forward by fascist regimes, but also under democratic capitalism, reached a point where they couldn't produce the type of authoritarianism and sexual repression that Fromm and Reich had analysed. However, the "desublimation" brought about by the capitalist penetration of these institutions was repressive. It produced new forms of an "unhappy consciousness,"[43] one where consumerism offered compensation for the alienation experienced at workplaces and through welfare state administration. Ironically, it was the new left that tried, drawing on Reich, Fromm and Marcuse, to initiate a politics of liberation which unleashed an authoritarian response that proved just how unhappy mass consciousness in advanced industrial society, the subtitle of Marcuse's *One-Dimensional Man*, had been. The "Fear of Freedom" that Fromm had diagnosed in the face of historical fascism came back with a vengeance and was successfully channelled into an authoritarian populism that, along with advocacy for market liberation, served as the ideological cover for the neoliberal counter-reform in its early stages.[44] Similar fears fuel the new right today. Compared to the 1970s, when welfare states were facing a crisis of legitimacy despite providing significant levels of social protection, the fear of freedom is continuously fuelled by fears of losing one's job, home or social status today because social protections have been cut to size during the neoliberal wave of accumulation.

Fears transformed into hate mark the faces of today's new right supporters, as they did during the transition from the Keynesian to the neoliberal wave of accumulation in the 1970s and before the breakthrough of Keynesian accumulation in the 1920s and 1930s. Unlike during those latter times, today's new right is divided between small neofascist gangs and populist parties with a significant electoral following. This is very different from the merging of storm troopers and voters that Mussolini and Hitler could organize. Moreover, the dominant factions of capital today see the new right with its calls for protectionism as a nuisance, if not a threat, to neoliberal globalization. Hence, their willingness to form alliances with this new right is limited. During the post-World War I period, by contrast, the dominant factions of the Italian and German bourgeoisies and significant currents of other countries' bourgeoisies were willing to surrender the exercise of political power to fascists in order to ward off the challenges of revolutionary and reformist socialism. They also used their alliances with fascism to continue the imperialist rivalries that had not been settled by World War I. Today's wars are more about maintaining imperial control over the peripheries and, to some degree, containing the rise of emerging economies, notably China, rather than rivalries between the centres. For these kinds of war, capitalists don't need fascist war dogs on the home front.

NOTES

Unless otherwise stated, URLs were last accessed on 8 October 2019.

1. Neil Young, "Light a Candle," recorded 2008–9, track #9 on *Fork in the Road*, Reprise Records, compact disc, © Neil Young/Silver Fiddle Music.
2. Francis Fukuyama, "The Populist Surge," *The American Interest*, 9 February 2018, www.the-american-interest.com/2018/02/09/the-populist-surge/; Cas Mudde, "Europe's Populist Surge," *Foreign Affairs*, November/December 2016, www.foreignaffairs.com/articles/europe/2016-10-17/europe-s-populist-surge; Chantal Mouffe, *For a Left Populism* (London: Verso, 1999).
3. Samir Amin, "Fascism Returns to Contemporary Capitalism," *Monthly Review* 66, No. 4 (2014): 1–12; John Bellamy Foster, "Why It's Not Populism," *Monthly Review* 69, No. 2 (2017): 1–24.
4. Max Horkheimer, "The Jews and Europe," in Stephen Bronner and Douglas MacKay Kellner, eds., *Critical Theory and Society* (1939; New York: Routledge, 1989), 92.
5. William Robinson and Mario Barrera, "Global Capitalism and Twenty-First Century Fascism: A US Case Study," *Race & Class* 43, No. 3 (2012): 4–29; Enzo Traverso, "Post-Fascism: A Mutation Still Underway," 17 March 2017, www.versobooks.com/blogs/3130-post-fascism-a-mutation-still-underway.
6. Samir Amin, "Fascism Returns to Contemporary Capitalism."
7. Bill Fletcher Jr., "Stars and Bars: Understanding Right-Wing Populism in the USA," *Socialist Register* 52 (2016): 296–311; Ingo Schmidt, "The Populist Race: Neoliberalism Falling Behind, New Right Forging Ahead, Left Stumbling Along," *Perspectives on Global Development and Technology* 18 (2019): 61–78.
8. For a different view see: Samir Gandesha, "Right versus Left Populism," *Zeitschrift für kritische Theorie* 46/47 (2018): 214–35.
9. Zbigniew Brzezinski and Carl Friedrich, *Totalitarian Dictatorship and Autocracy* (Cambridge, MA: Harvard University Press, 1956).
10. Vladimir Lenin, *Imperialism, The Highest Stage of Capitalism* (1916; London: Penguin, 2010).
11. Eugen Varga, *The Decline of Capitalism* (London: Communist Party of Great Britain, 1924).
12. Henryk Grossmann, *The Law of Accumulation and the Breakdown of the Capitalist System* (1929; London: Pluto Press, 1992).
13. Nikolai Kondratieff, "The Long Waves in Economic Life," *Review of Economics and Statistics* 17, No. 6 (1935): 105–15.
14. Rudolf Hilferding, *Finance Capital: A Study in the Latest Phase of Capitalism* (1911; London: Routledge, 2006).
15. Rudolf Hilferding, "Probleme der Zeit," *Die Gesellschaft* 1, No. 1 (1924): 1–17.
16. George Garvy, "Keynes and the Economic Activists of Pre-Hitler Germany," *Journal of Political Economy* 83, No. 2 (1975): 391–405; Bradford Lee, "The Miscarriage of Necessity and Invention: Proto-Keynesianism and Democratic States in the 1930s," in Peter Hall, ed., *The Political Power of Economic*

Ideas: Keynesianism Across Nations (Princeton, NJ: Princeton University Press, 1989), 129–70.

17. Werner Abelshauser, "Guns, Butter, and Economic Miracles," in Mark Harrison, ed., *The Economics of World War II* (Cambridge: Cambridge University Press, 2000), 122–76.

18. Franz Neumann, *Behemoth: The Structure and Practice of National Socialism* (1944; Chicago: Ivan R. Dee, 2009).

19. Frederick Pollock, "Is National Socialism a New Order?" *Studies in Philosophy and Social Science* 9, No. 3 (1942): 440–55.

20. Frederick Pollock, "State Capitalism: It's Possibilities and Limitations," *Studies in Philosophy and Social Science* 9, No. 2 (1941): 200–25.

21. Michal Kalecki, "Political Aspects of Full Employment," *Political Quarterly* 14, No. 4 (1943): 322–30.

22. Mark Blyth, *Great Transformations: Economic Ideas and Institutional Change in the Twentieth Century* (Cambridge: Cambridge University Press, 2002).

23. Ingo Schmidt, "Rosa Luxemburg's Accumulation of Capital: A Centennial Update with Additions from Long Wave Theory and Karl Polanyi's Great Transformation," *Critique: Journal of Socialist Theory* 40, No. 3 (2012): 337–56.

24. Robert Brenner, *The Economics of Global Turbulence* (London: Verso, 2006).

25. Benedict Anderson, *Imagined Communities: Reflections on the Origins and Spread of Nationalism* (London: Verso, 1983).

26. Neumann, *Behemoth*.

27. Gerd-Rainer Horn, *The Spirit of 68: Rebellion in Western Europe and North America, 1956–1976* (Oxford: Oxford University Press, 2008).

28. Stuart Hall, "The Great Moving Right Show," *Marxism Today*, January 1979: 14–20; Schmidt, "The Populist Race."

29. Hilferding, *Finance Capital*.

30. Ingo Schmidt, "Unmaking Neoliberal Europe and the Search for Alternatives," *Perspectives on Global Development and Technology* 12 (2013): 41–62; Ingo Schmidt, "The Populist Race."

31. Clara Zetkin, "Der Kampf gegen den Faschismus," in *Zur Theorie und Taktik der kommunistischen Bewegung* (1923; Leipzig: Reclam, 1974), 292. English excerpts: www.marxists.org/archive/zetkin/1923/08/fascism.htm.

32. Karl Marx, *The Eighteenth Brumaire of Louis Bonaparte*, accessed 12 April 2019, www.marxists.org/archive/marx/works/1852/18th-brumaire/; August Thalheimer, "Über den Faschismus," in Gruppe Arbeiterpolitik, ed., *Der Faschismus in Deutschland* (1930; Bremen: Gruppe Arbeiterpolitik, 1981), 28–46. English excerpts: www.marxists.org/archive/thalheimer/works/fascism.htm; Leon Trotsky, "Bonapartismus und Faschismus," in *Porträt des Nationalsozialismus* (1934; Essen: Arbeiterpresse Verlag, 1999), 336–43. English excerpts: www.marxists.org/archive/trotsky/germany/1934/340715.htm.

33. Otto Bauer, "Der Faschismus," in *Otto Bauer Werkausgabe*, Vol. 4 (1936; Wien: Europa Verlag: 1980), 136–59.

34. Zetkin, "Der Kampf gegen den Faschismus," emphasis added.
35. Georgi Dimitroff, "The Fascist Offensive and the Tasks of the Communist International in the Struggle of the Working Class against Fascism," accessed 12 April 2019, www.marxists.org/reference/archive/dimitrov/works/1935/08_02.htm#s2.
36. Marx, *The Eighteenth Brumaire*.
37. Chris Harman, "The Workers of the World," *International Socialism* 96 (2002): 3–46.
38. Ingo Schmidt, "The Downward March of Labour Halted? The Crisis of Neoliberal Capitalism and the Remaking of Working Classes," *Working USA: The Journal of Labor and Society* 14, No. 1 (2014): 5–22.
39. Nancy Fraser, "From Progressive Neoliberalism to Trump – And Beyond," *American Affairs* 1, No. 4 (Winter 2017), americanaffairsjournal.org/2017/11/progressive-neoliberalism-trump-beyond/.
40. Wilhelm Reich, *The Mass Psychology of Fascism* (1933; New York: Farrar, Straus and Giraux, 1970), 8.
41. Erich Fromm, *The Fear of Freedom* (1941; London: Routledge, 2001).
42. Jeffrey Herf, *Reactionary Modernism: Technology, Culture, and Politics in Weimar and the Third Reich* (Cambridge: Cambridge University Press, 1986).
43. Herbert Marcuse, *One-Dimensional Man: Studies in the Ideology of Advanced Industrial Society* (London: Routledge, 1964), 59–86.
44. Stuart Hall, "The Great Moving Right Show."

3

The Future of Futurism: From the Avant-Garde to the Neo-Avant-Garde, or, How to Imagine Communism by Other Means

Jaleh Mansoor

This chapter will offer a remapping of futurism's lost lineage along two lines of argumentation, one historical and one structural, in order to gain a better understanding of both history's unfinished business and its misrecognized alignments. My claim is that the contradictory structural determinants in present debates about the return of fascism might be freshly understood through a historical optic, one that might also offer a better account of the conditions of emergence of aesthetic contradictions between fascism and futurism now, long dormant and deferred. It will first aim to reconstruct the complicated and asymmetrical relationship between futurism and fascism through a return to primary sources, notably the poet F.T. Marinetti's declarations and missives to none other than Adolf Hitler himself, whom the artist challenged for his rejection of futurism in Nazism. These historical exchanges reveal the tensions among aesthetic and political wars of "position" and "manoeuvre." While the Futurists certainly subscribed to fascist politics, fascists failed to return the favour and were rather sceptical of the futurist programme. For fascism, futurism fell well short of their vaunted neoclassical ideal. The Futurists, in turn, dismissed as "passé" fascist aesthetic, historical, moral and existential ideals. Next, the chapter will explore the uncanny resonance of futurist discourse in the present not only to foreground its actuality, but also to understand what we confront now. These texts also echo Donna Haraway's discussion of the imbrication of biopolitics and technologies that cross the boundaries of the human in *A Cyborg Manifesto*.[1] Haraway locates the originary matrix of the cyborg in the same historical, geopolitical and cultural arena: the experimental state

Figure 3.1 F.T. Marinetti – *Zang Tumb Tumb*, Book Cover, 1914

formations of the early twentieth century and the economy of the present, the twenty-first century in this our era of Apple, Amazon, Google and Facebook. "The main trouble with cyborgs, of course, is that they are the illegitimate offspring of militarism and patriarchal capitalism, not to mention state socialism."[2] Suddenly, now, the singular conjuncture of displacement of human agency, the rise of automation, the hybrid fusion of abstraction and technology in the regime of the Internet, alongside the historically concomitant political swing to forms of authoritarianism in North America, Europe and many parts of the Global South at a time of economic austerity for the many and extreme gains for the one per cent, suggest the eerie relevance of the Futurist avant-garde. Technology, Haraway has argued, forms the very matrix of the political. At the same time, aesthetic mediation informs the "social nervous system" of the global capitalist network, in which the subject's very interiority is crushed under total instrumental domination, thereby portending a fundamental and imperative, if unrationalized, share of political consciousness. As I will suggest, the right seems to have intuited this political–cultural dialectical conjuncture. The left, in its tendency to insist on total demystification, failed to note the significance of aesthetic capacity for politics and therefore failed to note the urgent need for an aesthetics of a collectivized resource distribution and reversal of values, both symbolic and imaginary.

It will be necessary to continue asking after the structural relationship, if not identity, between aesthetics and politics, or aesthetics understood as a form of politics practised by other means. Existing readings of the avant-garde (futurism, dada and constructivism) fail to recognize the extent to which its complex entwinement of politics and aesthetics exceeds the Manichean binary frequently attributed to it by and in the aftermath of Walter Benjamin's famous statement on the "aestheticization of politics" (fascism) and "politicization of art" (communism) in "The Work of Art in the Age of its Technological Reproducibility."[3]

Borrowing a term from Jeremy Gilbert's preface to Maurizio Lazzarato's analysis of the Duchampian readymade, which he takes to be an avatar of the exponential mid-century rise of the non-value productive sector comprised of administration and management in the capitalist core, the avant-gardes *precognize* their future and our present, signalling a soon-to-be hegemonic logic *avant la lettre*.[4] Benjamin missed the fact that fascism and futurism were more inimical than identical, evidenced by the essay "Theories of German Fascism," in which he took fascism to be rooted almost exclusively in the German cultural and German linguistic contexts and which he saw symptomatized by expressionist writers like Ernst Jünger. Despite having essentialized fascism to Germanic language and culture, Benjamin then takes the extracted structure of his conclusions and projects it onto the Italian context.[5] Roman Jakobson, by contrast, addresses the proximity between F.T. Marinetti's and V. Mayakovsky's attention to the operations of the linguistic sign long after both the German and Italian rise to fascisms had come to pass, decontextualized of a historical, cultural matrix.

To bracket futurism off from the other international avant-gardes on aesthetic and political (if not ideological) grounds is to miss the prefiguration of their relation in our present.[6] First, the great majority of artists placed in the category of "futurism" – such as Balla, Boccioni, Severini and Carrà – joined the movement in 1910, as evidenced by becoming signatories to the *Manifesto of Futurist Painters* only in that same year.[7]

None of them had signed onto the 1909 *Manifesto*, nor is there any indication that they were solicited to do so. At this time, many among them were explicitly affiliated with either anarchism or socialism.[8] Second, a reason dating to the year after he got their signatures for the 1910 *Manifesto*, Marinetti was the only signatory to the *Manifesto in Support of War in Libya* in 1911, the year after they joined. Meanwhile, between 1911 and 1913, as Italian politics swung right, some of the earlier signatories, such as Balla, left the movement altogether. Others, like Boccioni, agreed to muzzle their political convictions to remain in what had by then become a kind of corporation in the interest of their careers and practices.

Figure 3.2   Umberto Boccioni – *Riot in the Gallery*, 1909

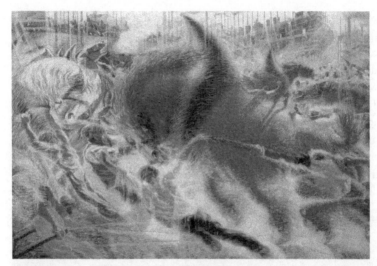

Figure 3.3 Umberto Boccioni – *The City Rises*, 1910

Figure 3.4 Umberto Boccioni – *The Riot*, 1911

By 1914, popular politics in Italy swung to nationalist chauvinism. This nonetheless contradicted the Futurists' participation in *internationalist* vehicles of dissemination which had marked their project from the start of the movement in 1911.

Historian Anja Klock has attempted to establish a direct link from Marinetti and the Italian futurism of the 1930s to the cyber technologies of the twenty-first century.[9] Ana Teixeira Pinto, writing in *Texte Zur Kunst* in June 2017, remarked on this resonance by drawing a comparison between the logic, language and rhetoric of the contemporary alt-right (which she locates in the triangulation between British accelerationism, American West Coast tech culture oriented to the "Singularity," and a perfervid allegiance on the part of both of those cultures to the capitalist libertarian legacy of Ayn Rand)[10] and aspects of the historical left most associated with the avant-garde. Pinto argues:

> The distinction between alt-right and the conventional far Right, on the other hand, is not so much a matter of content but of style, with the alt-right extolling nihilism, sarcasm, and anti-establishment sentiments, among other modalities of dissidence that were formerly the preserve of the Left, traditionally associated with the term "alternative."[11]

Teixeira Pinto locates the cultural and political emphasis on these qualities – nihilism, sarcasm, anti-establishment gestures – in the historical avant-garde across its geopolitical and aesthetic iterations (New York, Swiss and German iterations of dada, French surrealism, and the Russian and Soviet avant-gardes). In this regard, her claim is striking for how it transgresses the carefully delineated and, by now, sacrosanct subcategories of the historical avant-gardes. She notes, by contrast, the *continuities* among them, drawing this continuity into our moment, a synchronic entanglement shown to be diachronically tethered to the present.

The fifth item on Marinetti's list of "dictated intentions" in *The Founding and Manifesto of Futurism* states: "We intend to hymn man at the steering wheel, the ideal axis of which intersects the earth, itself hurled ahead in its own race along the axis of its orbit."[12] Evoking a planetary order in which the machine would at once mimic and align with a greater constellation to bring about another world within this one – victory over a reality principle involving gravity as much as bosses, or liberal capitalism, parliamentary democracy, or the value form; victory over material contingency – might recall that other paradigmatic moment within the historical avant-garde in which the sun itself was declared an object to be conquered and, more significantly still, conquered in such a way that man and the cosmic order itself would overcome division, poverty, even death. In the context of the Russian avant-garde (1912–28), Malevich's *Black Square* of 1915 and its twin, *Red Square: Or Painterly Realism of a Peasant Woman in Two Dimensions*, also from 1915, have stood prefiguratively as a space holder for the furthest aspirational limit of an anarcho-communism, prefiguring that which has not come to pass.[13]

Figure 3.5 F.T. Marinetti – *Parole in Liberta*, 1915

Both of these paintings emerged from the social fomentation of the moment leading to the 1917 October Revolution. Both carry the weight of textual supplements, titles which suggest radical acceleration from abject (gendered) peasantry to infancy of a higher communist order. *Red Square*, in particular, telegraphically addresses so many questions we might subsume – *pace* Lukács – under "the Marxism of Rosa Luxemburg," for the way in which it suggests how primitive accumulation constitutes the ground for proletarianization and therefore revolution in the Marxian account of revolution and necessity.[14] By offering as the "realism" of a "peasant woman" – after the African slave, the most exploited subject position in modernity and capitalism, formerly represented (*Woman with Bucket and Child*, 1910–11, Russian Museum, St. Petersburg, also by Malevich) in a primitivist idiom à la Gauguin – now as an abstract red square and as the very signifier of communist futurity, Malevich's gesture situates itself as a refrigeration of the temporal transformations necessary for its dream to come true. Malevich's peasant woman as "red square" might well and fruitfully be compared to Heidegger's famous reading of the "peasant women" in his analysis of Van Gogh's painting *A Pair of Shoes* (1886) to further tease out the vast divide between fascism and the historical avant-garde, or, at least, one pole of it.[15] Back to Malevich in 1915: this dream of a communism from the ground up, unconstrained by market or state, did not come to pass. However, both paintings have managed, throughout the twentieth century, and well into the present, to almost hieroglyphically symbolize the revolutionary moment, its failures and compromises, and finally serve, as though under the symbol of history, as the very letter of unfinished business, a kind of nod to futures as yet unrealized.[16]

On a more contextual level, however, the *Black Square* resulted from Malevich's agreement to design and construct a stage set for a theatrical production co-conceptualized by his friends, the self-identified "Futurist" poets, Velimir Khlebnikov and Mikhail Matyushin. The script heavily featured a telephone, which is situated as an object emblematic of modernity, an almost "theoretical" thing at that historical moment.[17] This modern object prosthetically extends the ear across space, opening onto another form of social (mis)communication enabled by electricity.[18] Jakobson's discursive association of Marinetti's post-humanist celebration with Malevich's radical vision of a true communism – one that had and has yet to exist, unconstrained by the state apparatus or a compromise to the market as had occurred in the Soviet context by 1920 under the auspices of the NEP (New Economic Policy) – is motivated by the numerous artists and writers who crossed international contexts. In other words, Jakobson simply hinges his argument on the contact among Futurists and Russian anarcho-communist artists such as Malevich and Khlebnikov, the poet with whom he collaborated on the opera *Victory Over the Sun*.

Walter Benjamin's clean binary wherein the politicization of art opens onto communism and the aestheticization of politics becomes fascism may be correct in many ways, but it fails to adequately address Italian futurism. Or, put another way, when applied axiomatically to Italian futurism, the dialectic collapses. The primary problem, here, is that the filiations among comrades across international and ideological lines (a revolutionary politics refusing ideological symbolization or final representation), or among several figures associated with the radical left and with the Bolshevik Revolution, shared a vision of a future to come with Marinetti. Only after the initial experiments with form did differentiated, and often opposing, orientations begin to become clear. One vision (revolutionary communism) initially focused on liberating productive forces in the service of breaking through extant property relations to liberate collective self-realization; the other (Italian futurism) sought to unleash a new humanity despite static property relations. In a long essay first published in the 2 August 1919 edition of the Moscow newspaper *Iskusstvo*, which is to say a full decade after Marinetti's *Founding and Manifesto of Futurism*, and, of course, two years after the Bolshevik Revolution, the linguist Roman Jakobson states that "the overcoming of statics, the discarding of the absolute, is the main thrust of modern times, the order of the day."[19] Citing Italian futurist manifestos, specifically the technical *Manifesto of Painting* from 1910 – which is to say long after Italian futurism's fascist tendencies might have become evident, as it had to some of the futurists themselves, such as Boccioni – Jakobson makes a curious argument that seems to have "stuck" as much as Benjamin's and yet contradicts it. The Soviet linguist elaborates a curious genealogy from cubism to a shared international avant-garde that he calls "futurism," a category encompassing Marinetti as much as the Soviet poet Vladimir Mayakovsky. With at least a decade in analytical hindsight, he not only conflates the Russians and Italians (or decides not to attend to their significant differences); he also seems to see both the communist and the supposedly Italian *fascist* futurisms as sharing a technique: "the canonization of a series of devices which thus also allows one to speak of cubism as a school."[20]

The shipping and commodities magnate Sergei Shchukin had begun travelling by train to Paris in the last decade of the nineteenth century to purchase paintings. He collected French Impressionists, with a decided preference for Claude Monet. By 1914, he had amassed a collection that included Cézanne and Matisse. His frequent trips to Paris and back were no doubt the privilege of the very wealthy. And yet his journey and its frequency are reflected in Jakobson's own occasional movement between Paris, where he met Picasso and Gertrude Stein, and Moscow. Jakobson's genealogy, born of a personal autobiographical narrative, seems motivated by more than a matter of access to the writers and poets he placed in the same category, all beginning from and expanding on cubism. Again, he seems to read a common operational mode or signifying strategy while curiously bracketing ideology: "Futurism brings with it practically no new pictorial devices, instead it widely utilizes Cubist methods."[21] Here, he explicitly posits a structural and operative (if not thematic or ideological) continuity, an almost technical affiliation, between both strands of futurism. Marcel Duchamp's *Nude Descending a Staircase, No. 2* of 1912 was similarly caught in the transitional moment, owing its formal influence to cubism but rejected by the Cubists for appearing futurist.[22] In this, his historical account could not differ more radically from Benjamin's. Jakobson's reading is erroneous at the level of the signifier, ironically his area of expertise. While Soviet Futurists practising across a variety of mediums from painting to poetry, such as Malevich and Mayakovsky, continued to query the signifier and to disarticulate it from its traditional mimetic and representational functions, Italian futurism was eager to recover mimesis by collapsing the sign and the purported real through a form of instrumentalized onomatopoeia in a battle call to technology and war.[23]

The (his)story nonetheless grows more complicated.

However odious a nationalist, masculinist project, the Italian Futurists neither shared nor even understood the commitments of German fascism. These qualities become ideological tenets include a glorification of the past, a desire for a triumphalist narrative rooted in classical antiquity and celebration of agrarian and proletarian identities or, we could say, "concrete" as opposed to "abstract" labour. In this regard fascist aesthetics are diametrically opposed to the Italian Futurists' vilification of history, their call for overcoming the fetishization of Italy's Roman imperial past and the fact that they were privileged urban dwellers, denizens of the modern metropolis. This model of temporality echoes the Marxian maxim that communism represents the domination of the present over the past, as in the *18th Brumaire* in which the past is said to "weigh like a nightmare on the brains of the living."[24] As such, this text is an anticipatory diagnosis of aspects of twentieth-century fascism. Above all, the Futurists wanted to dissociate themselves as much from Italy's post-unification agrarian identity as from its historical empires, in order to free Italy from the burden of the past to clear a future which finally entailed the domination of the industrial north over the agrarian south. If anything, war's role was to clear the field of the past, a kind of "scorched-earth" policy in which there would be nowhere to go but forward. It cannot be overemphasized the extent to which the Nazis, by contrast, wished to claim an ancient past to legitimate and justify their claim to racial superiority. If any one feature defines the avant-garde, it would be the compulsion to reach the furthest horizon of future time, by situating itself prefiguratively as though that longed-for future could be summoned directly through practice.

This places the Italian Futurists out of step with their time, abutting communism, on the one hand, and fascism, on the other, belonging finally to neither category and yet anticipating our own present. To repeat Haraway: "The main trouble with cyborgs, of course, is that they are the illegitimate offspring of militarism and patriarchal capitalism, not to mention state socialism."[25] The cyborg born of the triangulation of militarism and patriarchal capitalism (fascism) and state socialism seems to have had an older sibling in the Italian futurist fantasy of crossing man and machine. Hence, its trajectory lies in the "Singularity," in the possibility of uploading human consciousness into the digital network and also in colonizing Mars, evidenced by the fantasies of techno-entrepreneurs such as Elon Musk and Ray Kurzweil.[26]

But tucked in the pleats of context, F.T. Marinetti felt snubbed and misunderstood. Consequently, he confronted der Führer directly. He demanded to be taken seriously despite having been thrown into the category of *Entartete Kunst* (Degenerate Art),[27] co-created and organized by Adolf Ziegler and Joseph Goebbels in Munich in 1937. They included in it all idioms that might be associated with any of the avant-gardes including German expressionism, some dada and constructivism – in short: any artistic idiom that may have been understood to have issued from the aftermath of cubism. In their war on the avant-garde, the Nazis targeted the very techniques identified by Roman Jakobson as linking futurism across Italian fascist and Soviet communist politics: the autonomy of the signifier and the advent of abstraction. Taking umbrage at this survey exhibition convened at Hitler's behest, Marinetti wrote a response to Hitler addressing the Nazi leader directly. Entitled "Response to Hitler" (1937) and included in the main anthologies of the movement, Marinetti decried the Nazis' allegiance to a traditional symbolic and iconographic register despite the Nazis' own mobilization of new media such as radio and film.[28] Perhaps the friction and antagonism in this odd historical conjuncture suggests that aspects of history's contradictions must be revisited if any insight into the present might yet be gleaned. Marinetti opens his retort by associating futurism with cubism and dadaism. And yet, in the second point of his enumerated missive, he states, "I think that Hitler lapses into another very serious mistake when he regards the Futurist avant-gardes of Germany as either Jewish or Communist."[29] Marinetti displays the most transparent of reactionary defence mechanisms: displacement. For there is no German futurism; there is dada which from Heartfield to Schwitters had declared its sympathies with the radical left. Nonetheless Marinetti insists that futurism is "anti-communist by definition." In his own misunderstanding of what he perceives to be Adolf Hitler's misunderstanding – "Futurism is modernizing innovating accelerating" – he invites the German leader to reflect on the Italian artist Prampolini's sculptures on display in Berlin that same year at the Shell Building.

But the roots of the reciprocal misprision go deeper yet. Let us turn to Guillaume Apollinaire. It was Apollinaire who first applied the term "avant-garde," drawn from military jargon and imported into cultural discourse to denote those forms of articulation, pictorial and poetic, that broke radically with traditional representation, from the signifier's burden of duty to a stable referent in turn tethered to "reality."[30] Apollinaire and Marinetti met sometime between 1906 and 1909. Apollinaire embodies and personifies the complex lines of geological and formal affiliation that connect cubism, dada and Italian futurism. Having moved through the social constellations constituting each, he forged fierce bonds with first Pablo Picasso, who depicts him in *The Family of Saltimbanques* (1905), an homage to the bohemian urban life afforded by modernity. He subsequently undertook collaborations with the Italian Futurists, with whom he published his renowned cablegrams – the work for which he is perhaps best known in literary histories – before finally inspiring Marcel Duchamp who, for his part, immortalizes the artist in the work *Apolinère Enameled* (1916). Marinetti and the Italians

Figure 3.6 Guillaume Apollinaire – *Il Pleut*, 1916

included Apollinaire's textual experiments with theirs; Apollinaire's cablegrams were published in 1913 under the title *L'antitradition futuriste, manifeste-synthèse*. Apollinaire's fluid passage across the geopolitically and ideologically discrete branches (French, Italian and American) of the avant-garde has served as a source of contention for numerous generations of cultural historians, not least for the way in which it suggests

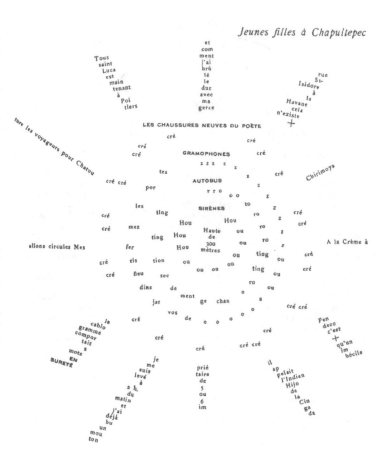

Figure 3.7   Guillaume Apollinaire – *Lettre-Ocean*, 1918

aesthetic and ideological continuity and filiations.[31] His trajectory, in short, challenges the maintenance of easy categories reticulated to clean ideological positions. Apollinaire's own contribution to the moment includes his extended poem "The Futurist Anti-Tradition. Manifesto = Synthesis" (1913), a year after his declaration that the artist wishes

Figure 3.8 Guillaume Apollinaire – *La Cravate et la Montre*, 1918

nothing other than to be "inhuman." Baker situates this fluidity in the contradictions in the battle for position characterizing the historical moment. Benjamin places the contradictions into tidy mutually irreconcilable, even transcendental categories. For instance, he notes the conflict within the left on which the avant-garde occasionally found itself. He recounts one incident in particular in which the long-standing

Figure 3.9   Guillaume Apollinaire – *Cheval*, 1918

antagonism between communists and anarchists, both to the far-left, surfaced in ways that offer the historian some clues into the complex imbrication of aesthetics and politics:

The Dadaists came to the club au fauburg seeking workers. They had been ill informed. Greeted, to their amazement, by an audience of one thousand people, the Dadaists quickly realized that this mass mostly excluded the working class. There were many socialists, who seemed eager to attack the Dadaists. But there were anarchists there too and the comedy of misunderstandings of this evening saw the debate devolve into a vigorous conflict between the socialists and the anarchists, with the anarchists putting up a brisk defense of the four men [artists] and siding with the Dadaists against socialism.[32]

In short, the artists' presence seems to have allowed for the difference among positions to surface, an illumination which begins to differentiate the left from within, suggesting once again a welded relationship between politics and aesthetics (on that no one could challenge Walter Benjamin), yet also suggesting a range of possibilities born of the moment lost to Benjamin's dialectic. The key question specific to Italian futurism, in distinction to both fascist aesthetics on the right and communist futurism on the left, then, becomes one of a question concerning technology. I will turn now to the current conjuncture to pose the question of whether we are witnessing an uncanny return of history's unfinished business or the monstrous return of fascism in our own time.

In our own time, a new hybrid of fascism takes some of its power and force from deeply conflicted historical forms of fascism. As Ana Teixeira Pinto has noted, the new far-right is comprised of the unlikely alliance of Silicon Valley, libertarian accelerationism, corporate nihilism and reactionary masculinist white supremacism, constituting a cultural constellation: "The [current] point of intersection between [the neoreactionary present], contemporary art, and the rhetoric of cyber utopianism, and cyber libertarianism, has been for several years now the *style* known as post-internet."[33] In what remains of this chapter, I will try to parse out the futurist dimension in the kind of fascism she describes. Note, first off, the word *style* and the unlikely conjuncture of a disparate cast of characters sharing no ideology, no immediate project, nothing but "style." And yet "style," as I have argued here, is precisely where futurism links to, yet parts ways with, left avant-gardes. This forms a kind of conjunctural contradiction. Teixeira Pinto states that her analysis is not reducible to saying the alt-right *results* from technology. But we are to understand that a "style" fills the gap left by ideology or technological determination. Steps are missing in the mediation.

The discussion to follow will proceed as an imagined conversation with Pinto's above-mentioned article "Art Washing: Nix (or Neoreaction) and The Alt Right," as a method of rethinking the way that the left has withdrawn from aesthetics altogether in light of the anxiety of Benjamin's account of the rise of Nazism in the late 1930s. Its aim is to imagine otherwise – and to hopefully seize once more on aesthetics as a means by which to fight back. A missing step in Pinto's argument is her tacit, but unargued, claim that aligns aesthetics with the realm of pre-subjective affect. "These overlappings do not imply a unified politics, but rather a shared libidinal investment in the triad of novelty/ technology/ potency." Without naming it, Pinto is summoning Kant's *sensus communis*, understood not only as common (as in commonplace) but in-common and communal (meaning with a sense of others and relation to others), now ossified by technology to the service of the right.[34] But in this she revisits Benjamin's words, reframing the "aestheticization of politics is fascism."[35] In a well-known passage from 1935 to 1936, Benjamin calls Marinetti by name, placing him in the category of fascism, a foregone conclusion:

> "Let art flourish, and the world pass away" says Fascism, expecting from war, as Marinetti claims, the artistic gratification of a sense perception altered by technology. This is the consummation of art for art ... its self-alienation has reached the point where it can experience its own annihilation as supreme aesthetic pleasure.[36]

Hence the question: how do we describe the nexus between aesthetics and ideology? In other words, Pinto *poses* the key question, one of mediation between the uncognized drives of the collective and the individual, and the forms of articulation that "precognize" and help to support or mobilize those drives, yet falls short of imagining how the contemporary left might also mobilize desires and drives. The right has recognized this capacity of aesthetics to operate in this pre-political mode by other means. But her answer is inscribed in the question. I take that question differently: how to describe the nexus between aesthetics and ideology, by placing an emphasis on the "aesthetics" side of the relationship. When Pinto asks "how to capture the imbrications of technological development, capital accumulation, and social formation without collapsing Silicon Valley, accelerationism and post-internet into one single bad object," she overlooks that this is what aesthetics is: a common sense of what is an acceptable horizon of imagination, what is conceivable, imaginable.[37]

Deferring to Shuja Haider's "The Darkness at the End of the Tunnel: Artificial Intelligence and Neoreaction," to connect the Singularity to capital accumulation, Pinto calls affirmation a "Warholian currency."[38] Here, she, at once, nods to and bests Adorno's claim that the culture industry embodies the logic of fascism, now locating it in that exemplary figure of capitalist realist high art: Andy Warhol. To drive the point home, she says, "The same state can address some as a social democracy and others as a fascist regime."[39] Aesthetics is a cognitive faculty constituting an *other* to reason, one which sets the condition for the possibility of a politics – any politics, libertarian or authoritarian, left or right, meta or enacted, imposed, electoral or spectacular – to emerge. Sadly, the right grasped what I provisionally call the "Kant with Sade" phenomenon to describe the mass effect of aesthetics while the left lost as a result of its fear of this faculty other to reason. I am not at all certain that what is these days called "affect theory" speaks to the saturation of aesthetics misunderstood as politics. Benjamin said that "Communism replies by politicizing art."[40] But the dream of communism, or any left formation, has not replied. While the left clung to an interpretation that shifted to ideology and ethics while simultaneously entrenching its belief in scientific rationality dialectically elevated to the status of religion, as evidenced already in World War II, the right, meanwhile, caring nothing for either ethics or science, understood Benjamin's provocation best. For any politics to prevail, aesthetics might be privileged as the primary terrain on which to resuture cognition and affect, a form of cognition independent of rational faculties, a cognitive faculty in its own right, just as Immanuel Kant had defined it in his 1790 *Critique of Judgment*, pendant to *Critique of Pure Reason* in 1781 and *Critique of Practical Reason* in 1788. The easy collapse of aesthetics with fascism, *tout court*, has only served to stoke the presence of the right and alt-right, to provide it with a vehicle of delivery, a Trojan horse long ago dismissed for its political inefficacy. It's time for a communist aesthetics if communism is to have a future.

The recursive conjuncture of fascism and techno-utopianism conditions our present, evidenced by alt-right sympathizers such as Peter Thiel, who is a Stanford graduate affiliated with, and active in, some of the most well-funded conservative think tanks in the United States. By contrast, the contemporary recrudescence of aspirational communism sees the liberation of the productive forces as materially central to the present,[41] as when Marx outlined it in the preface to *A Contribution to the Critique of Political Economy* (1859) and, before that, in his and Engels' *Communist Manifesto* (1848) as social capacities of rupturing the ever-more ossified relations of production;[42] socializing property, as well as labour power, while developing the latter's cognitive powers and capacities. Technology hangs in the balance. Aesthetic mediation, as the right seems to have intuited, tips socially determined political tendencies, collective orientation and shared desire toward one or the other: *either* a fascist centralized surplus value and resource extraction system or collectivized ownership of the means of production, de-alienation of political life and the abolition of the law of value.

At stake is the accelerated development of productive forces (technology) within property relations and the distributions of values and resources. Aesthetics mediates this in a form of consciousness initially autonomous but ultimately prefigurative and productive of political futures. We in the present bear the burden of these histories.

NOTES

Unless otherwise stated, URLs were last accessed on 15 September 2019.

1. Donna J. Haraway, "A Cyborg Manifesto," in *Manifestly Haraway* (1991; Minneapolis, MN: University of Minnesota Press, 2016). See Anja Klock, "Of Cyborg Technologies and Fascistized Mermaids: Giannina Censi's Aerodanze in 1930s Italy," *Theater Journal* 51, No. 4 (1999): 395–415.
2. Ibid., 9.
3. Walter Benjamin, "The Work of Art in the Age of Technological Reproducibility," drafted Dec. 1935–Feb. 1936, in *Collected Writing*, trans. Edmund Jephcott and Henry Zohn (Cambridge, MA: Harvard University Press, 2002), 122.
4. Jeremy Gilbert, "Experimental Politics: Its Background and Some Implications," Preface to Maurizio Lazzarato, *Experimental Politics: Work, Welfare, and Creativity in the Neoliberal Age*, ed. Jeremy Gilbert (Cambridge, MA: MIT Press, 2017), xxxv.
5. Although Benjamin spent a lot of time in Italy, in Naples in particular, with Alfred Sohn-Rethel and Asja Lācis, his discursive imaginary seems to have remained in Germany. See *Sur Naples: Walter Benjamin, Asja Lācis et Alfred Sohn-Rethel*, trans. Françoise Willmann and Alexandre Métraux (Paris: Editions La Tempete, 2019).
6. Christine Poggi, *Inventing Futurism: The Art and Politics of Artificial Optimism* (Princeton, NJ: Princeton University Press, 2009), ix–xi.

7. Umberto Boccioni, Carlo Carrà, Luigi Russolo, Giacomo Balla and Gino Severini, "Futurist Painting: Technical Manifesto," in Lawrence Rainey, Christine Poggi and Laura Wittman, eds., *Futurism: An Anthology* (New Haven, CT: Yale University Press, 2009), 62–4.

8. Ibid., 3.

9. Anja Klock, "Of Cyborg Technologies."

10. On this point, see the documentary series (comprised of three episodes) by Adam Curtis distributed by the BBC entitled *All Watched Over by Machines of Loving Grace*. The series was initially broadcast in May 2011 and is available on YouTube: www.youtube.com/watch?v=2XPGRmRCk4U.

11. Ana Teixeira Pinto, "Art Washing: On NRX and the Alt Right," *Texte Zur Kunst*, https://www.textezurkunst.de/106/artwashing-de/.

12. Ibid.

13. T.J. Clark, "God is Not Cast Down," in *Farewell To An Idea* (New Haven, CT: Yale University Press, 1999), 225–98. Clark argues that Malevich's *Black Square* functions, in its irreducible material flatness belied by its titling dynamism that opens onto virtual space, as a "Marxist dream of totality." To begin, see Daniel Spaulding, "Value-Form and Avant-Garde," *Mute* (27 March 2014): 1–14, www.metamute.org/editorial/articles/value-form-and-avant-garde.

14. Georg Lukács, *History and Class Consciousness*, trans. Rodney Livingstone (Cambridge, MA: MIT Press, 1971), 27–45.

15. The overlaps and breaks between futurism and fascism entail their technophilia – shared also by communism qua forces of production. Futurism and fascism celebrate technology without "altering property relations" as Benjamin formulates it. As Jeffrey Herf argues, Nazism is a reactionary modernism, a paradoxical lashing together of technophilia with a return to a hierarchical and deeply patriarchal social order. Jeffrey Herf, *Reactionary Modernism: Technology, Culture and Politics in Weimar and the Third Reich* (Cambridge: Cambridge University Press, 1986), 189–216.

16. The red square, for instance, became a signal of the student protests of Montreal in 2012, in which some 250,000 students antagonistically confronted the state for its proposed hikes in tuition and educational fees.

17. For a reference to the "theoretical object," see George Baker in *The Artwork Caught by the Tail: Francis Picabia and Dada in Paris* (Cambridge: The MIT Press, 2007), 11. Baker notes that he is "paraphrasing Rosalind Krauss in a different domain" when he calls the readymade *the* theoretical object of the avant-garde.

18. Malevich then moved the geometric shapes in stark black and white out of the temporary architecture he had constructed for these futurist literary and theatrical productions and back onto the canvas. This turn or re-turn to the medium of painting is no small irony given Rodchenko's declaration of the death of easel painting in 1920 and subsequent transition to design.

19. Roman Jakobson, "Futurism," in Bengt Jangfeldt and Stephen Rudy, eds., *My Futurist Years: Collected Essays*, trans. Stephen Rudy (New York: Marsilio, 1992), 147.

20. Ibid., 147. Again, Jakobson is arguing for technical continuity with almost a decade's hindsight into the trajectory of both histories, that of communism having become state communism in the USSR and the rise of fascism in both Germany and Italy.

21. Ibid., 147.

22. Yve-Alain Bois, Benjamin H.D. Buchloh, Hal Foster and Rosalind Krauss, "1909," in *Art Since 1900* (London: Thames and Hudson, 2004), 95–6.

23. Bois, Buchloh, Foster and Krauss, "1909," 96.

24. Karl Marx, "The Eighteen Brumaire of Louis Napoleon," in *Karl Marx and Frederick Engels: Collected Works*, Volume 11: *Marx and Engels 1851–53* (London: Lawrence and Wishart, 2010), 103.

25. Haraway, "Cyborg Manifesto," 9.

26. Both men envision a techno-scientistic future in which species extinction and climate collapse might be resolved by the occupation of other planets, specifically by those who can afford it in accordance with the logic and metabolic of capitalist value extraction. Neil Sahota, "Human 2.0 is Coming Faster Than You Think. Will You Evolve With the Times?" *Forbes*, 1 Oct 2018, accessed 12 August 2019, www.forbes.com/sites/cognitiveworld/2018/10/01/human-2-0-is-coming-faster-than-you-think-will-you-evolve-with-the-times/#2ad661db4284.

27. Neil Levi, "Judge for Yourselves: The 'Degenerate Art Exhibition' as Political Spectacle," *October*, No. 85 (Spring 1998): 41–64.

28. F.T. Marinetti, "Response To Hitler (1 August 1937)," in Lawrence Rainey, Christine Poggi and Laurie Wittman, eds., *Futurism: An Anthology* (New Haven, CT: Yale University Press, 2009), 297.

29. Ibid., 297–8.

30. Bois, Buchloh, Foster and Krauss, "1909," 95.

31. Ibid.

32. Ibid., 57. See also Susan Buck-Morss's *Dreamworld and Catastrophe: The Passing of Mass Utopia in East and West* (Cambridge, MA: MIT Press, 2000) which poses and dissects the tension between the politics of the Russian avant-garde and the Bolshevik vanguard. Finally, on the marriage of anarchism and communism in the context of the Soviet avant-garde, see Boris Groys, "Installing Communism," in Samir Gandesha and Johan Hartle, eds., *Aesthetic Marx* (London: Bloomsbury, 2017), 185–202. Groys looks at anarchism through the figure of Aleksei Gan.

33. Teixeira Pinto, "Art Washing," 162–9.

34. But under the *sensus communis* we must include the idea of a *communal sense* [*einesgemeinschaftlichen Sinnes*], that is, of a faculty of judgement, which in its reflection takes account (a priori) of the mode of representation of all other men in thought; in order as it were to compare its judgement with the collective reason of humanity, and thus to escape the illusion arising from the private conditions that could be so easily taken for objective, which would injuriously affect the judgement. Immanuel Kant, "Of Taste as a Kind of *Sensus Communis*," in *Kant's Critique of Judgment, Translated with Introduction and Notes by J.H. Bernard* (2nd edn revised)

(London: Macmillan, 1914), accessed 25 July 2013, oll.libertyfund.org/titles/kant-the-critique-of-judgement.

35. These are the oft-cited closing words of Walter Benjamin's "The Work of Art in the Age of its Technological Reproducibility," 126.

36. Benjamin, "The Work of Art in the Age of its Technological Reproducibility," 126.

37. Jacques Rancière, *The Politics of Aesthetics: The Distribution of the Sensible* (London: Continuum Press, 2005). See also Beth Hinderliter, William Kaizen, Vered Maimon, Jaleh Mansoor and Seth McCormick, eds., *Communities of Sense: Rethinking Aesthetics and Politics* (Durham, NC: Duke University Press, 2009).

38. Teixeira Pinto, "Art Washing," 162–9.

39. Ibid.

40. Benjamin, "The Work of Art in the Age of Technological Reproducibility."

41. Jodi Dean, *The Communist Horizon* (London: Verso, 2018). Consider the rhetoric around the 2020 presidential campaign in America, where Bernie Sanders is projected to have an advantage.

42. Karl Marx, "Preface to the Contribution to the Critique of Political Economy," in *Marx and Engels: Collected Works*, Vol. 29 (New York: International Publishers, 1987), 261–5, and, before that, his and Engels' *Communist Manifesto* in *Marx and Engels: Collected Works*, Vol. 6: *1845–1848* (London: Lawrence & Wishart, 1976).

4

The Aesthetics of Totalitarian Salvation

Alec Balasescu

In 1989 history was about to end – an end marked by the beginning of history as a reality show.[1] Giorgio Agamben observed how the change of the Romanian regime and the televised execution of the Ceauşescus, coupled with the "On Air Revolution," constituted the dramatic entry of the staged reality in becoming.[2] The revolutionary events unfolded in state TV studios and were transmitted via the airwaves to the citizenry in a way that seemed spontaneous, delivered by men who later became prominent holders of power in post-Ceauşescu Romania. A little reverse-engineering would easily re-establish the stage-managed character of the supposedly spontaneous addresses to "the people." Each instance of the broadcasting moment was preceded by the carefully directed spontaneity of the TV revolutionary men and occasionally, women.

At the tender age of 15, I was an extra in the show and I remember vividly how I quickly left the larger set of the streets when one of the speakers at the balcony – the microphone was up for grabs – received the loudest of ovations when he celebrated the newly acquired liberty by reminding the "people" that, now, they would be able to see the European Cup live on TV or even travel to see the games in person. How naïve of him not to realize, then, that the promised "free circulation" referred to *commodities* and *money*, and not to *human beings*! Even to this day, the unified European market refers more to goods and finance than to human beings. It is important to remember that there are still countries in the European Union, Romania included, that are not in the Schengen space – the space of truly unbounded, which is to say, "free movement of people." To his credit, the speaker on the balcony was visibly embarrassed after first trying to stir the revolutionary excitement with cultural signifiers. Freedom to travel to see the so-called "treasures of civilization" was top of his list; perhaps anticipating the populist wave, he reverted to the topic of footall when the masses did not react as expected. But before watching with docile fury the victories and failures of the Romanian national soccer team on the international stage, other images triggered the instant rage of the spectators of the Romanian Revolution and served to momentarily (though, for some, permanently) justify the summary execution of the Romanian dictatorial couple: the *sumptuous interiors of their residence.* The images of luxurious interiors played in an unending loop between the feverish announcements of the broadcasters updating the public about the pursuit, trial and ultimately the execution of Elena and Nicolae Ceauşescu. What seems to have caused the most outrage was not just any of the interiors, but the bathrooms with gold-plated appliances, in particular. One may be tempted to think that the crowd perhaps unconsciously channelled the Viennese Marxist architect and critic Adolf Loos, who argued that ornamentation constituted a kind of crime against the working class.[3] To complicate the image, those most outraged belonged to the materially impoverished but richly cultured Romanian middle class at the time.

In this chapter, I will explore the manner in which totalitarianism aesthetically projects its promise of salvation, and what the deeper meaning of such salvation may teach us about the sociopolitical conflicts of our own historical conjuncture. Fast forward ten years later after the Romanian Revolution, I had my first strangely familiar moment of recognition in southern California, when I visited the Trinity Broadcasting Center in the late 1990s – my ethnographic curiosity clearly knows no bounds! Located in the heart of Orange County, Trinity Broadcasting Center owns the eponymous TV channel and broadcasts news and movies of its own production. The architecture and interior design of the centre bears an uncanny resemblance to the "House of the People" – the initial name of the Ceauşescus' monstrous building in the heart of Bucharest that now houses the Romanian Parliament – and it is of utmost importance to experience the space from inside in order to fully grasp the effects of its layout. The references are clearly to Versailles, an anticipation of luxurious totalitarianism. However, it was the interiors that vividly reminded me of the recent history in Romania, with a twist. What the newly liberated "people" of Romania considered abhorrent, the free-born "people" of the United States took to be worthy of emulation, gold-plated washroom fixtures included. To complete the image, the gift shop of the Trinity Broadcasting Center offered for sale a fictional series of books and films about the rapture as imagined by American Evangelists, in which the main character is the Anti-Christ, also presented as the "Man of the Year" of the fictional *Newsweek*, the Secretary General of the United Nations: a certain Nicolae Carpathia. It was an interesting "creative" twist from the part of the series creators, in which the trope of a totalitarian *anti-globalist* figure – Nicolae Ceauşescu – is, paradoxically, transformed to signify the evils of coming *globalization*. My visit coincided historically with the introduction of the euro and I was surprised to find out that this currency, in the very same worldview, is apparently the financial vehicle of the devil himself. It was only after this that I discovered Kurt Vonnegut and reread Max Weber, which set me on a path of understanding the intimate link between money, the devil and salvation. The questions that stayed with me, and that I would like to explore in this chapter, are: What generates this display of worldly possessions? Is such an ostentatious display related to a totalitarian view of the world? Is it the expression of heavenly salvation? If so, salvation from what? And who will be there to lead us up the "stairway to heaven," where according to the woman in the iconic Led Zeppelin song, "all that glitters is gold"?

As there is no path without a guide, the providential leader accompanies by default a rhetoric of salvation – a prophet-like figure who commands love from the people. In fact, this explains the obsession of being the most loved by everybody, evinced in a multiplicity of forms from all those who aspire to power and believe it should be beyond a separation of powers, beyond the judiciary, beyond law itself, *limitless*. Following Tismăneanu's argument that *nationalism and populism propose a path to salvation*,[4] I propose that this salvation is from any form of perceived dependency – translated into debt – and the restoration of an idealized autarkic state consistent with a libertarian ideology or, more so perhaps, with a sedentary, farming type of patriarchalism. This path is meant to pave the way to self-determination as the practical expression of the construction of that very form of subjectivity. That subject – the subjectivity of the sovereign nation – is an extension of the "imagined community," or the self-determined individual at the centre of neoliberal discourse. Such a figure is strong, relates to himself and his powers as forms of property (he owns himself and his destiny), and, above all, is pure.

Impurity, in contrast, is equated with danger. It is, therefore, worth revisiting Mary Douglas's seminal work, *Purity and Danger*, in which the author explains how those categories intertwine:

> In general the underlying principle of cleanness in animals is that they shall conform fully to their class. Those species are unclean which are imperfect members of their class, or whose class itself confounds the general scheme of the world.[5]

Douglas goes on to argue that impurity represents danger, as it menaces the rigid order of the world. Those who are impure in a system of categories are deemed to be "dangerous." This passage extracted here refers to Leviticus and food impurity. In what I prefer to call the "nationalist (dis-)order of things,"[6] we can replace in this text "animals" with humans and "species" with ethnic, religious, racial or any other type of prevalent category that appears in nationalist discourses to categorize "other" groups. Thus:

> In general the underlying principle of cleanness [*in humans*] is that they shall conform fully to their class. Those[*groups*]are unclean which are imperfect members of their class, or whose class itself confounds the general scheme of the world.[7]

In these discourses, the pure national self must be protected from the threat of impurity, of contamination, for a very simple reason: impurity is framed as dangerous, as potentially diluting the ownership capacity of the pure self both in relationship with itself and with the world (see Chapter 8 in this volume). Politicians appealing to purity use thick brushstrokes to move freely from collective to individual notions of the self and back.As Trump stated in his 2017 speech to the United Nations General Assembly: "Strong sovereign nations let their people take ownership of the future and control their own destiny."[8]

This is a (not-so) subtle way of superimposing ethnicity or pre-existent group belonging onto state sovereignty, in that the nation-state comes to be identified less with an institutional structure governed by the rule of law and constitutionally defined citizenship, and more with a naturalized – albeit fictional – notion of a sovereign "people" taking ownership of its destiny. The current political division in countries that display the most resurgence of populism in Europe and in the Americas (i.e. the United

States and Brazil) becomes, thus, the division between the people: the natural pure sovereign and the outsider, "the other," however this other may be identified.

Ivan Krastev identifies this division as the separation between those "from everywhere" versus those "from somewhere,"[9] where the sense of locality is turned into a politics of exclusion. The political counter-discourse that sides with localism dismisses the global or cosmopolitan citizenship as an impossibility, as Theresa May (in)famously put it: "if you believe you are a citizen of the world, then you are a citizen of nowhere."[10]

Krastev superimposes this distinction on that between "open" and "closed" societies, and identifies two types of iconic outsiders that generate two types of attitudes in closed societies: the "tourist" and the "refugee." While the tourist is welcome because he or she comes and goes, the refugee is rejected because he or she is both a threat to the purity of the self and a reminder that nobody is "sheltered" from the forces of globalization. Hochschild makes a similar analysis for the American case, while observing that the prevalent feeling of mourning on the far-right of the American political spectrum is generated by the perception that the "land" and what it provides seems to have been swept from under the feet of its "entitled" occupants.[11] These occupants are then abandoned to consume the leftovers – and given clear instructions on how to do it, as the account of the "Protocol for Issuing Public Health Advisories for Chemical Contaminants in Recreationally Caught Fish and Shellfish" illustrates:

> The report was shocking but it also made a certain grim sense. If the companies won't pay for the clean waters they pollute, and if the state won't make them, and if the poverty is ever with us – some people need to fish for their dinner – well, trim, grill, and eat mercury-soaked fish. At least the authors of the protocol were honest in what was a terrible answer to the Great Paradox. "You got a problem? Get used to it."[12]

There is a third figure framed by politicians as a threat to those "from somewhere" – to use Krastev's term – and that probably concentrates even more the projected fear and anger. The "traitor," those from among "us" who becomes "them": the advocates for an open society that other-wise would qualify in the notion of the pure self (on group belonging criteria, ethnic or otherwise). In totalitarian rhetoric, this figure would correspond to Douglas's identification of a class that confounds the general, that is to say, *totalitarian* scheme of the world. The type of political discourse that characterizes a closed society implying an imaginary transfer of sovereignty from an institutionally based, and constitutionally limited, state to "the people," serves the politicians in two ways: it gives them carte blanche to act in their name and it also suspends the external accountability and possibly also normal legality.[13] The mechanism is well known, and has been used by totalitarian leaders repeatedly during recent history. Take, for example, this fragment from Nicolae Ceauşescu's address in 1980 in Moscow:

> Life demonstrates that we must act with full determination in order to assert, in the relationships between states, the principles of full equality of rights, respect for sovereignty and national independence, non-interference in internal affairs, renunciation of force and of threatening with force.[14]

Or, take the more recent defence of Qatar by Turkish leader Recep Tayyip Erdoğan, in June 2017: "Here we see an attack against a state's sovereignty rights … There cannot be such an attack on countries' sovereignty rights in international law."[15] What matters at this point is not necessarily the speaker, but the structure and the ideas they transmit:

> "Sovereignty is the shield that many governments use at the UN to defend against accusations of abuse," Maltz–ex-deputy chief of staff to former UN Ambassador Samantha Power, said. "When governments face criticism over imprisonment of dissidents, or persecution of minorities, or even sexual abuse by their peacekeepers on UN missions, they routinely cite sovereignty as the overriding concern, and justification."[16]

Purity, and the sovereignty of the pure, thus secures an arbitrary, and yet legitimate, power over the impure, without external checks. This power is transferred to the leader that embodies the will of "the people" and expresses its voice. It is perhaps time to remember that gold is sought for, and valued precisely by, its *purity*.

One of the important roadblocks in attaining the state of blessed autarky is debt. Not only because it creates a state of dependency on the creditor, but also because debt itself has a religious valence, and, while in debt, one is damned yet cannot be saved. Echoing Nietzsche, Deleuze and Guattari, David Graeber observes that in Christianity salvation is a salvation from the "infinite debt of sin":

> Since creditor and debtor are ultimately equals, if the debtor cannot do what it takes to restore herself to equality, there is obviously something wrong with her; it must be her fault. This connection becomes clear if we look at the etymology of common words for "debt" in European languages. Many are synonyms for "fault," "sin," or "guilt": just as a criminal owes a debt to society, a debtor is always a sort of criminal.[17]

In other words, monetary debt not only signals dependence, but also is, ultimately, a secular manifestation of sin. This may explain the obsession of totalitarian figures with being free of debt, and the recent independence campaigns in Europe, Brexit leading the way, that stress monetary calculations (misrepresented, but who cares in the "post-truth" era) over political and practical concerns. One can always choose to represent the self, freed from debt as a political achievement – because this self is presumably pure, free of sin, and worthy of salvation. The question regarding salvation at the beginning of this chapter is thus answered: the saving figure is the leader who will free "us" from debt. It is also what explains the entanglement of money, religion, and the hostility of totalitarians against that people who were historically prohibited from virtually all professions other than money-lending: the Jews.[18]

This is where things get really complicated, because there is an undeniable crossover between some of the left ideals and the rhetoric of nationalist sovereignty, arguably embodied in a figure such as Jeremy Corbyn, or the idea of a "Lexit" or left Brexit – a Brexit that would finally re-establish popular sovereignty in the state. The ideologues of new separatist or populist movements keep the left ideals of a strong state responsible for the well-being of its citizens and add a nationalist dimension to it – often through ostentatious deficit spending beyond EU-imposed limits, as in the proposed Italian budgets of 2019.[19] Their rhetoric limits the extent of the rights, benefits and responsibilities of citizenship to the pure ethnic definition of a citizen, and automatically suspends "the other" from access to such rights, benefits and responsibilities, subjecting them to pure sovereign power in an ongoing state of exception.[20] This state of exception is sometimes depicted as a state of animality, "zoe" or naked life, over "bios" or the authentic human life; it has happened before in history.[21] Populist discourses always depict "the other" as less than human, or downright part of the non-human animal kingdom – in other words, in a state of perpetual exception. Moreover, this type of discourse is rooted in a semantic slippage concerning the locus of sovereignty in liberal democracy: the people – both in need of and automatically generating those who are not "our people," the non-people.[22]

Let's go back to gold – if we have enough, not only do we pay our debts and become free, strong and "great again," but we can also use its surplus for ornamentation.[23] Recently, Trump's penthouse made headlines in conjunction with the release of Ivana Trump's book, *Raising Trump*.[24] The penthouse's interiors overflow with golden details and Louis XVI-inspired decorations (remember Versailles, which is also the signifier for German reparations and debt?). One fascinating detail about the decoration of Trump's penthouse is that it is his first wife, Ivana, who claims credit for it in her book, while humoristically drawing parallels between her personal taste and that of … Louis XVI.

One of the book reviews published in *The Atlantic* emphasizes the importance of Ivana's own biography and how this may have influenced both her taste and the family dynamic:

> Ivana Trump, née Ivana Zelníčková, was born in Czechoslovakia just after the Iron Curtain went down, the only child in a family rich in love and poor in most everything else. The Zelníčeks were not party members; the only chance they had of advancing, their daughter writes, was to keep their heads down and work – and work – and work some more. "Being less than the best was simply not an option, because, in a very real way, one mistake could doom your life," Ivana recalls. She adds: "We couldn't be sure who to trust outside the family."[25]

This upbringing, although not Protestant, breeds the conviction that success and wealth equals moral superiority, gold being the glittering material sign of grace. And the inverse: in this worldview, poverty may indicate a fallen state, view or even moral inferiority. But more so, what is to be retained from the above statement is the emphasis on the narrowness of the circle of trust. Beyond the family circle, no one is to be trusted. Does this explain, at least partially, the nepotistic composition of the current White House administration? Should we extend this to clan, tribe and ethnos? The seeds are there.

Since Louis XVI, the last King of France before the French Revolution, and his style is in discussion, let us think again of Versailles, outlandish style, and his predecessor, Louis XV. Let us do it via the Man of the Year 2016 award from *Time* magazine. Jake Romm provides a wonderful analysis of the cover image that portrays Trump sitting on a chair, from the position on the chair to the position of the camera, and passing through the red horns drawn by the letter M from the title of the magazine.[26] The chair, more so than its occupant, commands the central focus:

> The masterstroke, the single detail that completes the entire image, is the chair. Trump is seated in what looks to be a vintage "Louis XV" chair (so named because it was designed in France under the reign of King Louis XV in the mid-18th century). The chair not only suggests the blindly ostentatious reigns of the French kings just before the revolution, but also, more specifically, the reign of Louis XV who, according to historian Norman Davies, "paid more attention to hunting, women and stags than to governing the country" and whose reign was marked by "debilitating stagnation," "recurrent wars," and "perpetual financial crisis."[27]

Those lavish decorations and marks of excess are signs of reaching the state of grace, for a certain type of sensibility – the autarkic sensibility that fears interdependency. The middle ground, the equilibrium that fears excess, instantly rejects these representations as *mauvais goût* (taste of excess).

However, those representations do touch the sensibilities of the disenfranchised, who may dream of salvation in very earthly, material terms. And maybe, just maybe, what I thought were the Romanians' feelings of disgust towards the excesses of Ceaușescu was in fact envy. We may find an early critique of these dreams in Hieronymus Bosch's painting *The Garden of Earthly Delights* (1490–1510). Here is a figure that fascinates many commentators: some unknown being within a pit, in a psychoanalytical vein *avant la lettre*, who defecates gold coins. But what if the pit is also gold plated? The delight is supreme. Or should we say "total"? Those dreams, and their expression, are not to be taken lightly or viewed with derision. They do express a desire for something that perhaps some of us cannot fathom, and maybe we cannot do it because we, the relatively privileged, already live in Bosch's garden. Through derision, aesthetic smugness and moral righteousness we manage to push the underprivileged population "from somewhere" into the arms of politicians who, although from "everywhere," choose to profit from the state of the disenfranchised, mimicking their voices and venting their frustrations for political gains.

More than 20 years ago, in 1994, Isaiah Berlin received the title of Doctor of Laws from the University of Toronto. His speech is a clear call for moderation that seems to have been lost somewhere along the way:

> If you are truly convinced that there is some solution to all human problems, that one can conceive an ideal society which men can reach if only they do what is necessary to attain it, then you and your followers must believe that no price can be too high to pay in order to open the gates of such a paradise.[28]

The moral demarcation and righteous blaming may have little political effect in the democratic system – absent the awareness of Karl Popper's "paradox of tolerance"[29] – because in its internal logic, extremism is both morally coherent and morally superior (as any other type of religious system); or more so, for many, it appears to embody the essence of morality itself. Unless we understand the dreams of salvation of the disenfranchised, and the bottomless pit of desires that consumerism offers in exchange for dignity, we won't be able to save ourselves from a totalitarian dream – or another. Again, in Isaiah Berlin's words:

> The search for a single, overarching ideal because it is the one and only true one for humanity, invariably leads to coercion. And then to destruction, blood – eggs are broken, but the omelette is not in sight, there is only an infinite number of eggs, human lives, ready for the breaking. And in the end the passionate idealists forget the omelette, and just go on breaking eggs.[30]

ACKNOWLEDGEMENTS

I would like to extend my thanks to Samir Gandesha for inviting me to be part of this exceptional collective project, and for his invaluable suggestions and careful editing.

NOTES

Unless otherwise stated, URLs were last accessed on 15 September 2019.

1. Francis Fukuyama, *The End of History and the Last Man* (New York: The Free Press, 1992).
2. Giorgio Agamben, *Means Without End: Notes on Politics (Theory Out of Bounds)* (Minneapolis, MN: University of Minnesota Press, 2000).
3. Adolf Loos, *Ornament & Crime: Selected Essays* (1913; Riverside, CA: Ariadne Press, 1998).
4. Vladimir Tismăneanu, *Fantasies of Salvation: Democracy, Nationalism, and Myth in Post-Communist Europe* (Princeton, NJ: Princeton University Press, 2009).
5. Mary Douglas, *Purity and Danger* (1966; New York: Routledge, 2012), 55.
6. Alexandru Balasescu, "The National (Dis-)Order of Things, or the Reduction to Absurd of the Human Geography," in Alina Serban, ed., *Series. Multiples. Realisms* (Bucharest: Art Association Ilfoveanu, 2014).
7. Douglas, *Purity and Danger*, 55.
8. "Remarks by President Trump to the 72nd Session of the United Nations General Assembly," The White House Office of the Press Secretary, issued 19 September 2017, www.whitehouse.gov/briefings-statements/remarks-president-trump-72nd-session-united-nations-general-assembly/.
9. Ivan Krastev, *After Europe* (Philadelphia, PA: University of Pennsylvania Press, 2017).
10. Annabel Payne, "Why Being a Citizen of the World Matters in this Day and Age," *Glasgow Guardian*, 8 November 2016, glasgowguardian.co.uk/2016/11/08/why-being-a-citizen-of-the-world-matters-in-this-day-and-age/.
11. Arlie Russel Hochschild, *Strangers in Their Own Land: Anger and Mourning on the American Right* (New York: The New Press, 2016).
12. Ibid., 110–11.
13. See Chapter 6 in this volume.
14. Nicolae Ceaușescu, "Speech of Comrade Nicolae Ceaușescu at the Meeting of the Party and State Leaders of the States Participating in the Warsaw Treaty," Wilson Center Digital Archive (Speech, Warsaw Pact Meeting, Moscow, 5 December 1980), digitalarchive.wilsoncenter.org/document/112066.
15. "Erdogan Defends Qatar's Sovereignty," *Taipei Times*, 26 June 2017, www.taipeitimes.com/News/front/archives/2017/06/26/2003673307.
16. Zeeshan Aleem, "Trump's Message to the World at the UN: Every Country is on its Own," *Vox*, 19 September 2017, www.vox.com/world/2017/9/19/16332770/trump-unga-speech-north-korea-iran.
17. David Graeber, *Debt: The First 5,000 Years* (Brooklyn, NY: Melville House Publishing, 2012), 121.
18. For a further discussion of this see William Nicholls, *Christian Antisemitism: A History of Hate* (Lanham, MD: Rowman and Littlefield, 1995).
19. Angela Giuffrida, "Italy Defies EU Request to Present Revised Budget," *Guardian*, 13 November 2018, www.theguardian.com/world/2018/nov/13/italy-expected-defy-eu-request-present-revised-budget.

20. See Carl Schmitt, *Political Theology: Four Chapters on the Concept of Sovereignty* (1922; Cambridge, MA: MIT Press, 1985); and see Giorgio Agamben, *Homo Sacer: Sovereign Power and Bare Life* (Stanford, CA: Stanford University Press, 1998).

21. Agamben, *Homo Sacer.*

22. Samir Gandesha, "Editorial: The Political Semiosis of Populism," *Semiotic Review of Books* 13, No. 3 (2003).

23. See Adolf Loos, "Ornament and Crime," in Ulrich Conrads, ed., *Programs and Manifestos on 20th Century Architecture*, trans. M. Bullock (Cambridge, MA: MIT Press, 1971), 19–24.

24. See Ivana Trump, *Raising Trump: Family Values from Americas First Mother* (New York: Simon & Schuster, 2017).

25. Megan Garber, "The Biggest Winners: What Ivana Reveals About Trump Family Values," *The Atlantic*, 17 October 2017, www.theatlantic.com/entertainment/archive/2017/10/ivana-trump-book-review/543084/.

26. Jake Romm, "Why Time's Trump Cover is a Subversive Work of Political Art – Even a Year Later," *Forward*, 21 December 2016, forward.com/culture/356537/why-times-trump-cover-is-a-subversive-work-of-political-art-even-a-year-lat/.

27. Ibid.

28. Isaiah Berlin, "A Message to the 21st Century," *New York Review of Books*, 23 October 2014, www.nybooks.com/articles/2014/10/23/message-21st-century/.

29. Karl R. Popper, *The Open Society and its Enemies*, Volume I: *The Age of Plato* (1945; Princeton, NJ: Princeton University Press, 1969).

30. Berlin, "A Message to the 21st Century."

5

Are the Alt-Right and French New Right Kindred Movements?

Tamir Bar-On

The ND (*Nouvelle Droite* – French New Right) is a cultural school of thought which was created in 1968 and is centred around the think tank GRECE (Le Groupement De Recherche Et D'études Pour La Civilisation Européenne – Group for Research and Studies in European Civilization). It had its intellectual heyday in France in the late 1970s and early 1980s. Led by Alain de Benoist, the ND attempted to rethink the legacies of Nazism, fascism, Vichy collaboration and colonialism. Yet, ND intellectuals were dogged by accusations of fascism and cultural racism because they borrowed from German inter-war era Conservative Revolution thinkers such as Carl Schmitt (the crown jurist of the Nazis) and longed for ethnically homogeneous communities, even as they supported world-wide ethnopluralism and dropped their open support for violence, totalitarianism, the cult of the leader, racism and antisemitism.[1] Moreover, in attempting to outduel the liberal-left, the ND borrowed from Antonio Gramsci and the New Left in order to defeat liberalism and capitalism.[2] Some dubbed the ND "right-wing Gramscians."[3]

While the ND has been around for about 50 years, the AR (Alt-Right) is a more recent and largely Web-based cultural movement with few significant writings compared to the ND. The most important figure associated with the AR is Richard B. Spencer. Spencer noted that he coined the term "Alternative Right" in 2008 in order to differentiate himself from "mainstream American conservatism" and pass down European "ancestral traditions" to new generations.[4] The paleoconservative Paul Gottfried insists that both he and Spencer jointly created the term "Alt-Right," although the former thought it would be an antidote to the neo-conservative right and initially saw it as libertarian rather than racialist.[5] In contrast, for Spencer those "ancestral traditions" are racial preference for white Europeans and antisemitism – "old right" staples.[6]

Unlike Spencer, de Benoist is neither openly antisemitic nor racist. He even penned a piece attacking racism.[7] Nonetheless, the ND is anti-immigrant, promotes cultural racism,[8] and is criticized for wanting to build ethnically homogeneous communities.[9]

Like de Benoist, Spencer has been dubbed a "fascist," "neo-Nazi," "white supremacist" and "ethnic nationalist."[10] Like other white nationalists such as Jared Taylor,[11] Spencer believes that white racial consciousness and political solidarity can be attained without violence, continuing the ND's "right-wing Gramscianism." Yet, Spencer is openly racialist and antisemitic. His movement aims to stem the tide of liberal multiculturalism, advance the interests of the "white race" through concrete measures such as halting non-white immigration, and end so-called "Jewish influence" in politics.[12] He even longs for the creation of "white homelands" in the United States and other countries where whites live.[13]

This chapter poses the following question: Are the AR and ND kindred movements? Kindred connotes one's family, a relationship by blood, or even allied, connected or comparable. In 1959, Maurice Duverger categorized political parties as organizational types: cadre, branch or cell parties.[14] In 1985, von Beyme suggested that there were nine "familles spirituelles" (spiritual families) or "ideological groups" amongst the different political parties in Western Europe, including the "extreme right."[15] In 1995, Gallagher and his colleagues insisted that party families can be linked by "genetic" or historical circumstances with the goal of representing similar interests, transnational federations or links, and policies.[16] In 2007, Wolinetz noted that the "spiritual families" in Belgium were divided along four lines (i.e. liberal, Catholic, socialist and linguistic) and that the Netherlands had four "pillars" before the 1980s.[17]

Although used for political parties, von Beyme's notion of "spiritual families" might be appropriated for cultural movements like the ND and AR. Are the ND and AR part of the same "spiritual family"? We might view the ND and AR as cousins not based on blood, but in the ideological sense. Although there are different rights, the ND and AR are both within the ambit of the revolutionary right. They want to root and branch destroy liberal democracy, capitalism and multiculturalism. Both are led by charismatic intellectuals, viewed by some scholars as neofascist-like, focus on winning the "cultural war" against the "globalist" liberal-left elites, reject liberal multiculturalism, support homogeneous (white)

European identities, and desire a post-liberal, revolutionary order that is neither capitalist nor communist. Yet, there are important differences between the two movements: the differing ideological and historical trajectories and references, the significant intellectual pedigree of the ND versus the AR's Web-focused movement with little intellectual pedigree, and the advantages of the ND compared to the AR because of the presence of openly anti-immigrant political parties in Europe.

This chapter begins by tracing the diversity of right-wing currents of thought. In the next two sections, it analyses the manifestos of the AR and ND. It concludes by highlighting the similarities and differences between the ND and AR in terms of historical and ideological origins, strategies, and support in civil society and the state. It argues that the ND and AR are revolutionary right-wing ideological cousins, but that they are distinctive cultural movements.

MANY RIGHTS

The right and left are modern concepts, with origins in the French Revolution.[18] In the new liberal republican government, sitting on the right in parliament meant that you wanted to revive the *ancien régime* (old regime), the aristocratic system, and monarchy. If you sat on the left, you were for republicanism, secularism, the universal rights of the people, workers' rights, and an egalitarian social order.

If you want to establish a theocracy, you are more on the right than the left. In the 1920s and 1930s, the Cristeros were a more right-wing and traditionalist movement fearful of liberal republicanism and the loss of power for the Church in Mexico as a result of the secular Mexican Constitution (1917).[19] Other religious movements from the anti-abortion Army of God to Christian Voice have also been dubbed right-wing movements. Yet, there is a strange hesitation in the literature to label Islamists as "right-wing."[20]

The meaning of right-wing "varies across societies, historical epochs, and political systems and ideologies."[21] For one scholar, the right has included five different historical phases: (1) the reactionary right wanted a return to aristocracy and established religion; (2) the moderate right distrusted intellectuals and sought limited government; (3) the radical right called for a romantic and aggressive nationalism; (4) the extreme right proposed anti-immigration policies and did not favour explicit racism; and (5) the neoliberal right sought to combine a market economy and economic deregulation with traditional right-wing positions defending patriotism, elitism, and law and order.[22] Hardly any contemporary right is driven by theocratic or monarchical impulses. Some rights such as the ND, Italy's neofascist Casa Pound and even US paleoconservatives are "anticapitalist."[23] Other rights like the Anglo-American New Right are pro-capitalist, neoliberal, and critical of state bureaucratization and the welfare state.

Fascism and Nazism were special cases in the inter-war years. Although in public consciousness they are associated with the right, major fascist thinkers from Benito Mussolini to Oswald Mosley had intellectual roots on the left: socialism, the revisionist anti-Marxist left, and anarcho-syndicalism.[24]

Roger Eatwell and Neal O'Sullivan classify the right into five types: reactionary, moderate, radical, extreme and new.[25] In liberal democracies, the right generally opposes socialism and social democracy; and right-wing parties include conservatives, Christian democrats, classical liberals, nationalists, and anti-immigrant racists and fascists.[26] In France, there have been several right-wing traditions: counter-revolutionary, liberal, Orléanist and Bonapartist.[27] In Europe, after World War II, violent, revolutionary right-wingers included neofascists, Evolians and Third Positionists.[28] In the United States, there is a history of populist, radical right-wing movements that first came to the forefront in order to reject President Franklin Delano Roosevelt's "big government" agenda: pro-Nazi Father Charles Coughlin, Huey Long, the rabidly anti-communist Joe McCarthy, pro-segregationist Barry Goldwater, racist, neo-Nazi and militia movements, and the AR.[29] To these rights we should add the mainstream Republican Party and an anti-immigrant Trumpian right. In Latin America, there exists an anti-communist, authoritarian right led by military elites, the pro-fascist Peronist right, the Catholic right, the neoliberal right, the populist radical right,[30] and a more moderate right.

Thus, historically, there are different right-wing movements. While right and left are shifting concepts, Norberto Bobbio suggests that the right favours inequality (or hierarchy) and the left equality.[31] Bobbio also argues that the right is more inclined to authority and the left more towards liberty. In this respect, the ND and AR are both revolutionary right-wing movements because they reject administrative equality, attack the liberal legacies of the American Revolution and French Revolution, and see elites as crucial for destroying liberal democracy. In wanting to create homogeneous communities based on ethnic forms of belonging, both the ND and AR are revolutionary and challenge the multicultural ethos of liberal societies.

THE NOUVELLE DROITE MANIFESTO[32]

At this juncture, the chapter will highlight key aspects of the manifestos of the ND and AR. In 1999, the ND traced its vision for the new millennium in a manifesto entitled "The French New Right in the Year 2000." The manifesto was written by Alain de Benoist and Charles Champetier. It is split into three sections: (1) Predicaments; (2) Foundations; and (3) Outlooks.

What is striking about the ND manifesto is the concern with the creation of rooted ethnic communities. There is hardly any section in the manifesto that does not express a preference for homogeneous communities. The ND ultimately desires a pan-European empire cleansed of immigrants.

Section one: critique of modernity and theorizing modernity's demise

In clause 1, the authors critique modernity and theorize about modernity's demise. De Benoist and Champetier attack the Judeo-Christian tradition and its liberal, universal offshoot, which allegedly attempts to eradicate diversity worldwide and Europe's pagan past. Liberalism and socialism failed to liberate humanity, while also engendering totalitarian horrors. The "end of ideologies" phenomenon fuels a political crisis and crisis of meaning.

As belief in liberal and socialist myths fade, new myths are required for Europe. Jünger insisted that ultra-nationalism was the unifying myth, which could undermine the nihilism of the inter-war years and the loss of faith in progress spawned by modernity.[33] De Benoist and Champetier similarly seek the return of a European myth of "common origins." They desire the restoration of a hierarchical, elitist, pagan, aristocratic and roots-based Indo-European civilization, buried by the Judeo-Christian tradition and modernity.

In clause 3, liberalism is the main enemy. For the ND, this change from primary anti-communism to primary anti-liberalism pre-dated the fall of communist states after 1989. The authors reject both liberalism and Marxism as materialistic and "totalitarian" ideologies.

Section two: the ND's "premodern" conception of man

In section 2 of the manifesto, the authors trace the philosophical foundations of the ND's "premodern," anti-egalitarian conception of man. Modernity is held responsible for undermining "natural" inequalities between human beings. De Benoist and Champetier support an older biological concept of humans in order to erect homogeneous ethnic communities.

In clause 2, the ND highlights its obsession with rooted ethnic communities. Echoing Joseph de Maistre, the authors attack the "abstract" notion of humanity. Instead they promote worldwide ethnopluralism: the flowering of hundreds of "homogeneous" communities within the framework of a "heterogeneous" world. De Benoist and Champetier attack the notion of universal laws or rights in a world of diverse cultures. Such a drive for universalism is equated with totalitarianism and the West.

In clause 8, de Benoist and Champetier reject the proselytizing, ethnocentric zeal of the West, which de Benoist once defended in French Algeria.

Section three: a revival of homogeneous ethnic communities

In section 3, seven of the 13 positions are directly related to a revival of homogeneous ethnic communities. The authors call for the flowering of many homogeneous communities worldwide. While there is an attack on global capitalism, there is no real concern for rectifying social injustices.

In position 1, the authors invoke capitalism as the bogeyman responsible for the acceleration of ethnic conflict. Stressing the "primacy of differences" against universalist utopias, which undermine traditional identities, the authors embrace what ND thinker Guillaume Faye calls the "cause of peoples" against the liberal "New Class."[34] This "New Class" refers to the elites of the current global order. Faye, like de Benoist and Champetier, views the "New Class" as ethnocentric and neo-imperialist because it props up a dominant Western, capitalist model and imposes it on all cultures and civilizations. The "New Class" is attacked for undermining strong identities worldwide. Yet "the right to difference" cannot be used to exclude, which is disingenuous if we read position 3's arguments "against immigration."

In position 2, the ND claims to advance an "anti-racist" position. The ND co-opts the insights of anti-racist groups like SOS Racisme. The manifesto claims that people cannot be blamed for being racist if they choose their own ethnic groups in marriage to others. If people cannot be blamed for racism, the liberal, multiculturalist "New Class" is held responsible for sowing the seeds of racism by allegedly seeking to abolish cultural differences in a homogeneous liberal order.

However, racism is officially rejected in the manifesto in the spirit of the times. Yet, the twist is that "anti-racism" is a disguised form of racism. For the ND, race should not be jettisoned as a concept and both racism and anti-racism should be rejected. The struggle against racism is neither won by negating the concept of races, nor by the desire to blend all races into an undifferentiated whole. Rather, the struggle against racism is waged by refusing both exclusion and assimilation – or acceptance of the Other through mutual enrichment.

Claiming to support "true" multiculturalism, the ND co-opted the multicultural discourse of the liberal-left in a decidedly anti-racist age. However, the ND has not abandoned racism, even if it says it has. In position 3, we see the ND repairing its ties with the traditional, far-right-wing milieu, which in the 1980s thought it was becoming crypto-communist as it had been critical of Le Pen's Front National (FN) and flirted with the left. In line with most radical right-wing parties, immigration is seen as a negative process. The anti-capitalist mantra is different from the FN, which directly blames immigrants for all of France's ills. Yet the restrictive immigration calls are similar to the FN. Both the FN and ND argue that restricting immigration will benefit immigrant and host societies alike since both will be able to promote homogeneous ethnic communities.

Immigrants are too numerous and will not all of a sudden leave Europe. Thus, the authors propose a "communitarian model" – a "multi-culturalism of the right" that officially recognizes differences in order to exclude immigrants from public life through normal parliamentary channels or referenda.

In position 5, the ND thinkers sound like new leftists or old rightists. Globalization has produced the worldwide domination of Western elites. Elites are detached from the concerns of citizens, the "New Class" has no social responsibilities, and there is greater need for shared values and meaning between the lower classes and elites. Local communities rather than corporations, the New Class elites or EU bureaucrats must decide on the fate of their communities.

In position 6, the nation-state, so dear to the right in general, is rejected as outmoded. Belonging will be European and federal in nature. Federalism would allow for the protection of strong regions, nations and historical cultures, while allowing Europeans to "rediscover their 'common origins.'" It is significant that Europe as a federalized, sovereign power bloc would be tied with Russia against the United States, the key representative of liberalism. This is certainly part of a larger attempt to weaken the United States as a global superpower, while the alliance with Russia has historical echoes of the Nazi–Soviet Non-Aggression Pact of 1939 and the National Bolshevist tendency in Germany led by Ernst Niekisch (1889–1967). It is no accident that numerous radical right-wing parties today are pro-Russia and pro-Putin.[35]

In position 7, the *demos* (people) and *ethnos* (ethnic group) are united in a manner that valorizes homogeneous forms of community belonging, while rejecting the US and French democratic revolutions and the communist revolutions in the East. Democracy denotes a system whereby the people are sovereign.

In a key passage, the authors unite *ethnos* and *demos*: "The essential idea of democracy is neither that of the individual nor of humanity, but rather the idea of a body of citizens politically united into a people." "People" here does not imply all the people, but a circumscribed, homogeneous people rooted along ethnic lines. Is this not a disguised form of racism? In fairness to de Benoist, he has defended the right of Muslims to wear their Islamic garb in public spaces, but perhaps as a tactic to infuriate Europeans by telling them they have "lost" their rooted European cultures.[36] De Benoist's aim is a "multiculturalism of the right," one that recognizes public cultural differences in order to restrict immigration and give preference to white Europeans.[37]

The procedure of the referendum is invoked in order to allow the people the possibility to return to the *ethnos* and "counteract the overwhelming power of money" in political life. In 1961, de Gaulle organized a referendum on self-determination for Algeria. The implicit argument is that France has become the colony of uncontrolled immigration, the new Algeria is mainland France, and the "common sense" of the people can vote to democratically reverse this "ethnocidal" multiculturalism,[38] which is destructive of Europe's pagan past and historic regions and nations.

THE ALT-RIGHT MANIFESTO

This section will analyse the "Alt-Right Manifesto," or "What It Means To Be Alt-Right: A meta-political manifesto for the Alt-Right movement."[39] It was written by Richard Spencer and released on 11 August 2017, before the tragic events of Charlottesville, Virginia.

The "Alt-Right Manifesto" is an attempt by Spencer to create a broad white nationalist movement and influence the masses of white Americans wedded to liberal multiculturalism. It mimics the aforementioned manifesto written by the ND. Spencer likens his tract to the manifestos of the conservative and New Left movements of the early 1960s.[40] The manifesto consists of twenty points. The manifesto is dubbed "meta-political" as Spencer borrows from the ND in order to move towards an "Alternative Right." Spencer, like the ND, believes that the right must be more Gramscian – win hearts and minds.

The first point of the manifesto is about race: "Race is real. Race matters. Race is the foundation of identity." For Spencer, the United States should be a race-based ethnic state devoid of non-Europeans, non-whites, Blacks and Jews. Whereas historically many white nationalists might have excluded Latin and Slavic peoples from the United States, Spencer calls for the unity of all whites worldwide.

Race is made central for Spencer because both the mainstream political parties, he argues, deny the centrality of race, push for open borders and thus dilute the sanctity of the white race, and promote a multiculturalism that homogenizes white and non-white peoples. "As long as whites continue to avoid and deny their own racial identity, at a time when almost every other racial and ethnic category is rediscovering and asserting its own, whites will have no chance to resist their dispossession," states Spencer, echoing Wilmot Robertson.[41]

The notion of race is discredited today in the West. Spencer thus uses race in order to attack politically correct liberal-left discourses, which negate the importance of race. He wants to create racial ethnic states, which borrows from the ND's worldwide ethnopluralism. These ethnostates are seen in a positive light – forces against a "one-world civilization," globalization, multiculturalism and capitalism, all "destroyers" of peoples. Elites like Spencer must lead the drive towards white ethnostates. Spencer, like de Benoist, is Nietzschean in rejecting egalitarianism and valorizing heroic elites in history.

In point 2, Spencer writes the following: "Jews are an ethno-religious people distinct from Europeans" and they refuse assimilation. Spencer, thus, breaks one of the major taboos of post-World War II politics: anti-semitism. He also repeats what the Nazis and some fascists have opined about the Jews:

1) They are hostile to whites or Europeans since they support inter-nationalist ideologies.
2) Jews imposed egalitarianism on Europeans.
3) Like whites, Jews should have their own ethnostate (Israel). Despite his antisemitism, Spencer embraces "white Zionism." "Dispos-sessed" whites should be inspired by Zionism as it helped to create Israel – an unlikely dream come true.[42]
4) Jews should not be part of the body politic because they are a different race.

In point 3, Spencer demonstrates the power of the AR to create its own vocabulary. "Alt-Right" and "ethnostate" are terms used first by Spencer, then picked up by the mainstream media and spread to the public at large – part of the AR's cultural war against the liberal-left. Spencer also notes that racial or ethnic states are "legitimate and necessary."

In point 4, Spencer argues that the AR wages an ideological battle against the "decrepit values of Woodstock and Wall Street." Spencer sounds like Alain de Benoist, who rejects the liberal-left hedonism of the New Left generation and the pro-capitalist Anglo-American New Right. Yet, while Spencer condemned the killing of a liberal counter-protester at Charlottesville, he did march with a collection of racist and revolu-tionary right-wingers.

In point 5, Spencer calls for a "White America." He advances the notion that non-whites had no role in the foundation of the United States and that whites defined the United States. George Grant might have reminded Spencer that Canada and the United States includes Indigenous peoples and that North Americans (outside Mexico) are "Europeans who are not Europeans."[43]

In point 6, Spencer supports a discredited racist notion: "Europe is our common home, and our ancestors' bone and blood lie in its soil." For Spencer, Europe means:

1) The "blood and soil" of the ancestors.
2) White Europeans uniting around the world.

3) The refugee crisis, immigration and uncontrolled borders are threats to white European identity – "an invasion, a war without bullets."
4) Due to open borders, the Islamization of Europe and North America are probable.[44]

In point 10, Spencer abandons his conservative position of complete support for Israel, as highlighted in his piece in Paul Gottfried's edited volume *The Great Purge*.[45] Spencer's foreign policy positions include:

1) No "end of history" liberalism where the United States attempts to convert all states to liberalism.
2) A rejection of colonialism.
3) No "Jewish" or "foreign" influences in the country's foreign policy, a point highlighted by two realist thinkers.[46]
4) If US foreign policy is determined by "foreign" lobbies or corporate interests, the country is not really sovereign.
5) The foreign policy of the United States must protect white Europeans.

In points 15 and 16, Spencer echoes the ND idea that globalization and capitalism "threaten" rooted identities worldwide.

In short, the manifesto allows the AR to focus on the metapolitical as a prelude to a revolutionary, post-liberal and racial order; it borrows insights from the ND; and it is fixated on homogeneous, white identities.

CONCLUSION

At the outset, this chapter suggested that the ND and AR are ideological cousins. Von Beyme's idea of a "spiritual family" applies to the ND and AR. This chapter traced the diversity of right-wing currents of thought and then analysed the manifestos of the AR and ND.

The chapter posited that the ND and AR are both within the ambit of the revolutionary right because they want to destroy liberal democracy, capitalism and multiculturalism. In short, both movements are led by charismatic intellectuals, are viewed by some scholars as neofascist, focus on winning the "cultural war" against globalist liberal-left elites, reject liberal multiculturalism, support homogeneous (white) European identities, and desire a post-liberal, revolutionary order. Yet, there are some differences between the two movements: the differing ideological and historical trajectories and references, the significant intellectual pedigree of the ND versus the AR's Web-constructed movement with little intellectual production, and the advantages of the ND compared to the AR because of the presence of openly anti-immigrant political parties in Europe.

The ND and AR are ideological cousins, but they are different in terms of historical and ideological origins, strategies, and support in civil society and the state. In the first place, the ND has its origins in French revolutionary right-wing politics, the loss of French Algeria, the demise of the politics of white racialism, and debates about Vichy collaboration, fascism and Nazism. In contrast, the AR has more recent origins, related to the growth of the Web amongst the revolutionary right-wing milieux, the charismatic personality of Richard Spencer, and a racist and antisemitic worldview that is closer to white nationalism than the Republican Party.

Second, the ND is intellectually brilliant, as shown by de Benoist's vast body of works compared to Spencer's and the length and quality of the respective manifestos. De Benoist even won a prestigious French literary prize in 1978. Spencer is more known for his provocative YouTube videos and his "Hail Trump" speech.[47] As one scholar suggested, the AR "may be remembered as one more oddity of the Trump era" rather than "a permanent fixture of American political life."[48]

Third, it is true that the two movements share similar references and authors, including Nietzsche, Schmitt and Evola, some of which had clear connections to Fascist and Nazi regimes. The ND has been better at distancing itself from such Old Right authors, but both movements have been dogged by accusations of racism and neofascism.

Fourth, the ND had a very clear strategy to create a body of intelligent right-wing thought that would influence state and civil society actors throughout Europe. Two scholars note that the ND even attempted to influence political parties on the right (especially the FN), as well as military, state, educational and media elites.[49] The ND practised a thorough "Gramscianism of the right." For Spencer, the "Gramscianism of the right" was largely directed at educated university elites through lectures that generated controversy, AR websites, the respectable and non-violent image Spencer nurtured, marches like Charlottesville, and using President Trump's former chief strategist Steve Bannon to build links between right-wing radicals worldwide.

Fifth, if we examine the influence of the radical right on both sides of the Atlantic, the ND had a head start compared to the AR. Numerous factors have made the radical right-wing parties a force throughout Europe, including economic crises, the attack on the welfare state, the post-9/11 anti-terrorism discourses, the attack on multiculturalism by major European politicians, and the crises of the mainstream political parties. Yet, it is clear that the ND has provided the ideological and rhetorical inspiration for radical right-wing parties. Without the anti-immigrant rhetoric framed in an anti-racist veneer (borrowed from the ND), the radical right would not be the force that it is today. With the AR, we must see whether it is able to provide more Charlottesville moments in the future, increase its media coverage, and infiltrate the Republican Party or President Trump and thus change concrete policies related to immigration, race or multiculturalism.

In short, this chapter argued that the ND and AR are revolutionary right-wing ideological cousins, but that they are distinctive cultural movements. Nonetheless, this does not mean that revolutionary right-wingers cannot co-operate through exchange of personnel, messages of support (e.g. Bannon told FN supporters to take the charge of racism as "a badge of honor"[50]), and common disdain for liberalism, multiculturalism, capitalism and egalitarianism. Like the left, there are many rights. The ND thinker Tomislav Sunić once argued that not all those against something necessarily want the same types of ideal society and state.[51] Yet, the ND and AR have enough "anti-'s" in common, in order to make co-operation possible. After all, the members of a "spiritual family" might not agree on everything, but they tend to stick together on issues that matter most to them.

NOTES

Unless otherwise stated, URLs were last accessed on 8 October 2019.

1. Roger Griffin, "Fascism's New Faces (and New Facelessness) in the 'Post-Fascist' Epoch, and its Threats to Contemporary Democracy," *Erwägen, Wissen, Ethik* 15, No. 3 (Autumn 2004): 287–300; Nigel Copsey, "Fascism … but with an Open Mind: Reflections on the Contemporary Far Right in (Western) Europe. First NIOD Lecture on Fascism—Amsterdam—25 April," *Fascism* (2013): 1–17; Alberto Spektorowski, "The French New Right: Multiculturalism of the Right and the Recognition/Exclusionism Syndrome," *Journal of Global Ethics* 8, No. 1 (2012): 41–61; Roger Griffin, "German Nihilism" in Roger Griffin, ed., *Fascism* (Oxford: Oxford University Press, 1995), 351; Pierre-André Taguieff, "Origins and Metamorphoses of the New Right: An Interview with Pierre-André Taguieff," *Telos* 98–9 (Winter–Spring): 159–72.

2. GRECE, ed., *Le Mai 1968 de la nouvelle droite* (Paris: Le Labyrinthe, 1998).

3. Brigitte Beauzamy, "Continuities of Fascist Discourses, Discontinuities of Extreme-Right Political Actors? Overt and Covert Antisemitism in the Contemporary French Radical Right," in Ruth Wodak and John E. Richardson, eds., *Analysing Fascist Discourse: European Fascism in Talk and Text* (Abingdon: Routledge, 2013), 171.

4. Tamir Bar-On, "Richard B. Spencer and the 'Alt Right,'" in *Key Thinkers of the Radical Right* (New York: Oxford University Press, 2019), 222–41. Also, see *Radix Journal*, AltRight.com, accessed 1 October 2017, altright.com/author/radix/.

5. Jacob Siegel, "The Alt-Right's Jewish Godfather," *Tablet*, 29 November 2016, www.tabletmag.com/jewish-news-and-politics/218712/spencer-gottfried-alt-right; George Hawley, *The Alt-Right: What Everyone Needs To Know* (New York: Oxford University Press, 2019), 19–20.

6. Richard B. Spencer, "What It Means To Be Alt-Right," AltRight.com, 11 August 2017, altright.com/2017/08/11/what-it-means-to-be-alt-right/.

7. Alain de Benoist, "What is Racism?," *Telos* 114 (Winter 1999): 11–48.

8. Pierre-André Taguieff, "The New Cultural Racism in France," *Telos* 83 (Spring 1990): 109–22.

9. Alberto Spektorowski, "Ethnoregionalism: The Intellectual New Right and the Lega Nord," *Global Review of Ethnopolitics* 2, No. 3 (2003): 68–9.

10. "Richard Bertrand Spencer," Southern Poverty Law Center, accessed 13 October 2015, www.splcenter.org/fighting-hate/extremist-files/individual/richard-bertrand-spencer-0.

11. The author of *White Identity: Racial Consciousness in the 21st Century* (Oakton, VA: New Century Books, 2011).

12. See Spencer, "What It Means To Be Alt-Right."

13. Greg Johnson, *New Right versus Old Right* (San Francisco: Counter-Currents Publishing, 2013), xv.

14. Judith Bara, "Voters, Parties and Participation," in Judith Bara and Mark Pennington, eds., *Comparative Politics: Explaining Democratic Systems* (London: Sage, 2009), 244.

15. Cas Mudde, *The Ideology of the Extreme Right* (Manchester: Manchester University Press, 2002), 2–3.

16. Ibid., 3.

17. Stephen Wolinetz, "Belgium and Netherlands," in Colin Hay and Anand Menon, eds., *European Politics* (Oxford: Oxford University Press, 2007), 85–6.

18. Tamir Bar-On, "The French New Right Neither Right, nor Left?" *Journal for the Study of Radicalism* 8, No. 1 (2014): 3.

19. Jean Meyer, *The Cristero Rebellion: The Mexican People between Church and State, 1926–1929*, trans. Richard Southern (Cambridge: Cambridge University Press, 1976).

20. George Michael, *Confronting Right Wing Extremism and Terrorism in the USA* (New York: Routledge, 2003), 2.

21. Martha Augoustinos, Iain Walker and Nagire Donaghue, *Social Cognition: An Integrated Introduction* (2nd edn) (London: Sage Publications, 2006), 320.

22. William Roberts Clark, *Capitalism, Not Globalism: Capital Mobility, Central Bank Independence, and the Political Control of the Economy* (Ann Arbor, MI: University of Michigan Press, 2003).

23. Stanley G. Payne, *Fascism: Comparison and Definition* (Madison, WI: University of Wisconsin Press, 1983), 19.

24. Zeʾev Sternhell, with Mario Sznajder and Maia Asheri, *The Birth of Fascist Ideology: From Cultural Rebellion to Political Revolution*, trans. David Maisel (Princeton, NJ: Princeton University Press, 1995).

25. Peter Davies, ed., *The Extreme Right in France, 1789 to the Present: From De Maistre to Le Pen* (New York: Routledge, 2002), 13.

26. Iain McLean and Alistair McMillan, *The Concise Oxford Dictionary of Politics* (3rd edn) (Oxford: Oxford University Press, 2008), 465.

27. René Rémond, *Les droites aujourd'hui* (Paris: Louis Audibert, 2005).

28. Jeffrey Bale, *The Darkest Sides of Politics, I: Postwar Fascism, Covert Operations, and Terrorism* (New York: Routledge, 2018).

29. D.J. Mulloy, *Enemies of the State: The Radical Right in America from FDR to Trump* (Lanham, MD: Rowman and Littlefield, 2018).

30. Tamir Bar-On, "Brazil's Bolsonaro is the Latest Incarnation of the Radical Right in Latin America," *Rantt Media*, 2 November 2018, rantt.com/brazils-bolsonaro-is-the-latest-incarnation-of-the-radical-right-in-latin-america/.

31. Norberto Bobbio, *Left and Right: The Significance of a Political Distinction*, trans. Allan Cameron (Chicago: University of Chicago Press, 1996), 60–79.

32. This section borrows from: Tamir Bar-On, "Intellectual Right-Wing Extremism: Alain de Benoist's Mazeway Resynthesis Since 2000," in Uwe Backes and Patrick Moreau, eds., *The Extreme Right in Europe: Current Trends and Perspectives* (Göttingen: Vandenhoeck & Ruprecht, 2012), 333–58; Tamir Bar-On, "Richard B. Spencer and the Alt Right," in Mark Sedgwick, ed., *Key Thinkers of the Radical Right: Behind the New Threat to Liberal Democracy* (New York: Oxford University Press, 2019), 224–41.

33. Griffin, ed., *Fascism*, 351–54.

34. Guillaume Faye, *Le Système à tuer les peoples* (Paris: Copernic, 1981).

35. See, for example, Anton Shekhovtsov, *Russia and the Western Far Right: Tango Noir* (New York: Routledge, 2018).

36. John Veugelers and Gabriel Menard, "The Non-Party Sector of the Radical Right," in Jens Rydgren, ed., *The Oxford Handbook of the Radical Right* (New York: Oxford University Press, 2018), 290.

37. Spektorowski, "The French New Right," 68.

38. Robert Jaulin used the concept of ethnocide to describe the destruction of the Bari, an Indigenous group. Ethnocide has been employed by the ND to connote the slow destruction of various European peoples. See Robert Jaulin, *La Paix blanche, Introduction à l'ethnocide* (Paris: Éditions du Seuil, 1970).

39. Spencer, "What It Means To Be Alt-Right." In this section, I quote extensively from this manifesto.

40. That is, the Sharon Statement (1960) and the Port Huron Statement (1962) respectively.

41. Wilmot Robertson, *The Dispossessed Majority* (Cape Canaveral, FL: H. Allen, 1981).

42. Sam Kestenbaum, "Richard Spencer Touts Himself as 'White Zionist' in Israeli Interview," *Fast Forward*, 17 August 2017, forward.com/fast-forward/380235/richard-spencer-touts-himself-as-white-zionist-in-israeli-interview/.

43. George Grant, *Technology and Empire* (Toronto: Anansi, 1969).

44. Bat Ye'or, *Eurabia: The Euro-Arab Axis* (Teaneck, NJ: Fairleigh Dickinson University Press, 2005).

45. See Richard B. Spencer, "What is the American Right?," in Paul Gottfried and Richard Spencer, eds., *The Great Purge: The Deformation of the Conservative Movement* (Arlington, VA: Washington Summit Publishers, 2015).

46. John J. Mearsheimer and Stephen M. Walt, *The Israel Lobby and U.S. Foreign Policy* (New York: Farrar, Straus and Giroux, 2007).

47. Richard Spencer, "Who Are We?" National Policy Institute/Radix, 12 December 2015, www.youtube.com/watch?v=3rnRPhEwELo; "'Hail Trump!': Richard Spencer Speech Excerpts," *Atlantic*, 21 November 2016, www.youtube.com/watch?v=1o6-bi3jlxk.

48. Hawley, *The Alt-Right*, 216.

49. Anne-Marie Duranton-Crabol, "Les néo-païens de la nouvelle droite," *L'Histoire* 219 (March 1998), 217; Tom McCulloch, "The Nouvelle Droite in the 1980s and 1990s: Ideology and Entryism, the Relationship with the Front National," *French Politics* 4 (2006), 158–78.

50. CNN, "Wear 'racist' label as badge of honor," 10 March 2018, www.youtube.com/watch?v=SYysrAg8Yfo.

51. Tomislav Sunić, *Against Democracy and Equality: The European New Right* (New York: Peter Lang, 1990).

PART II

Theory

6

The Post-Democratic Horizon: Friend and Enemy in the Age of New Authoritarianism

Am Johal

Throughout his life, legal theorist Carl Schmitt was a ruthless critic of liberalism, parliamentary democracy and cosmopolitanism, especially in his notorious and controversial Nazi period when he was Hitler's crown jurist. In the twenty-first-century context of the proliferation of state and non-state practices such as torture (most notoriously at Guantanamo Bay), NSA surveillance, drone warfare, the rise of non-state actors such as ISIS, and the populist expansion of discriminatory legislation against immigrants and refugees, citations of Schmitt in the English-speaking world have accelerated since the attacks of 9/11 and, more recently again, following the rise of numerous neo-authoritarian political leaders worldwide. US president Donald J. Trump's inner circle have evoked Schmittian rhetoric unapologetically – it has become an essential part of the populist right's proverbial playbook.[1] Trump, during the nomination period in April 2016 when outlining his foreign-policy orientation, and also in his inaugural address in January 2017, drew directly on the friend–enemy distinction that argued that US foreign policy had lost its focus since Ronald Reagan in its willingness to go to war unnecessarily and its attempts to export democracy abroad. He further argued that Obama's policies confused friends and enemies, particularly citing the nuclear deal with Iran.[2] Even if former and current political insiders and outsiders with ties to the alt-right (like Steve Bannon, Darren Beattie, Stephen Miller and Richard Spencer to name just a few) haven't read Schmitt, they echo his ideas, both knowingly and unwittingly, and construct political strategies based on a de facto *friend–enemy* distinction.

Perhaps unsurprisingly, it is the far-right that has catapulted itself into the hallways of power in this time of economic crisis and ecological catastrophe as a paradoxical hardened avant-garde of an already conservative establishment. It has captured a distorted idea of political change *and* order simultaneously, and fomented anger and hysteria towards migrants, refugees, minorities and other vulnerable groups into a refined political project that is being self-consciously and deliberately replicated with varying degrees of effect and success internationally – such as in the EU elections of 2019, the rise of far-right figures such as Matteo Salvini in Italy, and Steve Bannon's attempt to create a neofascist international.[3] But the political mobilizations of resentment that have been launched with this toxic inertia seem to have had multiple successes on numerous fronts, particularly in consolidating ultra-conservative policy and appointments through the US Senate under the stewardship of hyper-partisan Republican Senate leader Mitch McConnell.[4] The progressive left has also fallen in on itself in its failure to articulate the root causes of the political moment. If Eric Hobsbawm once called Thatcherism "the anarchism of the lower middle class,"[5] Trumpism has taken this idea to an absurd new level.

The *post-democratic horizon* in this young century, I will argue, has Schmittian overtones and reverberations echoing throughout it. By considering Schmitt's work through key texts such as *Dictatorship* and *Political Theology*, this chapter will demonstrate that there is a lot that is *old* in the new authoritarianism that is emerging today.

But Schmitt should be approached cautiously. Matthew Specter poses the following question in his critique of the contemporary use of Schmitt on the left: can the former Nazi crown jurist be intellectual friend and political enemy simultaneously? Can we separate Schmitt's insights from his intentions? Specter argues that salvage operations often fail to deliver on their promise. Is the attempt to refashion Schmitt's ideas in such a way as to serve progressive critiques of the liberal order and, ultimately, class struggle, a Schmittian project?[6] For Schmitt, leaders like Mussolini represented the authentic politics of the strong leader – in contrast to parliamentary democracy's deliberative forms of political contestation and democratic claims; for the German legal theorist, liberalism ultimately evades the political.[7]

Specter argues that bringing Schmitt's insights into a leftist project is historically incoherent. The theorist of fascism and the ideologist of Nazi *Grossraum* is simply not worth the tendentious stretching and pulling necessary to turn him into a progressive and emancipatory egalitarian thinker – doing so would distort his actual theoretical project and personal politics. Yet the use of Schmitt carries a radical cachet in the post-9/11 world amongst certain segments of the progressive left. He has, at times, even been canonized as a genius political theorist. Others argue that he should be read carefully, but against the grain.[8] He is now being presented as relevant to our moment – a timeless classic that provides an important vision beyond the liberal state's self-presentation as a public good. The contemporary recirculation of Schmitt, particularly coming after the canonization of the Frankfurt School, may seem refreshing in redefining the political, especially insofar as (aside from figures like Pollock and Neumann) the first generation of Critical Theorists had precious little to say about the political.[9] But there's a danger, again, in reading Schmitt ahistorically. As Specter argues, the value of political antagonism in Schmitt can be found in Rousseau, Kant, Hegel and partly in many others, like Gramsci. Schmitt is an accomplished writer who traffics in seductive epigrams. It is in the search for something beyond the neoliberal political cul-de-sac, particularly post-9/11, that the present moment of the strongman and new authoritarian illiberalism opens itself up to a renewed potency in Schmittian ideas and rhetorics across the political spectrum. With these qualifications in mind, it is important to start with Schmitt's own work on the very concept of dictatorship.

DICTATORSHIP

Schmitt provided a book-length historical analysis of the legal concept of dictatorship in 1921. For Schmitt, dictatorship is a reasonable legal institution in constitutional law and has an avowed purpose. For him, the concept of dictatorship changed from the Roman period to the present through its integration into the theory of the constitutional state. Literally, for Schmitt, *dictator est qui dictat* (the dictator is one who *dictates*). However, in contrast to such a sovereign dictatorship, a *commissary dictatorship* becomes a mandate given by the people. The very move to a form of sovereign dictatorship is part of the process of dictatorship itself. In *Dictatorship*, Schmitt writes:

> The law, which is essentially a command, is based upon a decision related to the public interest; but the public interest only comes into being through the fact that the order has been given. The decision contained in a law is, from a normative perspective, borne out of nothing. It is, by definition, "dictated."[10]

Dictatorship is also something that fits firmly into a political matter; it solidifies processes of secularization. As Schmitt writes in *Political Theology*, "All significant concepts of the modern theory of state are secularized theological concepts."[11] Schmitt picks up this relationship between jurisprudence and theology from Leibniz. The very process of secularization for Schmitt means the dominance of reason over the authority of Scripture. The position of God has been replaced over time by secular principles like humanity, history, life, technology and others. For Schmitt, dictatorship is part of his *decisionism* – determining if the proper procedure has been followed by the appropriate authority – in which he builds on ideas from Machiavelli's *The Prince* and Hobbes's *Leviathan*. Schmitt is attempting to determine how decisionism can be understood in both a juridical and political context.[12]

The questions that Schmitt poses could certainly be asked in the present political moment with potency: "Who should be the guardian of the constitution in times of crisis? Who should be given extra-legal powers to save the constitution to restore public order and security when the welfare of the people is under threat? In other words, who is the *sovereign*?"[13] Who makes the decision? As Schmitt famously claims, the sovereign is the one who decides the state of exception. Schmitt writes:

Dictatorship is the exercise of state power freed from any legal restrictions, for the purpose of resolving an abnormal situation – in particular, a situation of war and rebellion. Hence two decisive elements for the concept of dictatorship are, on one hand, the idea of a normal situation that a dictatorship restores or establishes, and, on the other, the idea that, in the event of an abnormal situation, certain legal barriers are suspended in favour of resolving this situation through dictatorship. The concept of dictatorship has emerged during the last few centuries in state theory and in politics but the term has been generally used with great imprecision, in situations where an order is followed or a rule is being exercised. The concept develops from a legal Roman institution called dictatorship.[14]

Schmitt argues that "extraordinary conditions require extraordinary measures."[15] Dictatorship is the exercise of state power freed from any legal restrictions, for the purpose of a leader resolving an abnormal situation – in particular, a situation of war and issuing orders and executing them without having to obey traditional legal and parliamentary processes. Schmitt discusses Machiavelli's consideration of Aristotle – in the differentiation and parsing between the *coming to decision*, and its *execution*.[16]

Fare ogni cosa senza consulta (the right of the leader to do anything without consultation) has Roman origins as a concept.[17] Rational techniques of political absolutism were necessary for a leader to employ from time to time, particularly as an exception in a time of emergency. The state of exception is theorized as a legitimate tyranny because the decision to suspend the law is given freely to the leader as part of a constitutional process and order. For Schmitt, whomever rules over the state of exception ultimately rules over the state. He asks, through Machiavelli: should the king depend on the law, or the law depend on the king?[18] For Hobbes, "the law is not a norm of justice but a command, a mandate from the one who has supreme power and therefore wants to command the future actions of the members of the state."[19]

Schmitt writes that:

> The decision contained in a law is … borne from nothing. It is by definition "dictated" … sovereignty emerges from a constitutive act of absolute power, made through the people … But the question is: whose decision carries the day in the end, and by what authority? The matter does not depend on the ends, but rather on the decision about the means to those ends.[20]

Schmitt is particularly interested in the movement from the supreme command of war to an absolute parliamentary power that rules all other institutions in a centralized manner. In essence, this is the movement from *revolutionary* to *commissary* dictatorship. In the United States, for example, the President has "the football" close by, with nuclear codes and menu choices in order to launch various options of nuclear attack at a moment's notice without authorization required from the Senate or the House.[21] Delegated authority, dictatorship, constitutional norms and the law become entangled inside the emergency and its democratic and constitutional implications regarding the *decision*.

In the nationalist and illiberal contexts currently haunted by the spectres of fascism, sacrifice for the Nation becomes paramount as a faith-based exercise. The popular sovereign decides to enact violence or send people to death based on this subjective nationalist faith by not only maintaining a monopoly over violence, but also in determining when, how and why it gets used. It establishes and embodies a distorted and deliberately blurred "democratic" vision in matters of life and death. Liberal constructions like international law are not acknowledged as existing in real life, but as optional processes to consider in the realm of the political in this ultra-nationalist worldview. The friend–enemy distinction is the genie let out of the bottle again. Chantal Mouffe writes of Schmitt that he was of the view that liberalism negates democracy and democracy negates liberalism.[22] And, as Geoff Mann recently argued, since the state of exception has *become* the norm, it loses its critical purchase as a concept.[23]

Like Trumpism, Schmitt also believes in the homogeneity of a "people" in order to assert this political grouping as a norm of politics. Democracy can't exist for all humanity, but only for a people that is constructed on homogenous lines. Without an ethnonational, homogenous political unit, a strong state cannot exist in Schmitt's view.

Who belongs to the people then? In constructing a political context where the people rule, it is necessary to determine the identity of *the people*, and this for Schmitt can only be done by emphasizing the division between an *us* and *them*, or the *friend* and *enemy* distinction (see Chapter 5). Liberalism has a relationship to all humanity that Schmitt, like many anti-Enlightenment thinkers such as Burke, but also "reluctant modernists" such as Arendt,[24] views as failing to create a sufficiently specific political community. The very criterion of the political for many of these thinkers and current political leaders is based on the friend–enemy distinction. What is and isn't legitimate or allowable remains in the realm of the politically contestable. Schmitt argues that the state is not just another neutral arbiter between a plurality of communities, or accounts, of the "good life" as in liberalism. A weak state that acts as merely a referee is incapable of asserting political power on behalf of the people. For Schmitt, and for the neo-authoritarians of our present moment, pluralism leads to dangerous disunity and the potential for chaos.

Watching the slow, painful unravelling convulsions of the withering away of the Enlightenment project, aided by the speed of global-scale computation and its threats to traditional forms of sovereignty, it is unsurprising to see our contemporary version of the populist radio preachers, carnival barkers and "agitators" of the 1930s emerge in new, opportunistic forms today (see Chapter 8 in this volume).[25] To look at their specific local contexts and different political dynamics that have been mobilized in the name of the people, it is important that we do not conflate the figures of the moment like Erdoğan, Modi, Orbán, Putin, Trump and others. While there are some similarities in their mode of taking power and forms of centralization and varying commitments to neo-authoritarianism, their approaches have fit into their own specific nationalist contexts and some attempt to understand the mobilization of public support and historical resentment is necessary. What they do have in common is their capacity to create enemies both *within* and *without* in order to re-assert and re-articulate a new reactionary vision of the Nation and who constitutes it. Friend and enemy is also about the creation of winners and losers against a constructed establishment. The very real corruptions of the liberal state, both real and perceived, are a common denominator in calls for a purification of the Nation. For a progressive populism to exist, following Chantal Mouffe's *For a Left Populism*,[26] there must be an opposition constructed between the *demos* and the oligarchy. Reading Schmitt against the grain can possibly clarify the nature of the oligarchic enemy as the critiques of liberalism gain ground. We will now turn to Schmitt's work in *Political Theology*.

POLITICAL THEOLOGY

The state and political leaders ought to be concerned with the major question of the ever-present possibility of conflict, according to Schmitt. For Hegel, the state was the realization of the highest, most rational (*vernünftige*) form of existence. The role of the state was to secure the conditions where private citizens could actualize their public wills.[27] The state of exception and decision to enact such a moment is based on which authority in the state is competent to decide such a matter. For Hegel, the state was rational precisely because it mediated and reconciled the particular, the individual and the universal. Stability, order and political unity are the definitive goals of the state in this worldview. Schmitt was concerned with the question of which authority has the capacity to determine that these concepts have been restored. For Schmitt, it was only in the midst of crisis that sovereign power revealed itself. On that basis, sovereignty can only be determined in the borderline case and not with the normal routines of parliamentary democracy. Schmitt evokes the notion of a situational rather than universal law, whether to change or suspend laws according to the crisis at hand. For Schmitt, *all law is situational law*.

The stress on sovereignty reveals where true power resides; therefore, the study of emergency as part of a theory of the state is crucial to unpacking the concept of dictatorship. Schmitt famously writes:

> The exception is more interesting than the rule. The rule proves nothing; the exception proves everything: It confirms not only the rule but also its existence, which derives only from the exception. In the exception the power of real life breaks through the crust of the mechanism that has become torpid by repetition.[28]

For Schmitt, the exception thinks the general situation with intense passion and argues that every government is part of a continuum of dictatorship in its actual practices.[29] The state is governed by the ever-present possibility of conflict – the purpose of the state is to maintain its integrity to ensure order and stability. Schmitt's critique of liberalism centres on its attempts to depoliticize politics by avoiding fundamental existential decisions.

Schmitt argues, paradoxically, that because liberalism tries to serve *all* interests, it is not neutral. He contends that *all* forms of political authority are grounded in violence, and that despite the attempt of liberal political orders to cover over this inherent violence, the traces of it are increasingly visible.[30] Schmitt's critique of liberalism centres on its attempt to depoliticize political thought – in this it resonates uncannily with the almost universal legitimacy crisis of technocracy. Schmitt argues "today nothing is more modern than the onslaught against the political ... There must no longer be political problems, only organizational-technical and economic-sociological ones."[31]

For Schmitt, the notion of *the political* has four features:

1) The concept of the state presupposes the concept of the political;
2) The political precedes the state;
3) The political is a basic characteristic of human life;
4) The affirmation of the political is the affirmation of the state of nature.[32]

When the political emergency arrives, and the neo-Schmittians emerge inside the all-too-real institutions of power, they deform their very shape and eradicate universalistic, liberal-democratic norms with relative ease and absolute abandon. The political ground beneath our feet begins to shift and the *abnormal* contemporary political condition emerges into a state of hyper-normalization – the techniques of political combat become asymmetrical, the very grammar of political conflict is defiled and the capacity to resist becomes ever more compromised, perhaps to the point of becoming irretrievable.

A case in point is the 2019 formation of a bizarre "Unalienable Rights" Commission launched by US secretary of state Mike Pompeo, which will draw political distinctions between natural rights, and human rights imposed by the state. Due to the involvement of socially conservative figures in the formation of the commission, it is widely viewed as politically designed to roll back human rights into a narrower frame that will severely limit gender rights, gay marriage and trans rights. Besides being chaired by right-wing Harvard professor Mary Glendon, the Commission includes the involvement of prominent right Schmittians associated with *Telos* journal, such as Stanford professor Russell Berman and his protégé David Pan, a professor from the University of California-Irvine.[33]

The twenty-first-century forms of a post-democratic order and new authoritarian concepts emerge, take shape in real time, and are taking on particular features and contours of earlier periods of the twentieth century, particularly that of the strongman, the Nation, and enemies within and without. These nefarious forms of political border-keeping may not be a replication of the 1930s, but the pathetic re-appearance of the zombies like Trump, Mitch McConnell, David Duke et al. might just be the grotesque return of the 1980s on steroids, back with a vengeance. But will the future portend the continuation of this *new authoritarianism*, or will it be a return to a liberal order, or the formation of a robust and critical democratic socialist orientation? The present political culture seems to hinge on the very divisions of friend and enemy that liberal politics attempt to elide. What is inside or outside the polity is a perfectly Schmittian question that re-emerges in these sick times, and accelerates the assault on political reason that is the present-day fashion.

Trump seeks to clearly define the external enemy as "radical Islam" and the internal enemy as "'illegal' immigrants" (who are also always potential terrorists). It is a polemical rhetoric intended to put political adversaries on the defensive because of the overly wide net that it casts. In his attacks on judges and the judicial branch, Trump presents himself as a sovereign, above the law. This is further manifested in the pardoning of Arizona's Sheriff Joe Arpaio,[34] and references to neo-Nazis in Charlottesville as "fine people."[35] It is in the very vulgarity of the current public discourse that one can confidently declare the end of the end of history.[36]

The reality of the contemporary emergency is not about whether we *use* Schmitt or *lose* Schmitt, but that the political emergency has indeed already arrived. The state of exception has very much become the rule. We must, therefore, get back to the more central question: if we can't organize an agonistic politics of solidarity in *this* concrete political moment when everything – intellectually, spatially and temporally – is clearly at stake, *then when can we?*

NOTES

Unless otherwise stated, URLs were last accessed on 31 August 2019.

1. Mark Landler and Ashley Parker, "Donald Trump, Laying Out Foreign Policy, Promises Coherence," *The New York Times*, 27 April 2016, www.nytimes.com/2016/04/28/us/politics/donald-trump-foreign-policy-speech.html.

2. See "Transcript: Donald Trump's Foreign Policy Speech," *The New York Times*, 27 April 2016, www.nytimes.com/2016/04/28/us/politics/transcript-trump-foreign-policy.html; See also "The Inaugural Address," The White House, 20 January 2017, www.whitehouse.gov/briefings-statements/the-inaugural-address/.

3. Alexander Reid Ross, "Right Christian Army Is Marching on Liberal Europe – and on the Pope," *HAARETZ – Israel News*, 22 April 2019, www.haaretz.com/world-news/.premium-bannon-s-far-right-christian-army-is-marching-on-liberal-europe-and-on-the-pope-1.7151097.

4. Christopher R. Browning, "The Suffocation of Democracy," *New York Review of Books*, 25 October 2018, www.nybooks.com/articles/2018/10/25/suffocation-of-democracy/.

5. Eric Hobsbawm, *Interesting Times: A Twentieth-Century Life* (London: Allen Lane, 2002), 273.

6. Matthew Specter, "What's Left in Schmitt? Critique of an Academic Fashion," John Hope Franklin Center at Duke University, 3 April 2015, www.youtube.com/watch?v=-PhdIkq-rMc; See also Matthew G. Specter, "What's Left in Schmitt," in Jens Meirenrich and Oliver Simons, eds., *The Oxford Handbook of Carl Schmitt* (Oxford: Oxford University Press, 2017), 426–56.

7. Michael Lind, "Carl Schmitt's War on Liberalism," *National Interest*, 23 April 2015, nationalinterest.org/feature/carl-schmitt%E2%80%99s-war-liberalism-12704?page=0%2C2.

8. See Chantal Mouffe, ed., *The Challenge of Carl Schmitt* (London: Verso, 1999).

9. See Carl Schmitt's reception in *Telos*: David Pan and Russell A. Berman, "*Telos* 142 (Spring 2008): Culture and Politics in Carl Schmitt," *Telos Press*, 5 April 2008, www.telospress.com/telos-142-spring-2008culture-and-politics-in-carl-schmitt/.

10. Carl Schmitt, *Dictatorship*, trans. Michael Hoelzl and Graham Ward (Cambridge: Polity Press, 2014), 17.

11. Carl Schmitt, *Political Theology*, trans. George Schwab (Chicago: University of Chicago Press, 1985), 36.

12. Schmitt, *Dictatorship*, xxiii.

13. Ibid., xxiii.

14. Ibid., xxiii.

15. Ibid., 4.

16. Ibid., 4.

17. Ibid., 15.

18. Ibid., 15.

19. Ibid., 16–17.

20. Ibid., 17.

21. Michael Dobbs, "The Real Story of the 'Football' that Follows the President Everywhere," *Smithsonian Magazine*, October 2014, www.smithsonianmag.com/history/real-story-football-follows-president-everywhere-180952779/.

22. John P. McCormick, *Carl Schmitt's Critique of Liberalism: Against Politics as Technology* (Cambridge: Cambridge University Press, 1997).

23. Geoff Mann gave a public talk as part of the Vancouver Institute for Social Research series on Catastrophe on 4 March 2019. The talk can be accessed here: podcasts.apple.com/ca/podcast/geoff-mann-permanent-emergency/id1227965025?fbclid=IwARoZxzyftBkiW6cHotquwFCkE6-gXsg_NjXjYcN-ZOMrOYW_ZCwhuJjzIB8w&i=1000431150487&mt=2.

24. Seyla Benhabib, *The Reluctant Modernism of Hannah Arendt* (Lanham, MD: Rowman & Littlefield Publishers, 2003).

25. See the important work by Löwenthal and Guterman, *Prophets of Deceit: A Study in the Techniques of the American Agitator* (New York: Harper & Bros., 1949).

26. Chantal Mouffe, *For A Left Populism* (London: Verso, 2018).

27. Schmitt, *Political Theology*, 50.

28. Ibid., 15.

29. Ibid., 15.

30. See Walter Benjamin's 1921 essay "Critique of Violence", in *Reflections: Essays, Aphorisms, Autobiographical Writings* (New York: Schocken Books, 1986), 277–300.

31. Schmitt, *Political Theology*, 65.

32. Carl Schmitt, *The Concept of the Political* (Chicago: University of Chicago Press, 2007), 19.

33. See https://www.cbsnews.com/news/mike-pompeo-unveils-new-unalienable-rights-commission-amid-concerns-over-progressive-rollbacks/.

34. Julie Hirschfeld Davis and Maggie Haberman, "Trump Pardons Joe Arpaio, Who Became Face of Crackdown on Illegal Immigration," *The New York*

Times, 25 August 2017, www.nytimes.com/2017/08/25/us/politics/joe-arpaio-trump-pardon-sheriff-arizona.html.

35. Aaron Blake, "Trump Tries to Re-Write His Own History on Charlottesville and 'Both Sides,'" *Washington Post*, 26 April 2019, www.washingtonpost.com/politics/2019/04/25/meet-trump-charlottesville-truthers/?utm_term=.61862c5de18f.

36. See John M. Owen IV, "Not Melting into Air," *Hedgehog Review* 19, No. 3 (Fall 2017): 52–62.

Which Came First, Fascism or Misogyny? Reading Klaus Theweleit's *Male Fantasies*

Laura U. Marks

This chapter revisits Klaus Theweleit's landmark *Male Fantasies*, a massive and disorienting study of the journals of German Freikorps soldiers and related texts in the inter-war period. The book, appearing in English translation in 1987, contributed to the emerging scholarly topic of masculinity studies, still mostly grounded in psychoanalytic approaches. Theweleit intervened in the psychoanalytic discourse of the time by arguing that fascism lies in the pre-Oedipal fear of dissolution back into the mother. My reading of *Male Fantasies* tests what it is like to understand misogyny as a universal and ahistorical tendency, linked intimately to the terror of mortality associated with women and other subjects identified with their bodies. If that is the case, then fascism aligns with misogyny of necessity, as the armourization of the male self in the desperate quest to transcend mortality. Depressingly, this linkage holds fast today. However, my reading then backs off to study these questions historically, arriving at a somewhat more nuanced and politically workable understanding of the fascism–misogyny connection. At the end, I explain how Theweleit's book inspired me to diverge from his thesis as far as possible and to develop alternative theories of the subject as embodied and open to others.

Theweleit's two-volume *Männerphantasien* was published in West Germany in 1977, in the context of the first post-war generation's attempt to understand the cultural sources of Nazism.[1] (Theweleit returns to the topic in his recently published *Das Lachen Der Täter*.)[2] The University of Minnesota Press published the English translation, *Male Fantasies*, in 1987 in two volumes, comprising over 1,000 pages: Volume One, *Women, Floods, Bodies, History*, was translated by Barbara Ehrenreich and Chris Turner; Volume Two, *Psychoanalyzing the White Terror*, by Chris Turner, Erica Carter and Stephen Conway. A new edition is to be released imminently.

Male Fantasies examines the literature, both novels and journals, of German soldiers in the Freikorps (Free Corps) in the years after World War I. The Freikorps were volunteer paramilitaries composed of soldiers returning from the war in defeat, sensing themselves betrayed by the Weimar government, longing for the structure and meaning of military life. The Freikorps assassinated supporters of the Weimar Republic and Communists including Rosa Luxemburg and Karl Liebknecht. The Freikorps hated Bolsheviks, Jews and, importantly, the masses. Theirs was an elitism, not a populism.

Male Fantasies' literary analysis identifies, among the Freikorps soldiers, a pervasive terror of mortality expressed as misogyny, disgust with bodies and a desire for self-armourization. The second volume, *Male Fantasies: Psychoanalyzing the White Terror*, analyses the theme of hatred of women that recurs in the Freikorps literature. Women were divided into White and Red: the familiar virgin/whore dichotomy. The White woman was the sexless nurse, mother, sister. The Red woman was whore, Communist, Jew; an engulfing threat.

What is most striking in Theweleit's observations is that these soldiers didn't seek to dominate women sexually. On the contrary, they wanted to protect themselves from sex. The Freikorps soldier, Theweleit writes, feared "all of the hybrid substances that were produced by the body and flowed on, in, over, and out of the body: the floods and stickiness of sucking kisses; the swamps of the vagina, with their slime and mire; the pap and slime of male semen; the film of sweat ... the warmth that dissolves physical boundaries."[3] This is the terror of self-dissolution. Terror of the cunt, the swallowing wetness. Terror of losing one's boundaries in orgasm. Terror also of syphilis, associated in Freikorps literature with prostitutes, Jews and the masses.

Theweleit's study intervened in the psychoanalytic discourse of the 1970s and 1980s, bringing in theories of subjectivity from Wilhelm Reich, Gilles Deleuze and Guattari, and others. He argued that fascism lies not in Oedipal father-identification, as Theodor Adorno and others argued, but in pre-Oedipal fear of dissolution back into the mother. Terrifyingly, he raises the question of whether this particular kind of foundational misogyny is specific to the Freikorps, and perhaps identifiable in other periods, or whether it inheres in all men, or even all humans, throughout history. Patrice Petro identifies the problem: "Theweleit's notion of pre-Oedipality tends to make the dread of woman primordial (rather than cultural) by conjuring up some very archaic associations which link femininity and the maternal body to destruction and death."[4] Theweleit writes in a disorienting, almost nauseating style that evokes the very incontinence the Freikorps soldiers feared. The structure is loose and associative. A great number of quotations and loosely related pictures, with Theweleit's impressionistic responses, disperse the argument and allow it to dizzyingly envelop the reader.

WHICH CAME FIRST, FASCISM OR MISOGYNY?
THE AHISTORICAL ANSWER

The ahistorical answer is: fascism and misogyny are born together, inevitably and universally. I used to believe this and still do in weak moments; I repressed this belief for survival reasons. In this mood, I believe that misogyny is the deepest-held of human hatreds. I don't think sexism is a problem; misogyny is. It is a real hatred of women. Rape is universal: from war rape to date rape. Prison rape suggests rape is not about the woman – it's about the rapist needing to violate someone. But prison rape, in this logic, makes a man a woman. Because they've been fucked. In most of our societies, the definition of a woman is somebody who "gets fucked." The connotations are always negative – "This is fucked up"; "I'm so fucked!" In most societies, men who allow themselves to be penetrated are despised – because they've become like a woman. The worst insult you can say in Arabic is *charmout* (masculine), *charmouta* (feminine): literally, split like a log.

In this mood, I ask: "Why do people hate women so much?" Not only men. Women learn to hate women too, to despise each other and despise ourselves. Why? We know these simple answers. Because we're all afraid of mortality, and the female body reminds us of mortality more easily than the male body. Because the highest social values are "masculine" values like strength, individualism, competition, aggressiveness. Because in patriarchal societies women have to side with the men and turn against other women, to protect themselves and get ahead.

In this mood, reading *Male Fantasies* suggests an answer to "Which came first, fascism or misogyny?" that's both terrifying and, in a weird way, inspiring. Fascist ideologies actively transform personal fears into unifying worldviews. Most hatred is motivated by fear. Most people fear death more than anything else. At some point before that, people fear others who threaten their identities. People hate what reminds them of death. Theweleit reiterates the soldiers' terror and disgust when faced with bodies that have insides, wounds. This terror relates to Julia Kristeva's concept of the "abject" as that which should remain inside the body that appears outside it. *Male Fantasies* argues the "soldier males" hated women because women's bodies appear to be more material than men's bodies, more mortal, because women have vaginas, menstruate, give birth and (not mentioned by Theweleit) undergo menopause. Our bodies turn inside out, revealing the bloody insides. Sexual intercourse involves the inside of our bodies, an opening, which appears to the ignorant as a wound. (Though it is not a wound – it is a healthy orifice. In a cool way the cervix and vagina are not insides; they're folds, deep folds, and in fact our whole body is a very deeply folded surface. That is what I believe now.)

ARMOURED BODIES AND THE MYTH OF THE PHALLUS

In the section "The Mass and Its Counterparts," Theweleit demonstrates that "Red" women, Jews and the masses are all associated in the Freikorps literature with a threatening disintegration of bodily boundaries. Reflecting on one Ferdinand Brack's paranoid musing, in a Freikorps anthology, that enemy agents incite prostitutes to infect soldiers with venereal disease, Theweleit writes:

> The rebellious human mass gathering in the street is both an incarnation of all contagious diseases spawned by life-producing desire, and an incarnation of all the Red masses into which the man sinks and is lost: the embodiment both of pleasures that tempt and of pleasures that are dead. This may explain the soldier male's fascination with the decaying mass; for it appears to have all the features of his own externalized interior.[5]

A contaminating formlessness breaks down the boundaries between bodies, both killing them through disease and, interestingly, bringing them to life. The soldiers learned equally to repress their own desire, "life-producing desire," which threatened to break down their borders with threatening others.

So the Freikorps soldiers became ascetic, grew armour; effectively killed that part of themselves that desires. "Pleasure, with its hybridizing qualities, has the dissolving effect of a chemical enzyme on the armored body."[6] Theweleit adapts Reich's theory of psychology of fascism. It is the familiar project of making men into soldiers. First, they are individually hardened, oblivious to pain, rejecting any awareness of their insides, thinking of their bodies as "sacks." Second, they are hardened and anonymized into the phalanx or de-individualized soldier unit. We need to mourn the damage military service, especially conscription, does to men, and increasingly to women as well. It breaks them, makes them despise the weakness of their own and others' bodies, and spits them back into the world to do harm to others.

Most cultures dignify their leaders by disguising their bodies, making them appear godlike – or, at least, hiding their human bulges in a suit so that they appear to be minds, not bodies. The suit as armour, the power suit, the uniform. It's weird when you think about it: that, in our culture, when a couple dresses up, the man disguises his mortality in a suit, while the woman enhances hers in a revealing dress.

Hence the male soldiers' desire to be armoured, hard-surfaced and invincible allowed them to indulge their hatred of those who appear weak, and their desire to murder the weak. Fascist cultures categorize some humans as identified with the body, not the mind, and thus deeming them subhuman. Recall the detailed Nazi anthropological hierarchy that places near the bottom Jews, Africans, homosexuals and the disabled. The Freikorps created a special place at the bottom for "Red" or non-disembodied women.

Theweleit states that his study is part of a larger history of "the ways the European male ego develops in opposition to woman."[7] This statement suggests that the Freikorps books are simply one case study of millennia of misogyny. As in the Freudian and Lacanian psychoanalysis in which Theweleit's study is grounded, the suggestion is that the ego – which, for Freud and Lacan, was by definition male – can only build itself by seeing others as opponents to be assimilated through identification (other men) or taken as objects (women, the weak, foreigners etc.).

When I started out studying film in the late 1980s, Lacanian psychoanalytic theory still dominated the field. The theory of the gaze, a potent concoction of selected Lacanian and apparatus theory, postulated that a (implicitly and necessarily male) viewer can occupy the position of power offered by a film, propping his mere mortal look on a mythical phallic gaze. The theory states that males can identify with the illusory phallic power only to the extent that they deny their own physical and mortal bodies, as the Freikorps soldiers did. The generation of scholars and popularizers who received this theory tended to forget that actual males *never* in fact possess this phallic power. This mistake ravaged our field. Generations learned that men possess the gaze: "Stop looking at me with your male gaze!", "She's a victim of the male gaze." In this way, a later generation repeated the Freikorps' identification with a deathless power at the expense of their mortal bodies.

But in fact, nobody possesses the gaze. To have a body, to be mortal, means not having the phallus, ever. So why don't people talk more about the vulnerability of the male body, the exposed sexual organs? Why do people say phallic when they mean penis-like?

WHICH COMES FIRST NOW, FASCISM OR MISOGYNY?

Above, I noted that, according to Theweleit's analysis, the Freikorps soldiers avoided sexual intercourse because of their inordinate fear of self-dissolution. This attitude does not contradict the use of rape as a weapon of war, for millennia and in our own time. Burmese soldiers have gang-raped thousands of women in their attacks on Rohingya villages.[8] Saudi and UAE military personnel have raped Yemeni women and men in the ongoing Saudi–Yemeni war.[9] I do not even want to think about the psychology of the rapist, but I'm pretty sure it does not entail fear of self-dissolution as a man might feel with consensual sex. Rape is torture. Again, the fact that soldiers and prisoners rape men as well as women underscores that power lies in the ability to render the other person effectively just a body. This aligns with the hierarchy of disembodied–embodied that characterizes fascism.

Meanwhile, note the correlation between the ideas about gender among the far-right of our day and the Freikorps' division of women into virginal Whites and whorish Reds. For example, after James A. Fields, Jr., ran over and killed activist Heather Heyer at the infamous confrontation between white nationalists and counter-demonstrators on 12 August 2017, the neo-Nazi website *The Daily Stormer* devised the headline "Heather Heyer: Woman Killed in Road Rage Incident was a Fat, Childless 32-Year-Old Slut."[10]

Theweleit's study reveals that male desires to dominate and subjugate women rest upon an abject fear of the body. On this point, *Male Fantasies* might not seem to describe US President Donald J. Trump's particular brand of misogyny. Trump is a very embodied character, constantly referring to his and others' bodies and penises, boasting about grabbing women by the "pussy," claiming to be always ready for sex. Unlike the Freikorps, the US president does not revile sexual contact. There are, however, a couple of points of contact. Trump refers specifically to the length of his erect penis, not his flaccid penis; he attempts to assimilate himself to the phallic ideal. He appears terrified of female bodily functions, as when he referred to Fox News anchor Megyn Kelly bleeding from all her orifices, and seemed obsessed with Hillary Clinton's bathroom break during one of the presidential debates.[11]

However, if we subtract Trump from the current platform of the US Republican Party (which will happen if he is impeached), we get a much less colourful, less masculine display of power. Instead, we get policies to protect the rich and corporations, armourize the country, and, importantly, punish people for having bodies by cutting Medicare and Medicaid, destroying Obamacare and illegalizing abortion. Punishing women for having sex. The virgin/whore, White woman/Red woman dichotomy in full effect, in the full-throated misogyny of Vice President Mike Pence.

I have to say there is something galvanizing about the renewed visibility of the far-right in Europe, the United States and Canada in its most reptilian form: racist, misogynist, anti-immigrant, anti-Indigenous – especially in Canada, with the ongoing scandal of missing and murdered Indigenous women and the high number of Indigenous children abducted into foster care (see Chapter 12). It is a big relief to see all that hatred finally on display instead of hidden behind liberal appearances. I think repressed misogyny is much more dangerous than expressed misogyny; and the same with homophobia and racism. That is the danger of liberal discourse that tries to repair politics on the level of representation alone, clearly motivated by many fears.

Nevertheless, we need to keep alert for a blander form of fascism that I still suspect is more dangerous than overt fascism, and whose motives are economic control. This one is a fascism seemingly without ideology, concerned only with consolidating political and economic power. It holds in many nations; for example, as Zeinab Abul-Magd argues, the Egyptian military has been able to remain united over seven decades because it is not divided by ideology: all it wants to do is maintain power.[12] We can also see fascism without ideology functioning in the mega-media corporations that are establishing unprecedented power all over the globe. The new global empires like Alphabet (owner of Google),

Amazon, Facebook and Alibaba have successfully foisted their monop-
olies through ideological blandness and control of modern-day shipping routes: powerful servers.[13] If Amazon decided to arm itself and buy
some aircraft carriers, it could easily conquer nations and consolidate
global military power. I think we need to remain vigilant about these
fascist powers that are insidious because they operate without ideology.

WHICH CAME FIRST, FASCISM OR MISOGYNY?
THE HISTORICAL ANSWER

Above I quoted Theweleit's statement that his book is part of a larger
history of "the ways the European male ego develops in opposition to
woman."[14] The grimy glimmer of hope in this statement is his reminder
that the study *is* a history and does not make universal claims (though
the scholarly disavowal of other cultures makes me suspicious). There
is some comfort in Theweleit's reference to the history of this supposed
development of the male ego in opposition to women, because it invites
us to study periods when this tendency rises and falls, and to look for its
end. A historical view requires those of us interested in this question to
examine the other ways that egos develop at the expense of designated
others: we can examine how racism, homophobia and imperialism inter-
weave with misogyny but do not overlap. It requires alertness to new
forms of domination.

More excitingly, seeing the male ego as a *historical* phenomenon
creates the opportunity to examine the existence and emergence of
cultures whose idea of the self is not a fortress. There are ways to live that
acknowledge mortality. There exist cultures and subcultures around the
world, including among the young, that cultivate a way of being that is
open, not armoured; a self that is okay with its borders being indistinct,
that is oriented to others with care, perhaps built not on an individual,
but some kind of open network or ecosystem.

In a way these values constitute the despised "feminine" practices of
the daughter who never differentiated fully, the female that knows she
is castrated, and other feminine ego models psychoanalysis offered us.
It would be nice not to think of them as negations of the fully differentiated, hardened, successful ego. I don't believe the world can improve
until these values are placed equal to, and perhaps higher than, the
"masculine" values that have led us into ruin. Again, I reject the idea
that "masculine" values are inherently male qualities. They are ideals that

boys are supposed to develop, and for which females too are rewarded with money and status. Remember liberal feminism and the claim that women are as good as men? Instead, this is a time to celebrate that we humans are all mortal, all vulnerable, and therefore all need to cultivate care, openness, vulnerability and other cunty characteristics. Let us all be cunts! Let us embrace the pan-human capacity to be fucked.

There are lots of cultures and subcultures of men who don't culti-vate or reject the armoured ideal. In North American societies, there are slackers, dropouts, "sensitive men" (sometimes). Bears and puppies who push back against the gay hard-body cult. Born males who reject the gender and try out a third path. "Lesbian boys." Stylish men. Men who grow old gracefully. Men at ease with their sexuality. Gentle fathers. Gamers who manage to balance the imaginary body adventuring in virtual space and the soft, flabby, physical body at the console. There are so many kinds of lovely men.

Meanwhile, the erstwhile "feminine" but disembodied values of self-effacement and putting others first resonate a little too much with the White women revered by the Freikorps. What about pleasure, seduc-tion, sluttiness, "decadence"? Let's value "Red" women. A shout-out to Elizabeth Grosz's beautiful emphasis, in her rereading of Darwin, on sexual selection, which she opposes to natural selection (though we can understand it as a type of natural selection). The popular notion that the fittest are the ones who survive, where fitness indicates the ability to fight, has received far too much press in the 160 years since Darwin published *The Origin of Species*. If we turn our attention to Darwin's less-repeated disclosure that peacocks, roses, coffee plants, the male stickleback fish and the male bowerbird do all they can to delight and entice potential pollinators and mates, we quickly recognize that these dances of pleasure and seduction – *not* "fitness" – are how species carry on. Delight, beauty, colours, scents, the shimmer of the male stickleback are *necessities* for us living beings, not decadent treats to enjoy after we've slain the enemies and battened down the hatches. This shift of focus embraces the powers of seduction in all creatures – and notably celebrates male (non-human) splendidness.

Theweleit's books had a large influence on my work as a writer and film programmer in the late 1980s and early 1990s – a negative influ-ence, as I mentioned above. If I was to live, I had to find alternatives to theories that the ego cannot bear others different from it and must anni-hilate them. I was looking for ideas of subjectivity by which rather than identifying with destructive power one identifies with dissolution, or more positively, with the creative destruction of desire. I worked through alternatives couched within feminist Lacanian theory. I entertained Kaja Silverman's proposal that the dominant form of identification, homeo-morphic identification on the basis of similarity with the self, should give way to heteromorphic identification, or identifying with another that is different.[15] Heteromorphic identification undermines the ego's efforts to maintain a coherent identity. It tends toward death, or accepts a "reduced existence." Theories of masochistic identification, from Gaylyn Studlar and Gilles Deleuze, also interested me.

Moving away from the psychoanalytic theories that seemed irremedi-ably tragic, I built the idea that one's relationship to others need not be one of mastery, but of self-loss, openness or curiosity. I looked for alter-native images of men: embodied, vulnerable, okay with being fucked; I included some of them in a film programme, "Men We Love," in 1997. I adopted a theory that it is okay to occupy a state of near-dissolution some of the time. This became my theory of haptic visuality. I looked away from the painting of important subjects to the curly gilt frame, to abstractions that allow you to lose yourself. I looked at broken-down, demagnetized, glitchy images to see how we take the glitchiness into ourselves and accept the way it connects us materially to others, draws us out of ourselves and into a shared and pleasurable mortality.

I know that the armoured, disembodied, hateful subjectivity Thewe-leit analysed thrives on and cannot be theorized away. But I must believe that it is an artefact of history.

NOTES

Unless otherwise stated, URLs were last accessed on 20 April 2019.

1. 1977 was the year of the so-called "*der deutsche Herbst*" (German Autumn) that capped a decade of increasing student radicalism and violence and culminated in the deaths (state-sponsored liquidation?) of leading members of the Rote Armee Fraktion, Gudrun Ensslin, Andreas Baader and Jan-Carl Raspe, on 18 October 1977, in the notorious Stammheim Prison. I thank Samir Gandesha for this historical context.
2. Klaus Theweleit, *Das Lachen Der Täter* (Salzburg: Residenz Verlag, 2018).
3. Klaus Theweleit, *Male Fantasies*, trans. Barbara Ehrenreich and Chris Turner (Minneapolis, MN: University of Minnesota Press, 1987), 1:410.
4. Patrice Petro, "Review of *Male Fantasies. Volume I: Women, Floods, Bodies, History* by Klaus Theweleit," *SubStance* 17, No. 3 (1988): 77.

5. Theweleit, *Male Fantasies*, 1:17.
6. Ibid., 1:7.
7. Ibid., 1:384.
8. "'All of My Body Was Pain': Sexual Violence against Rohingya Women and Girls in Burma," Human Rights Watch, 16 November 2017, www.hrw. org/report/2017/11/16/all-my-body-was-pain/sexual-violence-against-rohingya-women-and-girls-burma.
9. "Yemen: United Nations Experts Point to Possible War Crimes by Parties to the Conflict," United Nations Human Rights Council, 28 August 2018, www.ohchr.org/.
10. Andrew Anglin, "Heather Heyer: Woman Killed in Road Rage Incident was a Fat, Childless 32-Year-Old Slut," *The Daily Stormer*, 13 August 2017, dailystormer.name/heather-heyer-woman-killed-in-road-rage-incident-was-a-fat-childless-32-year-old-slut/.
11. Elizabeth Schambelan, "Pseudo-Conservatism, the Soldier Male, and the Air Horn," *Los Angeles Review of Books*, 18 April 2016, lareviewofbooks.org/article/pseudo-conservatism-soldier-male-air-horn/.
12. Zeinab Abul-Magd, *Militarizing the Nation: The Army, Business, and Revolution in Egypt* (New York: Columbia University Press, 2018).
13. Jaron Lanier, *Who Owns the Future?* (London: Allen Lane, 2013).
14. Theweleit, *Male Fantasies*, 1:17.
15. Kaja Silverman, *The Threshold of the Visible World* (New York: Routledge, 1996).

8

"A Composite of King Kong and a Suburban Barber": Adorno's "Freudian Theory and the Pattern of Fascist Propaganda"

Samir Gandesha

There can be little doubt today that, after a long period of dormancy, authoritarian and, at times, downright fascistic elements have returned to public life with a vengeance; not just throughout Europe, the United Kingdom and the United States, but globally, most notably in Turkey, India and Brazil. The most visually shocking image of such a return are the migrant detention centres that litter southern Europe and, more notoriously, those of neglected, terrified Central American children, allegedly subject to psychical and sexual abuse, housed in concentration camps on the United States' southern border with Mexico.[1] However, today's fascism, for the most part, does not take the form of a mass movement geared to the violent overthrow of democracy, the installation of a one-party state, and the incarceration and liquidation of its "enemies." Rather, it entails the gradual but steady erosion of the institutions of the liberal-democratic order consisting of, inter alia, the rule of law, the separation of powers, and, in particular, the independence of the judicial branch, the freedom of the press and the right to dissent. Taken together, such an erosion amounts to what has been called by both defenders and critics alike "illiberal democracy."[2] Against the backdrop of social and economic crises, such illiberal democracy is justified by supposedly strong leaders purporting to embody the will of an ethnonational "community" allegedly besieged by "floods" of migrants from below, and a nefarious, abstract logic of finance from above. Occasionally, as in the case of figures such as George Soros, these two forces are sounded, in a paranoid key, as locked together in secret complicity.[3]

The return of fascistic elements to politics today within the context of a neoliberal capitalism, a social order in which the state has become fully marketized, in which the figure of *homo politicus* has been eclipsed by *homo economicus*, requires some explanation.[4] As Michel Foucault has shown in his lectures on biopolitics in the late 1970s, one of the dominant currents of economic thinking in the newly formed Bundesrepublik (Federal Republic of Germany) was the ordoliberal economic doctrine of the Freiburg School. This doctrine held that the most effective way of preventing the return of the authoritarian state was by giving the rationality embedded in the market full reign, thus enabling it – in a kind of Keynesianism in reverse – to limit and regulate the state.[5] So, how could it be that, rather than forestalling authoritarianism, neoliberalism has in fact created a salubrious environment for it to take root and flourish?

One way of explaining the relationship between authoritarianism and neoliberalism is through a reading of Theodor W. Adorno's essay "Freudian Theory and the Pattern of Fascist Propaganda" (hereafter "Freudian Theory"). While there is now a veritable "academic cottage industry" in studies on Trump and political authoritarianism,[6] such studies have largely failed, in my view, to connect up their analyses with the larger problem of the specifically "damaged life" of neoliberal society (see Chapter 11 in this volume).[7] The reason for this is that they focus rather too much on Trump himself – and figures like him – while overlooking the socioeconomic conditions that make such figures so attractive to a significant proportion of the electorate. This is precisely why Adorno's synthesis of socioeconomic and social-psychological perspectives is so apposite and timely.

In "Freudian Theory," Adorno principally engages with two texts: the first is Löwenthal and Guterman's *Prophets of Deceit: A Study of the Techniques of the American Agitator* (1949);[8] and the second is Sigmund Freud's *Group Psychology and the Analysis of the Ego* published one year before Mussolini's Partito Nazionale Fascista's March on Rome and seizure of power in 1922.[9] The first represents a content analysis of the speeches of "agitators" or far-right demagogues such as Father Coughlin and Gerald Smith, whom Löwenthal and Guterman situate in relation to a typology of responses to socioeconomic problems. The second seeks to show how the individual's orientation to the reality principle can be short-circuited via the sense of power and security afforded by virtue of membership in a mass.

How is it, as Adorno glosses Freud, "that modern men [and women] revert to patterns of behaviour which flagrantly contradict their own rational level and the present level of enlightened technological civilization"?[10] In order for such reversion, or *regression*, to be fostered, an *artificial* social bond must be created based upon the pleasure principle, which is to say, "actual or vicarious gratifications individuals obtain from surrendering to a mass."[11] Freud helps to *explain* what most other forms of social psychology merely *describe*: the potentiality for "short-circuiting" the relation between "violent emotions" and "violent actions." The particular nature of the social bond, in Freud's view, enables the individual to throw off the "repression of his unconscious instincts."[12] Insofar as Freud points to the interpenetration of the archaic and the modern, the mythical and enlightened elements of social psychology, he anticipates the argument of *Dialectic of Enlightenment*. Archaic myth and modern enlightenment converge in the idea of *sacrifice*. The key difference is that the process of enlightenment through disenchantment and rationalization entails the increasing "introjection" or internalization of sacrifice understood as "self-renunciation" or repression.[13] This means that in order to survive the individual must adjust to external imperatives and as a result renounce the aspiration to happiness or sensuous fulfillment.

Therefore, it is the civilizing process, or "second nature," that produces the revolt of "first nature." In recent decades, Freud's supposedly "negative" account of repression has been challenged by such figures as Jacques Lacan, Gilles Deleuze and Felix Guattari.[14] Nowhere has this account been more forcefully criticized than in Foucault's introductory first volume of *The History of Sexuality*. Here, Foucault takes Freud's "repressive hypothesis" to task as a purely negative account of power positing that social and historical forces restrict the expression of "instinct" or "nature" from a position exterior to it; implying that, for resistance, "nothing less than a transgression of laws, a lifting of prohibitions, an irruption of speech, a reinstating of pleasure within reality, and a whole new economy in the mechanisms of power will be required."[15] Adorno, in contrast, shows the way in which Freud's own account of repression is much more subtle and entails the interpenetration and mutual conditioning of nature and history in the very operation of the psychical agencies. As Adorno suggests in his gloss of *Civilization and its Discontents*: "As a rebellion against civilization, *fascism is not simply the reoccurrence of the archaic but its reproduction in and by civilization itself.*"[16]

Returning to the question of the nature of the social bond, it seems doubtful, however, that an account of such a bond grounded in libido could provide a convincing account of Nazism insofar as Hitler replaces the *loving* with a *threating* and *punishing* father. While there is a connection here to Freud's conception of the primal father in *Totem and Taboo*,[17] it is necessary to explain the nature and content of fascist propaganda which deliberately aims to re-activate the individual's "archaic inheritance"; that is, it is manufactured and constantly reinforced. If under modern conditions in which the guiding principle of public life is individualism, how is it that individuals can be induced to relinquish their own individuality and therewith their rational interests including, in extreme cases, their interest in *self-preservation* itself? This is a question that becomes especially pertinent under the hyper-individualistic conditions of the neoliberal order. The question is: how do people become a mass?[18] The answer that Adorno provides, via Freud, is that this happens through the mechanism of *identification*.

Drawing on Erik H. Erikson's work, Adorno suggests that the agitator appears to be the "enlargement" of the subject's own personality rather than the image of the father, whose authority had already started significantly to diminish in the inter-war period.[19] Contemporary fascist leaders, then, are not simply the manifestations of an ambivalent image of the father nor the domineering head of the "primal horde" who, through the threat of violence, establishes a monopoly on women, but, rather, are what Adorno calls "great little men."[20]

The process of *identification* is inextricable from that of *idealization*. In *Prophets of Deceit*, the authors emphasize the way in which the agitator exploits the negative affects of his followers. Löwenthal and Guterman argue that "Unlike the usual advocate of social change, the agitator, while exploiting a state of discontent, does not try to define the nature of that discontent by means of rational concepts. Rather does he increase his audience's disorientation by destroying all rational guideposts and by proposing that they instead adopt seemingly spontaneous modes of behavior."[21] Adorno explains more specifically how these frustrations and anxieties emerge in the first place and how fascist propaganda exploits them by promoting identification through idealization.

In the crux of his argument, Adorno suggests that frustration has to do with the "characteristic modern conflict between a strongly developed rational, self-preserving ego agency and the continuous failure to satisfy their own ego demands."[22] In other words, the conflicts stem from the contradiction lying at the heart of bourgeois or liberal-democratic society between the *political* ideal of individual autonomy or self-determination through democratic institutions, on the one hand, and a purely negative conception of freedom that characterizes capitalist relations of production, on the other. As Adorno presciently suggests in *Negative Dialectics*:

> The more freedom the subject – and the community of subjects – ascribes to itself, the greater its responsibility; and before this respon-sibility it must fail in a bourgeois life which in practice has never yet endowed a subject with the unabridged autonomy accorded to it in theory. Hence the subject must feel guilty.[23]

As a result of this contradiction between the *ideality* and the *actuality* of freedom, the promise of and failure to realize a self-determined life, the individual experiences frustration and discontent resulting from the face of her own ego ideal or idealized sense of self often deriving from the imago of a parent. Such a conflict constitutes a key aspect of the "damaged life" of late capitalist societies, the anatomy of which Adorno lays bare in *Minima Moralia*.[24] "This conflict," Adorno argues, "results in strong narcissistic impulses which can be absorbed and satis-fied only through idealization as the partial transfer of the narcissistic libido to the object."[25] The collective adulation and love of the leader is the way in which frustrated modern subjects overcome their negative self-images resulting from the failure to approximate their ego ideal – the gap between ego and ego ideal becomes, in other words, unbearable. The leader's seductive aura of omnipotence, therefore, owes less to the "archaic inheritance" of the primal father and more to the individual's narcissistic investment in collectivity resulting from this failure.

In order for such collective identification through idealization to be successful, the leader must be "absolutely narcissistic," that is, someone who *is loved but does not love in turn*. This is what explains the agita-tor's disinterest – in contrast to revolutionary and reformer alike – in presenting a positive political programme outlining concrete policy proposals, as Löwenthal and Guterman point out. In place of the latter, which would suggest some minimal concern for the needs of the followers, there is only the "paradoxical program of threat and denial."[26]

At the same time, the leader embodies a contradiction between, on the one hand, appearing to be a super-human figure and, on the other, an average person – as Adorno puts it memorably, in reference to Adolf Hitler, "a composite of King Kong and the suburban barber."[27] This is key to understanding the seductive psychological structure of fascism: these two dimensions mirror a split in the followers' own narcissistic egos – one part of which attaches to "King Kong" and the other to the "suburban barber" – and are retained by them. It is thus that the leader represents the followers as their *enlargement*. Fascist propaganda is constructed around the basic concept of the "'great little man,' a person who suggests both omnipotence and the idea that he is just one of the folks, a plain, red-blooded American untainted."[28]

It is in this way that Adorno provides an account of the guiding concept of *The Authoritarian Personality*: that personality type characterized both by subordination to the "strong" (suburban barber) and domination over the "weak" (King Kong). In this, the structure of social character reproduces the contradiction lying at the heart of bourgeois society between the theory of autonomy or freedom and the practice of heteronomy or unfreedom. The image of the "great little man", therefore, according to Adorno, answers:

> [The follower's] twofold wish to submit to authority and to be the authority himself. This fits into a world in which irrational control is exercised though it has lost its inner conviction through universal enlightenment. The people who obey the dictators also sense that the latter are superfluous. They reconcile this contradiction through the assumption that they themselves are the ruthless oppressor.[29]

This is perfectly expressed in Hitler's slogan, which lays bare the essence of the ambivalence of the authoritarian or sadomasochistic personality type: "*Verantwortung nach oben, Autorität nach unten*" ("responsibility towards above, authority towards below").[30] Or, as Adorno writes in Chapter 19 of *The Authoritarian Personality*, "The identification of the 'authoritarian' character with strength is concomitant with rejection of everything that is 'down.'"[31]

The more superfluous the idea of the dictator within formally democratic and egalitarian – though substantively unequal – societies based on private ownership and control of the means of production, the more emphasis will be placed precisely on the dictator's ersatz quality. Such phoniness is maintained in the form of the hollow shell of the "artificial group" of the religious institution. The hierarchy of religion, stripped of its spiritual essence, is taken over by fascism, in particular its emphasis on the distinction between "sheep and goats," insiders and outsiders, and also, therefore, on its deployment of negative libido. In other words, the emphasis on love within the Christian religion, which was, nonetheless, also based upon hatred towards those who remained beyond the faith, is now divested of even the appearance of *agape* or fellowship, transformed into an almost exclusively *negatively* integrating function.[32] This enables fascism to play its "unity trick," which is to say, it elides differences *within* the group (other than the extant hierarchy) by emphasizing differences *between* the group and those who remain outside it. Such a trick culminates in what Adorno terms a "regressive egalitarianism" – all members of the "national community" should *equally be denied* individual pleasures. The social bond is, as it were, solidified through a shared introjection of sacrifice or the renunciation of the aspiration to a sensuously fulfilled life. The Nazis' repeated and hyperbolic demands for sacrifice for the "Fatherland," which echo every form of nationalism particularly when it comes to war, bear this out.[33]

Adorno touches upon a key technique by which fascist propaganda emphasizes the difference between insider and outsider groups: namely the repeated use of images of lower animals such as insects and vermin to characterize foreigners, in particular Jews and refugees. Drawing not only on Freud but also Otto Rank's observations that in dream symbolism insects and vermin signify younger siblings, in fact, babies, such symbolism scarcely conceals negative cathexis. Yet, at the same time, such brothers and sisters have identified with one another through a shared love object, namely the leader, and therefore must direct or project this negative cathexis outward beyond the group.

Here, one might argue, as Horkheimer and Adorno suggest in *Dialectic of Enlightenment*, that it is not just the displacement of contempt experienced by the followers themselves that is projected outwards in the image of lower animals, but also a direct evocation in propaganda of powerful and affectively charged tropes of abjection. As Julia Kristeva suggests, this has, ultimately, to do with the pre-Oedipal relation to the maternal body and, in turn, with the transgression of a boundary and the ensuing production of disgust.[34]

But anything natural which has not been absorbed into utility by passing through the cleansing channels of conceptual order – the screech of the stylus on slate which sets the teeth on edge, the *haut goût* which brings to mind filth and corruption, the sweat which appears on the brow of the diligent – whatever is not quite assimilated, or infringes the commands in which the progress of centuries has been sedimented, is felt as intrusive and arouses a compulsive aversion.[35]

The abject and "compulsive aversion" it evokes have to do with a fear of self-dissolution. This constitutes the drive to eliminate the non-identical or that which cannot be conceptually grasped without remainder; in the attempt to bring nature under the sway of technical control and mastery, whatever residue of uncontrolled or uncontrollable (non-identical) nature remains elicits an automatic response of revulsion.[36] The very signs of destructiveness that fascism substantively embodies are projected outwards onto its victims; fascism, in this sense, is the paranoid performance of the victimizer who compulsively assumes the role of victim.

Abjection is employed as a propagandistic technique, in other words, to portray the other as a dangerous contagion who threatens the health and the very life of the body politic and must be both spiritually and physically excluded, by force if necessary. Traces of offensive yet secretly desired "nature" are projected onto the stranger that become his stigma. Once so projected, the "other" can then be contained, excluded and in extreme cases, ultimately "liquidated" or "exterminated" like pests or vermin. Through the process of extirpating the non-identical, the identity of the ethnonational "community" is confirmed and stabilized.

Adorno addresses the question of how the agitators came to such precise knowledge of group psychology without having the intellectual wherewithal to access it. The answer is that, given the psychological identity between the leader and the led, the agitator accesses mass psychology through his *own* psychology. The key difference, though, is that the former evinces "a capacity to express without inhibitions what is latent in them, rather than by any natural superiority."[37] The authoritarian leader is an "oral" personality type who, according to Freud, seeks gratification through eating, drinking and other oral activities including speaking. The *aggressive* oral type is hostile and verbally abusive toward others. The agitator evinces a "capacity to speak incessantly and to befool the other."[38] The incessant nature of such speech leads it to void itself of sense and become magical; it casts a spell over its listeners and plays on the follower's "archaic inheritance." The power he exercises is, paradoxically, indicative of his powerlessness insofar as it intimates ego weakness rather than strength laying bare his unconscious drives. Yet, at the same time, this plays into the very image of the leader as the enlargement of the follower's own ego. "In order successfully to meet the unconscious dispositions of his audience," Adorno argues, "the agitator so to speak simply turns his own unconscious outward."[39]

The fit between the agitator's techniques and the "psychological basis of their aim" is assisted by larger transformations in society that also contribute to the increasing passivity of the individual, which is to say, the decline of her capacity for experience through the consolidation of the culture industry as a whole.[40] The standardization that lies at the heart of the culture industry harmonizes perfectly with a key attribute of authoritarian personalities, namely: "stereotypy" and "their infantile wish for endless, unaltered repetition."[41] The link between European high culture and the culture industry, for Adorno, can be located in the easily recallable leitmotiv, originated by proto-fascist composer Richard Wagner, which he likens to "component parts of factory-assembled products: musical Fordism."[42] In order to mobilize the masses against their very own interests, fascist propaganda tends to circumvent "discursive thinking" and "mobilize[s] irrational, unconscious, regressive forces."[43] In this, it is aided greatly by the culture industry that already has greatly diminished the human capacity for autonomy and spontaneity.

What are we to make of Adorno's social-psychological account of fascist propaganda today? There are broadly three areas in which Adorno's reflections are illuminating: (1) populism; (2) the analysis of contemporary "agitators"; and, finally, (3) the culture industry. Before addressing these in turn, however, it is important to consider the limitations of such reflections as well. As I have argued elsewhere, the sociological assumptions of Adorno's appropriation of Freud, specifically Pollock's concept of "state capitalism" – according to which the state's role is to manage the crisis tendencies of capitalism – must be rethought in the period characterized by the obsolescence of Keynesianism.[44] Moreover, Adorno's unmediated reliance on the orthodox Freudian account of drive theory and concept of the Oedipal conflict require rethinking and reconstruction insofar as Freud's atomistic, Hobbesian ontology does not sit particularly well with a *social* ontology indebted to Hegel and Marx.[45]

What remains of enduring importance, however, is Adorno's discussion of the basic contradiction lying at the heart of capitalist democracy, and the way in which authoritarianism today re-emerges as a powerful, if false, response to it in the face of a paucity of viable alternatives that comprises what Marcuse called one-dimensional society.[46]

The objective condition for the stubborn persistence of authoritarianism is the contradiction lying at the heart of liberal-democratic society between the democratic principle of *egalitarianism*, on the one hand, and the liberal conception of *negative freedom*, on the other. The neoliberal, financialized form of capitalism, which has been in place roughly since the mid-1970s, has dramatically sharpened this contradiction insofar as the *citoyen* (Brown's *homo politicus*) has become eclipsed by *homo economicus*, understood now as the "entrepreneur of himself."[47] The latter is forced to take more responsibility for himself, yet, at the same time, has access to fewer resources with which to *actualize* this responsibility in any meaningful sense. On average, rates of growth in high-income countries have dropped precipitously since the 1960s (4.3% p.a.), falling to 2.8% in the 1970s, 2.3% in the 1980s, 1.8% in the 1990s and 1.2% in the 2000s.[48] Accordingly, since the 1970s, wages for the vast majority have remained stagnant, not even keeping pace with inflation,[49] while welfare state provisions have declined considerably and social services as well as higher education have become more costly. What has filled this vacuum is growing financialization and debt.[50] Individuals constantly fall short of their ego ideals as a result of which there is a corresponding proliferation of guilt, anxiety, frustration and ultimately anger.[51]

Ironically, rather than forestalling authoritarian tendencies, as West German ordoliberalism maintained it would, the advent of neoliberalism has proven to be particularly fertile ground for the germination of neo- and post-fascist political movements.[52] In a way that echoes Moishe Postone's analysis of the implicit antisemitism at the heart of one-sided criticisms of finance capital (abstract labour) from the standpoint of the working class (concrete labour),[53] Neel argues that:

As one of the poorest generations in recent history, debt and rent are the defining features of our lives. It is this fact that makes the current incarnation of the far right an actual threat, because it increases the probability that some variant of present-day Patriot politics might actually find a mass base, as a program formulated specifically to oppose the extraction of rents from an unwilling population in the far hinterland is translated into a more general opposition of rents as a primary form of exploitation in contemporary capitalism.[54]

The contradiction between autonomy in the "political" realm or formal structures of representative democracy, and increasing heteronomy within the "economic" realm becomes ever more unbearable. As Adorno states in "The Meaning of Working Through the Past":

Fascism essentially cannot be derived from subjective dispositions. The economic order, and to a great extent also the economic organization modeled upon it, now as then renders the majority of people dependent upon conditions beyond their control and thus maintains them in a state of political immaturity.

He goes on to argue that:

If they want to live, then no other avenue remains but to adapt, submit themselves to the given conditions; they must negate precisely that autonomous subjectivity to which the idea of democracy appeals; they can preserve themselves only if they renounce their self ... The necessity of such adaptation, of identification with the given, the status quo, with power as such, creates the potential for totalitarianism.[55]

The idealization and identification with the aggressor can be regarded as a (false) solution to this contradiction. In the "great little man" the follower is mesmerized by an enlarged image of himself before which he bows down.

Populism emerges as a response to the ensuing legitimacy crisis of the neoliberal order.[56] Rather than dismissing and vilifying this political formation *tout court*,[57] it is worthwhile distinguishing between left and right versions of populism. Adorno helps us arrive at criteria that enables us to do precisely this, by emphasizing that the process by which "people become a mass" is of vital importance – insofar as the foregoing discussion, as we have seen, is geared to understanding the role of the agitator in contrast with the reformer or revolutionary who, like contemporary left populists such a Jeremy Corbyn and Bernie Sanders, seek genuinely to outline concrete policy objectives and in the process respond to their followers' democratic demands, by specifically taking aim at *socioeconomic inequality*. In contrast, the agitators obviate such interests by emotional appeals to racist and exclusionary conceptions of the people and in the process transform them into a mass.[58]

Adorno's account of the mechanism of *identification through idealization* is especially helpful in understanding a host of right-populist leaders who appear to embody the oxymoronic idea of a "great little man," such as the Filipino President Rodrigo Duterte, Indian Prime Minister Narendra Modi, Brazilian President Jair Bolsonaro, and British Prime Minister Boris Johnson. However, no one embodies this oxymoron more clearly than the current President of the United States: Donald J. Trump exemplifies the "great little man" and is consequently regarded by his supporters as a larger-than-life version of themselves. But, could it be said that their followers have internalized the logic of self-sacrifice or renunciation? Isn't it the case that they are aggressively standing up to the "elites" that have sacrificed them at the altar of globalization? Trump may not explicitly demand self-sacrifice, but in supporting him most, though perhaps not all, of his supporters nevertheless sacrifice their own interests – for example, in the continued viability of the Affordable Care Act- at the altar of "Making America Great Again." The massive tax cut for the ultra-rich will materially harm them. To this one could add the opioid crisis that keeps deepening among poor whites and, as a result, dropping their life expectancy rapidly.[59] Trump's supporters could be called "self-sacrificing" in a very literal way. Yet, when the political establishment attacks him for his somewhat tenuous grasp of the English language, sartorial faux pas, gustatory blunders, fake hair etc., it backfires and only reinforces the idea of the establishment's contempt not only for the President but the *demos*, the people who idealize and identify with him; it reinforces their identification with the aggressor. So, despite being presented with evidence that his presidency has harmed them materially, their support remains as more or less unabated.[60] At the same time, Trump supporters' love for the President is matched only by the hatred and occasional violence they direct towards the "other": "*Verantwortung nach oben, Autorität nach unten*"!

Trump is clearly an aggressive oral type who tweets incessantly, often issuing threats to his own political rivals such as Hillary Clinton ("Lock her Up")[61] or, perhaps more disturbingly, encouraging his followers at a recent rally to direct the chant "Send her Back!" at the Somali-American representative from Minnesota, Ilhan Omar, as well as Alexandria

Ocasio-Cortez, Rashida Tlaib and Ayanna Pressley who were all born in the United States.[62] The incessantly contradictory nature of Trump's speech eviscerates language as the genuine medium of truth-claims – this violence enacted on language itself is key to understanding our increasingly post-truth era perhaps even more than the rise of far-right media outlets such as Breitbart News. The slogan of "Make America Great Again," moreover, draws upon the rhetoric of an *authentic*, falsely concrete American life, liberated from frighteningly abstract, inscrutable, global processes signified by the barely concealed antisemitic trope of "the swamp."

The fetishization of the wall on the United States' southern border with Mexico represents an extreme expression of authoritarian populism globally, manifesting a heightened hysteria directed at those driven to migrate by geopolitical and political-economic catastrophes. Despite his claims that climate change is a hoax or conspiracy, Trump seems to be preparing for a worsening crisis of climate refugees. So, people are transformed into a mass by virtue of a common object of affection that is inextricable from the negative libido generated by way of projection of strangeness, which is to say, illness, contagion and ultimately danger (the abject) onto the outsider. Such negative libido is bolstered by references to "shithole countries" and statements that "all Haitians have AIDS."[63] Moreover, in addition to demonizing refugees as an "invasion," telling four non-white members of Congress to go back to the "broken and crime infested place from which they came,"[64] Trump referred to Baltimore, the home of the late Rep. Elijah Cummings (D-Md.) as a "disgusting, rat and rodent infested mess" that was "far worse and more dangerous" than the conditions at the southern border.[65] The French author Jean Raspail, who has profoundly influenced Trump's former advisor Steve Bannon (see Chapter 13), portrayed a Europe in the near future overrun by the dispossessed of the Third World, symbolized by defecating and fornicating Indian migrants, in his racist dystopian novel *Le Camp des Saints* (*The Camp of the Saints*).[66] One can see in Trump's rhetoric not only overt misogyny ("Grab 'em by the pussy") but also the hatred of ambiguity which might explain the ferocity of attacks on LGBTQ+ communities, transgendered people in particular.

Perhaps most presciently, Adorno (with Horkheimer) draws attention to the elective affinity between the authoritarian personality and the culture industry. The condition for the possibility of people being transformed into the mass is the passivity that follows from the gradual but steady weakening of the critical function of the ego. In their account of the culture industry, Horkheimer and Adorno show the way in which the former replaces what Kant called the "transcendental schema," according to which the sensible manifold is related to concepts through the activity of the imagination, by:

> Ready-made thought models, the termini technici which provide them with iron rations following the decay of language. *The perceiver is no longer present in the process of perception.* He or she is incapable of the active passivity of cognition, in which categorial elements are appropriately reshaped by preformed conventional schemata and vice versa, so that justice is done to the perceived object.[67]

Today, we can see this in the digitization of the culture industry in recent decades. The algorithm has come to replace the transcendental schema in organizing the manifold of sensible intuition. In place of Fordist mass production and standardization it now generates difference and heterogeneity tailored specifically to the whims and tastes of each individual. Yet the algorithm is a code that also nonetheless locks into place a logic of repetition and stereotypy, often confirming, deepening and reinforcing the subjective prejudices mentioned above through the creation of so-called "echo chambers" or unconscious manifestations of confirmation bias.

Just as twentieth-century fascists used radio and film to spread their propaganda, contemporary agitators evince a predilection for the use of Twitter, Facebook, Instagram and WhatsApp which, amongst other things, enables them to effectively bypass the putatively rational and critical scrutiny of serious journalists, intellectuals and academics, and communicate often unconscious wishes and desires directly to their followers themselves. While social media has been taken up by progressive forces to organize and mobilize against authoritarian regimes – for example in Iran in 2009, then subsequently in the Arab Spring and Occupy movement – it has become the means by which the far-right has successfully manipulated voters, as the Cambridge Analytica scandal has shown, wherein the British consulting firm engaged data-mining of personal information by accessing millions of Facebook profiles without their will for the purpose of political advertising.[68] The Wiki-Leaks release of hacked emails in the final stage of the 2016 election, as the Mueller Report has shown, was not inconsequential to its outcome.[69] Social media, moreover, has provided the infrastructure for right-wing populist parties and movements to spread fake news and misinformation. It could be said to create new types of what Freud called "artificial groups" that undermine the reality-testing capacity and therefore critical capacity of the ego.[70] It is both the medium and expression of a "turning outward" of the unconscious.[71]

Furthermore, online message boards, such as 4chan and 8chan, make possible precisely the "short-circuiting" of the relation between "violent emotions" and "violent actions." Taking inspiration from the far-right mass murderers Anders Breivik and Brenton Tarrant (the Christchurch mass murderer), copycat white supremacists in Europe and North America, particularly the United States, have discussed and planned their attacks on these message boards before executing them in the real world. Participants discuss topics such as "Target Selection" (most effective ways to maximize body counts) and the online group compares and celebrates the numbers of casualties from shooting to shooting in what *The New York Times* calls "a gamification of mass murder." Attackers often post manifestos, and in the case of Christchurch provide a live feed of the attack in real time. The aim is to appeal to the unconscious aggressive impulses of others who form part of the virtual artificial group.[72]

Adorno's examination of the stubborn persistence in the post-war period of the authoritarian personality type was oriented towards articulating "a new categorical imperative after Auschwitz" – so that the Holocaust would never repeat itself.[73] Key to this, for Adorno, was the Kantian idea of enlightenment understood as *Mündigkeit*, which means political maturity or the notion that the citizen must be empowered to speak for herself as an *autonomous* subject.[74] This means the capacity to break the compulsion to repeat embodied in the culture industry. The citizen is capable of speaking for himself, according to Adorno, "because he has thought for himself and is not merely repeating someone else; he stands free of any guardian."[75] *Mündigkeit* is vital, moreover, for the citizen's capacity to resist conformity to prevailing opinion and stands in a close relation to what Kant called reflective judgement. At the same time, Adorno emphasizes, with Nietzsche (and, later, Kristeva), that we are all "strangers to ourselves." This means that aspects of our experience, for example pain, trauma and suffering, can never be made fully transparent, can never enter into concepts without some excess or remainder escaping their grasp. In this, as the psychoanalyst Christopher Bollas has suggested, the genuine plurality of democracy must echo the plurality within the mind.[76] Such a plurality, however, will not truly come into its own until the opposition between liberalism and democracy is transcended and overcome.

NOTES

Unless otherwise stated, URLs were last accessed on 15 September 2019.

I would like to thank John Abromeit, Ian Angus, Rosemary Bechler, Hilda Fernandez-Alvraez, Martin Jay, Claudia Leeb and Harriet Olivette Wills for helpful comments on previous drafts of this chapter. An earlier version was presented at the Institute of Philosophy at the Czech Academy of the Sciences in Prague in June 2019. Thanks to Joe Grim Feinberg and Pavel Siostrzonek for their insightful questions and interventions.

1. Mathew Haag, "Thousands of Immigrant Children Said They Were Sexually Abused in U.S. Detention Centres, Report Says," *The New York Times*, 27 February 2019, www.nytimes.com/2019/02/27/us/immigrant-children-sexual-abuse.html.

2. See Ruth Ben-Ghiat, "Trump's Twinship with Orbán Shows 'Illiberal Democracy' Has a Home in the US," *Guardian*, 16 May 2019, www.theguardian.com/commentisfree/2019/may/16/trump-orban-democracy-us-hungary; and see Christopher R. Browning, "The Suffocation of Democracy," *New York Review of Books*, 25 October 2018, www.nybooks.com/articles/2018/10/25/suffocation-of-democracy/.

3. A good example of this is Hungary's anti-migrant legislation called the "Stop Soros Law." "Hungary Pursued by EU over 'Stop Soros' Migrant Law," BBC News, 19 July 2018, www.bbc.com/news/world-europe-44887638.

4. See Wendy Brown, *Undoing the Demos: Neo-Liberalism's Stealth Revolution* (Cambridge, MA: MIT Press, 2015). Apparently, Brown was caught off guard insofar as there is little indication of the authoritarian populism that would be spawned by precisely this neoliberal order. In a sense, the undoing was also, as it were, an unleashing of the *demos* (the people). Brown's Foucauldian account of neoliberalism, while one of the best, fails to discern the populist backlash it engenders. She does attend to this later via a reading of Nietzsche in her essay "Neoliberalism's Frankenstein: Authoritarian Freedom in Twentieth-First Century 'Democracies,'" in Wendy Brown, Peter Gordon and Max Pensky, *Authoritarianism: Three Inquiries* (Chicago: University of Chicago Press, 2018). Chapter 11 in the current volume provides a fascinating account of the intertwining of neoliberalism and fascism in the Latin American context with a particular focus on Chile and Brazil as laboratories of an authoritarian neoliberalism that have ramifications beyond this context.

5. Michel Foucault, *The Birth of Biopolitics: Lectures at the College de France 1978–79*, trans. Graham Burchell (Basingstoke: Palgrave Macmillan, 2008): 129–84.

6. Richard Wolin, "Our 'Prophet of Deceit': WWII-era Social Scientists explained Trump's Appeal," *Chronicle*, 30 October 2016, www.chronicle.com/article/Our-Prophet-of-Deceit/238176. See the section "The Frankfurt School and the New Right," *Logos Journal* 16, No. 1–2 (2017), logosjournal.com/2017-vol-16-nos-1-2/, as well as that found in *Public Seminar*. One of the best essays of the latter happens to be by Jay M. Bernstein in which he suggests that Adorno's "Freudian Theory" reads as "if it was written precisely in order to address the Trump phenomenon." Yet, what he tends to de-emphasize is that the Trump phenomenon is made possible by a distinctive set of socioeconomic arrangements that are global. Jay M. Bernstein, "Adorno's Uncanny Account of Trump's Authoritarian Personality," *Public Seminar*, 5 October 2017, www.publicseminar.org/2017/10/adornos-uncanny-analysis-of-trumps-authoritarian-personality/. See also Brown, Gordon and Pensky, *Authoritarianism: Three Inquiries*, and the excellent article by Claudia Leeb, "A Festival for Frustrated Egos: The Rise of Trump from an Early Frankfurt School Critical Theory Perspective," in Marc Benjamin Sable and Angel Jarmillo Torres, eds., *Trump and Political Philosophy: Patriotism, Cosmopolitanism and Civic Virtue* (Cham, ZH: Palgrave Macmillan, 2018): 297–314.

7. This has been recently described with tremendous eloquence and insight by Phil A. Neel in *Hinterland: America's New Landscape of Class and Conflict* (London: Reaktion Books, 2018).

8. Leo Löwenthal and Norbert Guterman, *Prophets of Deceit: A Study of the Techniques of the American Agitator* (New York: Norton, 1949).

9. Sigmund Freud, *Group Psychology and the Analysis of the Ego* (New York: W.W. Norton, 1990).

10. Theodor W. Adorno, "Freudian Theory," in Eike Gebhardt and Andrew Arato, eds., *The Essential Frankfurt School Reader* (New York: Continuum, 1982), 121.

11. Ibid., 122.

12. Ibid., 122.

13. As, for example, analysed by Max Weber in his *Protestant Ethic and the Spirit of Capitalism* (Oxford: Oxford University Press, 2010), his study of the crucial role of puritanism in the emergence of capitalism in western Europe.

14. See for example Félix Guattari and Gilles Deleuze, *Anti-Oedipus: Capitalism and Schizophrenia*, trans. Robert Hurley and Mark Seem (London: Penguin, 2009).

15. Michel Foucault, *The History of Sexuality Volume I: An Introduction*, trans. Robert Hurley (New York: Pantheon Books, 1978), 5.

16. Adorno, "Freudian Theory," 122, emphasis added.

17. Sigmund Freud, *Totem and Taboo* (New York: W.W. Norton and Company, 1990).

18. On this question, see Siegfried Kracauer's 1938 essay on fascism: Siegfried Kracauer, *Totalitäre Propaganda*, ed. Bernd Stiegler (Frankurt: Suhrkamp, 2013) as well as John Abromeit, "Siegfried Kracauer and the Early Frankfurt

School's Analysis of Fascism as Right-Wing Populism," in Pierre-François Noppen, Gérard Raulet and Iain MacDonald, eds., *Théorie critique de la propagande* (Paris: Editions de la Maison des science de l'homme, forthcoming).

19. As Horkheimer, Marcuse and Fromm had already suggested in their research on the family in the 1930s, and social psychologists such as Alexander Mitscherlich would subsequently emphasize in the 1960s *Society Without The Father: A Contribution to Social Psychology* (New York: Perennial Press, 1992).

20. This diminution of individual agency is accelerated through the war and is a phenomenon that can be understood today with transformations in the displacement of the industrial by the service sector and the ensuing "feminization" of labour, leading to a profound crisis of heterosexual masculinity. Such a crisis is key to understanding the return of a misogynistic far-right today and the appeal of its spokespersons such as Carl Jung-influenced psychologist Jordan Peterson. See Nellie Bowles, "Jordan Peterson, Custodian of the Patriarchy," *The New York Times*, 18 March 2018, www.nytimes.com/2018/05/18/style/jordan-peterson-12-rules-for-life.html. See also: Harrison Fluss, "Jordan Peterson's Bullshit," *Jacobin*, February 2018, www.jacobinmag.com/2018/02/jordan-peterson-enlightenment-nietzsche-alt-right.

21. Löwenthal and Guterman, *Prophets of Deceit*, 6.

22. Adorno, "Freudian Theory," 126.

23. T.W. Adorno, *Negative Dialectics*, trans. E.B. Ashton (New York: Continuum Books, 1981), 221.

24. T.W. Adorno, *Minima Moralia: Reflections on Damaged Life*, trans. E.F.N. Jephcott (London: Verso, 2008).

25. Adorno, "Freudian Theory," 126.

26. Ibid., 127.

27. Ibid., 127.

28. Ibid., 127.

29. Adorno, "Freudian Theory," 127–8.

30. Ibid., 128.

31. T.W. Adorno et al., *The Authoritarian Personality* (New York: Norton Library, 1950), 762.

32. In the *Genealogy of Morals*, Nietzsche saw this dynamic very clearly, referring to it as the *ressentiment* lying at the heart of the "slave morality" which Christianity took over from Judaism, whereby the identity of the insider group is constituted by the pure negation of the outsider group.

33. While it would be mistaken to draw too close a parallel between fascism and contemporary identity politics of the left, the "unity trick" can certainly be seen in the latter. See Samir Gandesha, "Not Only the Difference Between Identities but the Differences Within Them," *openDemocracy*, 19 November 2018, www.opendemocracy.net/en/not-only-difference-between-identities-but-differences-within-them/.

34. Julia Kristeva, *The Powers of Horror: An Essay on Abjection*, trans. Leon S. Roudiez (New York: Columbia University Press, 1982).

35. Max Horkheimer and Theodor W. Adorno, *Dialectic of Enlightenment*, trans. E.F.N. Jephcott (Paolo Alto, CA: Stanford University Press, 2002), 147–8.

36. The experience of women's bodies as fundamentally abject as expressed in the writings of the Freikorps played an important role, according to Klaus Theweleit in his two-volume *Males Fantasies*, trans. Christ Turner, Erica Carter and Stephen Conway (Minneapolis, MN: University of Minnesota Press, 1987). See also Chapter 7 on Theweleit in this volume.

37. Adorno, "Freudian Theory," 132.

38. Ibid., 132.

39. Ibid., 133.

40. While Adorno doesn't mention it, there was a direct line of transmission of psychoanalysis to the culture industry precisely through the figure of Edward Louis Bernays – Freud's nephew. Bernays was the originator of psychoanalytically informed propaganda techniques for modern industry. This propaganda was called advertising. See Adam Curtis's film *Century of the Self* (2002).

41. Adorno, "Freudian Theory," 133.

42. T.W. Adorno, *Essays on Music*, ed. Richard Leppert (Berkeley, CA: University of California Press, 2002): 534.

43. Adorno, "Freudian Theory," 134.

44. Samir Gandesha, "Identifying with the Aggressor: From the 'Authoritarian' to the 'Neo-Liberal' Personality," *Constellations* 25, No. 1 (2018): 147–64. See also John Abromeit, "Frankfurt School Critical Theory and the Persistence of Right-Wing Populism in the United States," in Jeremiah Morelock, ed., *Critical Theory and Authoritarian Populism* (London: University of Westminster Press, 2018), in which he discusses in some detail the shift from the Fordist-Keynesian to the neoliberal period and how this has created conditions much more propitious for RWP.

45. See the work of Jessica Benjamin which challenges normative assumptions of the thesis of the "society without fathers" and, more recently, Chiara Bottici's contribution to *Public Seminar*'s Roundtable on "Freudian Theory": Chiara Bottici, "Adorno with Freud, Adorno Beyond Freud: Part 4," *Public Seminar*, 19 October 2017, www.publicseminar.org/2017/10/adorno-with-freud-adorno-beyond-freud/.

46. Herbert Marcuse, *One Dimensional Man: Studies in the Ideology of Advanced Industrial Society* (London: Routledge, 1991), 87–126.

47. Foucault, *Birth of Biopolitics*, 226.

48. Neel, *Hinterland*, 14.

49. See Thomas Piketty, *Capital in the Twenty-First Century* (Cambridge, MA: Belknap Press, 2017) in which he shows that the average return on capital far outstrips the increase in the rise of wages leading to a logic of widening socioeconomic inequality, which reverses the anomalous trend of *les trente glorieuses*.

50. See Costas Lapavitsas, *Crisis in the Eurozone* (London: Verso, 2012) and Maurizio Lazzarato, *The Making of the Indebted Man: An Essay on the Neoliberal Condition* (Cambridge, MA: Semiotext(e) Books, 2012) and *Governing by Debt* (Cambridge, MA: Semiotext(e) Books, 2015).

51. As Jay Frankel and Lynne Layton have argued, this also leads to shame – a common response to trauma that results from the feeling that there is something wrong with oneself. See Jay Frankel, "The persistent sense of being bad: The moral dimension of identification with the aggressor," in Adrienne Harris and Steven Kuchuck, eds., *The Legacy of Sandor Ferenczi: From Ghost to Ancestor* (New York: Routledge, 2015), 204–22.

52. On the idea of "post-fascism" see Enzo Traverso, *The New Faces of Fascism* (London: Verso, 2019).

53. Moishe Postone, "Zionism, Anti-Semitism and the Left: An Interview with Moishe Postone," *Krisis*, 27 June 2010, www.krisis.org/2010/zionism-anti-semitism-and-the-left/.

54. Neel, *Hinterland*, 44.

55. T.W. Adorno, "The Meaning of Working Through the Past," in *Critical Models: Interventions and Catchwords*, trans. Henry W. Pickford (New York: Columbia University Press, 1998), 98–9. See also T.W. Adorno, *Aspekte des neuen Rechtsradikalismus* (Frankfurt am Main: Suhrkamp, 2019), 39.

56. See Adam Tooze, *Crashed: How a Decade of Financial Crises Changed the World* (New York: Viking, 2018).

57. See Eric Fassin's *Populism Left and Right* (Chicago: Prickly Paradigm Press, 2019) which considers populism of both left and right to be fundamentally a politics of resentment.

58. Samir Gandesha, "Understanding Left and Right Populism," *Zeitschrift für kritische Theorie* 46/47 (2018): 214–35. Reprinted in Jeremiah Morelock, ed., *Critical Theory and Authoritarian Populism* (London: University of Westminster Press, 2018), 49–70.

59. Josh Katz and Margo Sanger-Katz, "'The Numbers Are So Staggering': Overdose Deaths Set a Record Last Year," *The New York Times*, 29 November 2018, www.nytimes.com/interactive/2018/11/29/upshot/fentanyl-drug-overdose-deaths.html.

60. John Harwood, "Trump's core supporters are about to be handed the bill for tax reform," CNBC, 16 November 2017, www.cnbc.com/2017/11/16/trumps-core-supporters-are-about-to-be-handed-the-bill-for-tax-reform.html.

61. Uttered not just in the 2016 presidential campaign but re-iterated in Trump's re-election announcement in Florida. Maggie Haberman, Annie Karni and Michael D. Shear, "Trump, at Rally in Florida, Kicks Off His 2020 Re-Election Bid," *The New York Times*, 18 June 2019, www.nytimes.com/2019/06/18/us/politics/donald-trump-rally-orlando.html.

62. "Crowd Chants 'Send Her Back' as Trump Attacks Ilhan Omar—Video," *Guardian*, 18 July 2019, www.theguardian.com/global/video/2019/jul/18/crowd-chants-send-her-back-as-donald-trump-attacks-ilhan-omar-video.

63. Ibram X. Kendi, "The Day 'Shithole' Entered the Presidential Lexicon," *Atlantic Magazine*, 13 January 2019, accessed 19 August 2019, www. theatlantic.com/politics/archive/2019/01/shithole-countries/580054/.

64. Jennifer Rubin, "Trump's Speech Would be Laughable if it Weren't So Infuriating," *Washington Post*, 5 August 2019, www.washingtonpost.com/opinions/2019/08/05/im-too-busy-watching-what-hes-doing-hear-what-hes-saying/.

65. Spencer Kimball, "Trump Calls Baltimore a 'Disgusting, Rat and Rodent Infested Mess' in Attack on Rep. Elijah Cummings," CNBC, 27 July 2019, www.cnbc.com/2019/07/27/trump-calls-baltimore-a-disgusting-rat-and-rodent-infested-mess-in-attack-on-rep-elijah-cummings.html.

66. Jean Raspail, *Camp of the Saints* (Petoskey, MI: Social Contract Press, 1994).

67. Adorno, *Dialectic of Enlightenment*, 167, emphasis added.

68. See "The Cambridge Analytica Files," *Guardian*, accessed 21 July 2019, www. theguardian.com/news/series/cambridge-analytica-files.

69. Julie Hirschfeld Davis and Mark Mazzetti, "Highlights of Robert Mueller's Testimony to Congress," *The New York Times*, 24 July 2019, www.nytimes.com/2019/07/24/us/politics/mueller-testimony.html.

70. Richard Seymour has this to say about the new Brexit Party led by Nigel Farage: "Unlike older party models, it doesn't invest in lasting infrastructure. It is nimble-footed, expert at gaming social media—the stock market of attention. It won the battle for clicks, and made a killing in this election. Such online frenzies are akin to destabilizing flows of hot money, forcing legacy parties to adapt or die. But when Parliament is so weak, its legitimacy so tenuous, they can look like democratic upsurge." Richard Seymour, "Nigel Farage is the Most Dangerous Man in British Politics," *The New York Times*, 28 May 2019, www.nytimes.com/2019/05/28/opinion/nigel-farage-brexit.html.

71. See the work of Christian Fuchs, in particular *Digital Demagogue: Authoritarian Populism in the Age of Trump and Twitter* (London: Pluto, 2018).

72. "We Have a White Nationalist Terrorist Problem," *The New York Times*, 4 August 2019, accessed 5 August 2019, www.nytimes.com/2019/08/04/opinion/mass-shootings-domestic-terrorism.html.

73. Adorno, *Negative Dialectics*, 365.

74. Immanuel Kant, "An Answer to the Question: What is Enlightenment?" in *What is Enlightenment? Eighteenth Century Answers, Twentieth Century Questions* (Berkeley, CA: University of California Press, 1996), 58–64. This is also where I disagree with Vladimir Safatle's interpretation: autonomy in Adorno's sense has little if anything to do with the ego psychology of the neo-Freudian revisionists such as Karen Horney (the *bête noire* of the Lacanian school to which Safatle is sympathetic). In fact, Adorno had little more than scorn for such revisionism. Vladimir Pinheiro Safatle, "Adorno's Freud in the Age of Trump: Part 1," *Public Seminar*, 2 October 2017, www. publicseminar.org/2017/10/adornos-freud-in-the-age-of-trump/.

75. T.W. Adorno, "Critique," in *Critical Models: Interventions and Catchwords*, trans. Henry W. Pickford (New York: Columbia University Press, 1998), 281.

76. Christopher Bollas, "The Democratic State of Mind," in David Morgan, ed., *The Unconscious in Social and Political Life* (Bicester: Phoenix Books, 2019): 27–39.

9

So, You Want a Master? Psychoanalytic Considerations on the Intellectual's Responsibility in Light of Traumatic Repetition

Hilda Fernandez-Alvarez

Man is an animal which, if it lives among other of its kind,
requires a master

Kant, *On History*[1]

For the only master, it has to be said, is consciousness

Lacan, *Seminar XXIV*[2]

Today we face the worst crisis of displaced and stateless persons of modern times; palpable climate change that is causing ecological disaster; neoliberal financialization as the new regime of accumulation within capitalism; and an overall deterioration of the public sphere, commanded by right-wing political movements in different regions of the world. In contemporary neoliberal capitalism, new geopolitical relations are enabling far-right values, such as bigotry, racism, misogyny and greed, to claim wider allegiance. The actualization of these values relies upon naturalistic accounts of inequality and gender that have disastrous effects on the most vulnerable among us: refugees, Indigenous people, women and children, particularly from the poorest countries of the Global South.

The new right has gained growing numbers of followers by criticizing the establishment and capitalizing on strategies historically associated with revolutionary movements, such as humorous transgression, vitalism and youthfulness. These strategies have succeeded in the ascension of right-wing populisms that, as Gandesha describes, work through a form of authoritarianism that, via the signifier "the people," invokes allegiances by exploiting insecurities and fears of the "strange other" and by "personalizing" the enemy (refugees, terrorists etc.).[3] Meanwhile the left, for its part, seems to be primarily focused on contesting cultural issues and policing political correctness, in the process strengthening identity politics, and thus it has been unable to gain a propitious space for a truly effective critical and political response. There are important exceptions such as the increase in popularity of the Labour Party in the United Kingdom, commanded by Jeremy Corbyn; the new grassroots progressive democratic movement represented by Alexandria Ocasio-Cortez and other strong women of colour, who are joining efforts with Bernie Sanders in the United States; or the recent election in Mexico of a left coalition "Morena," with López Obrador as its candidate, which won the vote of about 30 million people hoping for a change of regime. The enduring dialectics of political oppositions has always historically existed. Today, however, we appear to be tilting towards the right, which requires a profound self-examination on the part of the left.

In this chapter I employ logical principles extrapolated from psycho-analytic clinical practice, which aims at subverting the compulsion to repeat, to account for the ways in which the unconscious participates in the political realm. The compulsion to repeat is understood by Freud as a manifestation of the death drive, a force stronger than pleasure, which seeks to reproduce some prior condition – repetition as an end in itself – despite the suffering it generates.[4] It is my intention to signal ways in which the left is, itself, marked by the compulsion to repeat in light of the current spectre of fascism.

The political is defined, here, as the possibility of making a social link – negotiating conflicts and antagonisms with others – in the presence of both an excess and a residue of the "Real." Far from meaning "reality," the Real is that which exceeds, and therefore constitutes, the crisis of symbolization. The political significance of the Real ought not to be underestimated because it is the very negative force that structures social relations. This chapter is in dialogue with what has been referred to as the "Lacanian left," which, according to Stavrakakis, is gaining prominence in political theory.[5]

In light of this tradition and stemming from clinical practice, the thrust of this chapter is to propose a Lacanian reading of politics that descales the concept of political action from a presumed social totality to the level of the individual act in the immediate social cell of the institution (couple, family, friend group, workplace, university, creative practice etc.). I propose:

a) To think of politics as an endeavour of inscription and re-inscription, which are mechanisms that arrest the repetition of the traumatic emergence of the death drive;
b) That these socially healthful processes are blocked by the effects of the Master signifier, whose "symbolic efficacy" is increasingly displaced by mechanisms of what Lacan calls the "imaginary" that not only fail to correspond to the universal, but also strengthens identity politics; and, finally,
c) That the politics of inscription inquire the ethical responsibility of the contemporary intellectual, who can be thought of as a Gramscian counter-hegemonic analyst who grasps opportunities to stop the compulsion repetition and takes this desire to its logical conclusion.

Inscription refers, here, to the process of partial symbolic assimilation, or legibility, of *that which can't be written* (the impossible); re-inscription, in contrast, refers to the process of resignification of overdetermined "writings" that have maintained things the way they are; thus, it is a new and different writing of *the already written* (the necessary).[6] These processes of inscription and re-inscription are only known by the consequent effects, which pertains to a cessation of the destructive insistences of the death drive and a transformation via a creative act, which partially cease alienation and suffering, and thus, are of emancipatory nature. My approach is based on Lacan's theory of discourse;[7] his deployment of the three categories of modal logic discussed in *Seminar XX*: the necessary, the contingent and the impossible;[8] and his later work around the material impact of the letter, which partakes of the Real and whose insistence in the imaginary and symbolic reality influences modes of desire, enjoyment and suffering.[9]

THE POLITICS OF THE REAL: INSCRIPTION AND RE-INSCRIPTION OF THE DEATH DRIVE

Let's start from the inarticulable impossible. Every political instance brings about a traumatic residual excess, inaccessible to representation, which manifests today in the overwhelming emergencies of humanitarian, ecological, sociological or economic nature. Such residues correspond to the insistence of the death drive idly circulating around *objet petit a*, understood by Tomšič as the negative *Undinge* of the Kantian transcendental aesthetics, the "*nonthing*" or the "nothing as something;"[10] and it is also akin to Adorno's "non-identity."[11]

Can we imagine the everyday experience of a child living in households that make a living out of extreme violence (e.g. narco-cartels, gangs, terrorism etc.)? Can we imagine the hardship of a displaced new mother seeking asylum? A seriously ill person who can't afford proper health care? A grandfather picking up the remains of a grandchild after a bomb has hit her? What about imagining the experience of a live animal in a food factory or a fish tangled in plastic in the ocean? Those instances are the unconscious residue of an excess "which does not cease to not be written,"[12] and thus, is a manifestation of the death drive of our late capitalist system, whose dehumanized cost falls harder onto the most vulnerable through a sanctioned naturalization of history. By the fact that media and social media are obscenely transparent, these events appear as all too visible, writable and legible, but it does not mean these traumatic moments ever cease. The mediatic depiction of ongoing residues of larger ruptures of the social link might contribute to their desensitization, but such representation does not, in any way, involve a cessation of the effects of bare life, human indignity or puzzlement. Similarly, when a person who has suffered a traumatic event keeps remembering the disturbing content of the trauma, it does not necessarily translate as a gain of any relief from their suffering; they have not found a way to inscribe the destructive insistence, as to do away with the traumatic residue, a creative emergence is needed.

Any lifestyle, exchange and interaction among humans produce debris that, in Walter Benjamin's famous account of history, corresponds to the historical and cultural piling wreckage of "progress." Those residues need to be accounted somehow; yet the emergence of this Real residue, in its geo- and sociopolitical particularity, traditionally has materialized in hardship for the most vulnerable. "One reason why Fascism has a chance is that in the name of progress its opponents treat it as a historical norm."[13]

The death drive is the entropic derivation of the sexual drive that generates jouissance and sanctions its compulsive repetition via the superego's injunction to "Enjoy!" Jouissance is the production of "what shouldn't be," but that simultaneously "could never fail" (*qu'il ne faudrait pas*).[14] Death drive mechanisms possess the quality of what Freud called "the uncanny" (*das Unheimliche*), particularly with regards to the apparent occurrence of fatal destiny: at the individual level, that is, people's idea that their personalities are unchangeable or suffering the repetition of circumstances perceived as almost identical (e.g. accident-proneness, ending up in the "exact" same disastrous relationships etc.); and, at the social level, the politically naturalized repetition of dispossession and suffering of the most vulnerable. Freud defined the drive as a concept "on the frontier between the mental and the somatic, as the psychical representative of the stimuli originating from within the organism and reaching the mind."[15] Contra naturalistic readings of the Freudian drive, Lacan brings his aphorism "the unconscious is structured like a language" to render such a concept as primarily language bonded and thus historical (diachronic), subjected to the capitalist structure of sociopolitical determination (synchronic). Could the death drive fully be assimilated by Eros, as Marcuse suggests? In Lacanian terms, the drive does not disappear through the course of an analytic treatment; it is the change of object, raised "to the dignity of the Thing," which transforms the very signification and effects of the drive on the subject, through an act of sublimation.[16] Jouissance, although less deadly, will remain beyond the termination of analysis because, as Žižek points out, "the very renunciation of jouissance brings about a remainder/surplus of jouissance."[17] We are left with the tasks of dealing with the unconscious as residual death drive in its possibility of inscription and/or re-inscription in the social. How do we transform the death drive? How do we pay for its residue? How do we subvert the Real, which is the (im)possibility of conceiving things otherwise? In my view, this is the only meaning of politicization of psychoanalysis and its realization is an ongoing struggle. For example, the acceleration of anthropogenic climate change is striking, despite the Kyoto Protocol of 1997 and the Paris agreement of 2015. This profound global problem hasn't been able to radically alter political apathy at most levels. One wonders if such apathetic denial of this real threat is partially sustained by the assumption – impossible to question – that the poor, specifically the Global South, will continue paying the higher price; thus, providing the Global North with a fantasy of being protected.

THE UNCONSCIOUS IS ETHICAL

Lacan defines the unconscious as a troubling disruption – parapraxes, symptoms, dreams – whose status is not ontic or ontological, but ethical;

"its status of being, which is so elusive, so unsubstantial, is given to the unconscious by the procedure of its discoverer."[18] In other words, there is no unconscious, as such, until a subject, in their "thirst for truth,"[19] inquires into that which he has stumbled upon. Consequently, the Real unconscious – understood as such by Lacan since the late 1960s – resists knowledge, yet it is not irrational as it tests the subject in their ability to articulate such ruptures.

Psychoanalysis, by its engagement with the unconscious, is a negative endeavour, not so much for a misperceived pessimism, but rather because, in principle, it concentrates on the Real – that which does not work, that which is "ugly,"[20] shameful or guilt ridden, and continues appearing repeatedly, leaving effects that can't be signified. With Lacan, the central question of civilization would not be so much how to liberate the repression of the sexual drive – sanctioned by the state apparatus, as it appears in the traditional Marxist reading of Freud in Marcuse or Reich – but rather how to inscribe the insistence of the death drive within a possible social link. An example of a successful inscription is instantiated by Chandler and Lalonde's epidemiological study with about 200 Aboriginal groups in British Columbia, Canada. They tried to understand why suicide among First Nations youth was, in some groups, up to 800 per cent higher than the national average. They found that the groups with more markers of cultural continuity, such as land claims and self-governance in matters of health, education, police, fire services and cultural facilities, presented lower suicides in youth, to such an extent that in communities with the highest cultural continuity, the phenomenon of suicide was practically absent. They claimed that cultural continuity allows a sense of temporal self-continuity in youth, lowering significantly the incidence of suicide.[21] In our words, those Indigenous groups which successfully have preserved life among their youth have *inscribed*, partially, the brutally devastating colonizing effects through a political achievement that preserves their own cultures.

Alongside ethics beyond identity (Lacan's criticism of the imaginary, akin to Adorno's "negative dialectics") or ethics of signification, Lacan interrogates the experience of unconscious disruptive residues, and frames the ethical act in terms of the question of *responsibility*, on one's chosen *response*, to the perplexing experience of the Real. Such response corresponds, at the individual level, to the symptomatic constellation and the act; on the larger scale of the social, it corresponds to the field of politics.

Ethics, as the branch of philosophy that deals with the nature of the Good (virtue ethics), the maximization of human happiness (utilitarianism) or the nature of binding maxims or duty (Kant), is, for Lacan, an imperative of not ceding "ground relative to one's desire."[22] The latter involves releasing the full force of the drive, whose transformed object has channelled it into creation and pleasure, rather than destruction, or as Fink puts it, "once the drives have managed to find an outlet to satisfaction, they tend to flow repeatedly in the same pathways."[23] This process involves paying a price; not only a renunciation of any ideal of totality, perfection, full harmony or absence of crises, but also the articulation of the ethical law sustaining one's desire in an act that involves the social dimension. Ethics is, then, the channelling of the drive into desire and the partial object into the Other.

Psychoanalytic clinical practice, in its singular way to advance dialectics in the analysand–analyst dyad, shows us that inscribing *something* of the death drive is possible and allows the cessation of its destructive insistence. In the clinic, unconscious inscription is extremely challenging work, however, which does not eliminate or fully contain the death drive; it demands patience and moderation, and also ethical determination on the part of the analyst for carrying through the inquiry until its last consequences and articulations. Can we translate the same mechanism of inscription and re-inscription from the individual scale to the sociopolitical? The short answer is: No. We are faced with the inability to represent the ways in which individual logics and multitude of methods of enjoyment are complicit, one by one, in sustaining structures and institutions of power. We would go so far as to say sociopolitical critique, per se, radically sanctions the foreclosure of the individual unconscious, even though the latter's participation – as I have already suggested – inheres in the very shaping of social reality. In approaching the relationship between the social and the individual we can see the rope of the collective but not the quality of each of its fibres. Notwithstanding a key aspect of the Frankfurt School's critique of fascism of the twentieth century connecting sexual and political repression,[24] the procedures of how those supposed repressions work are intractable in the total aggregate of the one by one. Such lack of representation of the subject cannot be approached by psychology (the categorical and futile organization of individual motives), but rather through elucidation of the organizational mechanisms of the social link; as, for example, in the Lacanian theory of discourse,[25] proposing to think the social bond as constituted by a group sharing a certain positionality regarding variables such as desire, Other, truth and the object of traumatic jouissance.[26] This approach affords to map the topological relation between modes of production and its representation.[27]

MASTERS ARE NEEDED

Gandesha and Hartle consider that a new political ontology has emerged post-9/11, constituted through a tripartite constellation of commodity-reification–spectacle; such an ontological shift "unleashes profound and troubling anxieties within societies."[28] Alongside this line of thought, the Lacanian left agrees that the conditions brought about by the neo-liberal discourse have created a crisis of the Master signifier. Lacking the ability to sustain identifications within the symbolic order, the social bonding has shifted in isomorphic movement from the relationships of commodities to social relations between objects, rather than between subjects. Braunstein calls this the "pestilent discourse of the markets"[29] as Lacan had foreseen a "post" discourse that will affect psychoanalysis: "A discourse that would finally be truly pestilent, wholly devoted, finally, to the service of the capitalist discourse."[30] This subjective/ontological crisis, brought about by late capitalism, has produced a society ontolog-ically orphaned, and thus it enhances the longing for a master, such as in the voters of Trump and Bolsonaro; consequently, the Master signi-fier re-asserts itself even more adamantly to partially ease the condi-tions of social isolation, while simultaneously producing its weakening, becoming more imaginary and less symbolical. As Braunstein explains, the subject becomes atomized and isolated, excluded from the social link, relying on ineffective imaginary identities in hopes of replacing a needed Master signifier that can name them.[31]

To provide "ontological security" from unwritable traumatic residues, we lean on "masters": racists, patriarchal, neoliberal or ableist; revolu-tionaries, feminist, antifa. Right, liberal, left, even the anarchist's claim "Ni Dieu ni Maître" harbours a master, as those signifiers organize all further significations. We lean on masters to gain a sense of identity, orientation, consensus, love and recognition, and we relate to them, Freud signalled, with "the same sanctity, rigidity and intolerance, the same prohibition of thought – for its own defence."[32]

The Master, as signifier, is at the core of our identity because, on the one hand, it is what gives us *the trait* to identify with, and on the other, it provides a function of securing signification. In Lacanian theory, the Master signifier refers to the "signifier function,"[33] brought about by the signifier of the Other (parents, culture, institutional ideals) and which has contoured the subject's primary identity by introducing a "unary trait," single element or minimal mark, that allows the entrance into the symbolic and thus the naming of herself. The Master signifier (S1) represents the subject for all other signifiers (S2) and is akin to the Lacanian concepts "Name of the Father" and the "phallus."[34] The Master signifier voices, at the social level, the core of the superegoic demand to "belong" to a group or ideology. The superego is commanded by the Master signifier, whose symbolic identification originated in an idealized father whose castration the subject aims to conceal with the purpose of safeguarding her own lack and the subjective split from emerging. When the Master signifier increasingly relies on imaginary strategies – mirroring others, fascination, rivalry etc. – the superego becomes necessity because instead of an ethical law, an internalized lawless ideal of wholeness and total harmony prevails, which rejects castration, lack or disarrangement. After God – the quintessential *idealized father* – is dead "nothing is permitted anymore,"[35] and so oppressive guilt and shame emerges in place of the subject's articulation of her ethical law. Miller opposes the incompatibility between civilizations that allow social insertion through ideal ego and the current forms of injunction to consume based on the superego.[36]

The Master signifier constitutes an apodictic necessity – it does not require demonstration and is beyond dispute – builds social reality and sustains the repetition of "what cannot be otherwise," thus it "does not cease to be written."[37] Although Imaginary, Symbolic and Real orders are always entwined, the Master signifier (S1) is at the core of our symbolic identities, similar to how the image of oneself stands for the imaginary identity.[38] Social action based on symbolic identifications is a progression of consciousness from those actions formed through imaginary identifications, yet the Master signifiers are becoming more imaginary, increasing rivalry and hindering action. A sustained transformation of the social conditions requires an articulation of symbolic identifications in an act that impacts the Real, in the same way that the radical cure claimed by psychoanalysis works beyond the *exclusivity of* meaning and towards the emergence of a subjective act.

What masters are we serving? When Lacan was contested by enraged radical students for his apparent passivity in the context of May 1968 in

Paris, he answered this: "What you aspire to as revolutionaries is a master. You will get one."[39] That was a milder version of what he had voiced ten years earlier about the intellectual left suffering from a sort of metaphysical "knavery."[40] Why would Lacan say such thing? Firstly, although he probably would not deny that May 1968 involved an action of organized labour that brought the whole of France for a period of time to a standstill,[41] Lacan sees this movement, perhaps prophetically, as Boni points out, as a "redistribution of tasks and places in the system" in which the "revolt against the master's discourse just means its translation into a 'capitalist discourse.'"[42] Secondly, Lacan links it to hypocritical altruism: "The good of others [resides] in the image of my own,"[43] thus, what is unthinkable for the revolutionary activist or intellectual is that their own impotent jealousy, envy or self-righteousness will undermine transformative politics. Another way of saying this is that the intellectual/activist of the left, hooked into a discourse of certainty and all knowledge, will deny the oppressiveness of his anti-oppressive stands, because his superego commands. This is the soil in which fascism thrives; this is the logic of failed revolutions.

We see many examples of the "oppressiveness" of "anti-oppression politics" today. There seem to be heated controversies about a whole branch of left politics focusing on policing statements that relate to identitarian qualities (race, gender, ability etc.). While these "call out" cultures are important to legitimize struggles for recognition and equality as "in the political domain it is precisely through the coherent articulation of subjugated narratives that oppressed groups become empowered,"[44] the movement often regresses into inflammatory and puritanical demands – the imaginary order – occluding the more crucial, material forces that shape our world: the domination of the law of value, the privatization of the commons and ensuing ecological destruction.

The far-right gains ground and becomes more effective, lending voice to widespread dissatisfaction with the material reality of unlivable conditions at present, which has favoured their political advancement in elections. The left, in contrast, is naïve about the limits of what should be acceptable to say in public speech to gain recognition, or, as Mark Fisher has pointed out, there is a bourgeois-liberal appropriation of the energy of the left movements they appear to be fighting, but in reality "It is driven by a *priest's desire* to excommunicate and condemn, an *academic-pedant's desire* to be the first to be seen to spot a mistake, and *a hipster's desire* to be one of the in-crowd."[45]

The left searches for the precise signifier to organize around, as we see, for example, in Jain's diatribe against *Jacobin* magazine for their dismissiveness of the term "identitarian Leftism."[46] Jain argues that instead of only focusing on a class struggle, the magazine has the responsibility of diversifying victories and struggles of particular groups, such as Indigenous, Black, queer, feminist, disability and migrant movements. While, at first sight, the idea of diversifying the Master signifier of the left from socioeconomic class to other signifiers (race, gender etc.) might appear attractive, the problem of imposing *any* Master signifier as an authentication of political struggles is not only that this modality serves identitarian purposes rather than subjectification ones, but also that Master signifiers are not universals. Is there a way to rescue the concept of universality as a means of forestalling the threat of an always already arbitrary and capricious Master signifier? McGowan insightfully suggests that not all Master signifiers are universal, but all universals function as Master signifiers.[47] The ideas of love, freedom or happiness are certainly pursued in every spectrum of the political, yet the significations of such instances are disparate and often radically opposed. For example, on the one hand, "freedom" signifies the liberation of humanity from the violence of closed borders, discriminatory policies or poverty – in an emancipatory project – and, on the other, the neoliberal freedom of the markets and what Wendy Brown has called the "authoritarian freedom" to actualize racist and misogynist fantasies of violence and domination.[48]

We are aware of the vastness of philosophical discussions about the universal and the particular; however, two authors allow us to distinguish universality in relationship to the Master signifier: Badiou situates the universal in the act primarily, as an "incalculable emergence rather than a describable structure";[49] the universal is an event of thought of radical singularity that, as is intrinsic to any "event," appears while disappearing and is only known by its effects of subjectification. Thus, the universal for Badiou is a singular emergent event that isn't defined by positive "identificatory predicates"[50] or preregistered knowledge and, by means of an act, it states a valence for something that was previously undecidable, uncertain or anonymous; by doing so, such an event reaches an inaugural subjectification.

For Todd McGowan, the "key political struggle" today is a recuperation of the universal and its distinction from the Master signifier, as "weakening the universal is always, in the last instance, a conservative project."[51] McGowan explains that the Master signifier is a structural necessity, empty of meaning, even though we endorse it with all sorts of identitarian substance. The fact that we use signifiers to designate the universal – freedom, equality etc. – does not imply that we have an actualization of such an idea, so he concludes "we never have the universal, which means that politics must be nothing but the fight on its behalf."[52] A genuine left acts *on behalf of a universality to be achieved*, on the principle of its negativity, while the far-right or even fascist right *sees the universal as always already the actualization of the ethnonationalist particular*.

The negative quality of the universal, as above described, evidences the crucial difference between the Master signifier's aspirational universality and its actuality. We attest that those instances of the traumatic residue of the Real, its location outside of signification, and the strife undergone by peoples and communities, corresponds to the universal, to the lack that we all share and struggle to articulate and acknowledge. This corresponds to the notion of Marx's class, in Rancière's terms, regarding universal equality, "the part of those who have no part."[53] Class doesn't function in the same way as other Master signifiers, insofar as it isn't a positive but a negative term which is to be dissolved rather than maintained. As Gandesha states: "The realisation of proletarian identity is, ultimately, negative rather than affirmative; proletarian 'identity,' unlike most other identities, has an interest its own self-dissolution along with that of class society as a whole."[54]

The fact that class is a universal concept does not prevent, by its very negative quality, the potential of being reified as Master signifier by those who interpret it. And here is where the rope of the social requires a magnifier to investigate how those singular fibres conforming the social might transform a universal concept into an oppressive Master signifier. What is key is the way in which the Master signifier, an unquestionable necessity, is produced; this will be approached in the last section. For now, let's explore the potentialities of possibility and contingency.

POSSIBILITY AND CONTINGENCY

According to Parker, masters "function as anchors of representation in a text through rhetorical tropes such as 'this is the way things are,' that is not subjected to challenge or dissent."[55] It is true that, as Bistoen claims, "when a new master signifier surfaces, this changes the meaning of those prior anchoring points,"[56] such as a "hard" Brexit of the United Kingdom from the EU; Trump's wall excluding immigrants; Bolsonaro threatening Indigenous peoples of the Amazon basin or López Obrador unsettling the political class under the signifier "Fourth Transformation." Those emerging new masters, as Stavrakakis suggests, work as "the contingent dislocation of a pre-existing discursive order, through a certain resurfacing of the traumatic real which shows the limits of the social."[57] The latter means that the new Master signifier attempts to respond to an emergence of the Real, without successfully inscribing it: for the Brexiteers, Trump or Bolsonaro, the traumatic consists in the emergence of the figure of the migrant labourer (the Muslim, Black, Mexican or Indigenous) that upsets the capitalist symbolic order; those political strategies of exclusion aim at concealing the illegibility of the excluded by validating new signifi-cations that preserve the exclusion through strategies that privilege the particularity of race or ethnicity. But Master signifiers play a similar role for the left and, in the case of López Obrador's initiative, it introduces new Master signifiers that disrupt or challenge the corrupting modes of past governments, yet it will still need to prove whether those new Master signifiers will be imposed by him (as "Leader") or be produced collectively by the body politic.

Thus, the change of Master signifier does not necessarily reincor-porate traumatic material; to heal such trauma, the hope of the left movements, it must be inscribed in a new social bond. This has been the privilege of cultural and aesthetic endeavours (art, ritual, myth, humour etc.), yet the question remains as to exactly how the traumatic could, at least partially, be integrated into the pragmatic field of politics. I propose to follow the two pending logical modalities: the *possible*, corresponding to an evental disruption, and the *contingent* which consists in the decid-ability of such event.

The possible is the occurrence of a rupture that transforms the refrac-tory sameness through a logical re-uptake by a subject who partially writes anew the traumatic residue in the symbolic order. In the clinical setting, the emergence of the possible often impacts both the analysand and the analyst, and its decidability – meaningful value – occurs in the space between the two actors.[58] By deciding, through an assumption of the subjective truth hidden in the enunciation,[59] or through an act of sublimation,[60] on the value of the Real with its impossible truth, on the one hand, and the overdetermined insistences of the symbolic, on the other, the subject might transform the symptomatic constellation into socially bonded pleasure. These are exclusive ways in which structural conditions of suffering can be addressed. Yet, it is important to note that the actualization of the *possible* in analysis occurs in the context of trans-ference, which is to say, within a field of trust, by the positioning of the analyst outside the rival imaginary condition. Could the left develop such trust within itself? This would imply a left on the side of the *impossible* rather than on the side of *impotence*.

Badiou tells us that "everything will depend on the way in which the possibility proposed by the event is grasped, elaborated, incorporated and set out in the world."[61] This is what Lacan refers to as contingency, what "stops [not] being written."[62] The delicate processes of inscription (a temporal cessation of the insistence of the traumatic) and rein-scription (the emergence of a new embodied signification) in the clinic demand from the analyst that they bear the anxiety of the traumatic, holding the space for its unfolding and resignification through silences and interventions, and to acknowledge negativity, which we automat-ically deny at the level of the social. I argue that in a civic society this is the function of the intellectual, who comes to occupy the function of the analyst in the processes of inscribing the residue of the Real. Thus, the intellectual needed today is one that has been an analysand and is able to produce the Master signifier of her own ethical law, which – while continuing to serve the purpose of securing signification, identification and access to the symbolic field – comes from the acknowl-edgement of her own historical production. Again, such a production is an *ongoing process* of universalization as opposed to a supposedly *completed* universalization of a given, reified particular.

DO YOU WANT TO HAVE OR TO BE A MASTER?

In an old essay, Chomsky interrogates the responsibility of US intellec-tuals to speak about crimes in which they are implicated, such as the war in Indochina. He reflects on the history of the term "intellectual," going from Brunetière's definition of "ridiculous pretentious eccentrics" to the neoliberal ideal of the intellectual as "technocratic and policy-oriented" experts, to the avant-garde would-be "anarchist of the lecture-platform."[63] This was before the advent of new alt-right pseudo-intellectuals, who quote great thinkers to encourage crowds of disaffected young men to embrace misogyny and bigotry.

From a psychoanalytic perspective, I argue, the intellectual should become an analyst, not as an external critic but one that carries out an immanent critique by taking responsibility for their own unconscious at two levels. The first is hermeneutic, which is to say, the signification of their own symptomatic constellations; and the other is heuristic, or that which socially addresses the perplexity of that which falls outside of signification. Such an intellectual is required to produce their own Master signifiers, that is, that are "produced by the subject rather than imposed upon the subject from outside."[64] Such a signifier is less absolute, less rigid, less exclusive and totalitarian, *renouncing any will to mastery*, because it is aware of its own limit.

Human beings are subjected to a form of internalized, unconscious and unacceptable enjoyment: racist, patriarchal, or ableist, catastrophic thinking, narcissistic desire for others to be a reflection of us, or rigid antagonistic disposition. The seeds of this unconscious jouissance, if veiled to the hypocritical comrade, will bear impotent fruits. As the subject finds himself exposed to these unacceptable contents, it recurs to the lawless superego. By ideologically imposing a superegoic demand that expects all actors to share the same Master signifier to be connected to a social milieu, we prohibit thought and encourage exclusion, and in the process, we become complicit in the building of social structures that remain oppressive, because they deny the seed of jouissance that the social has brought on to our very intimate way of enjoyment. In *Group Psychology and the Analysis of the Ego*, following LeBon, Freud shows the power of identification among members of a group, which "wants to be ruled and oppressed and to fear its masters. Fundamentally it is entirely conservative and it has a deep aversion to all innovations and advances and unbounded respect for tradition."[65] So, do you want a Master?

The sort of ethics and politics offered by psychoanalysis, contrary to what many people believe, does not uphold a pessimistically hopeless view of human subjectivity, à la Schopenhauer (the stoic denial of the will); otherwise, it would not be a transformative treatment in the interest of the freedom of human subjects. But Lacanian left politics, as it were, might frustrate because:

a) It offers an ethical practice of the Real, which highlights the difficulty for the human subject to write their own history by articulating their symptom and acknowledging the truths of those aspects veiled to consciousness (castration, traumatic residue, subjective division etc.);

b) It upsets epistemologically because it confronts us with the impotence of not being able to fully transform our world with only the power of the will, reason and intellect, as we yet need to deal with what falls outside of consciousness and signification.

As Bistoen quite precisely articulates: "the act in the face of the traumatic Real is an injunction for the other/Other to take up a position ...
rewriting the rules of what is possible and what is not."[66] This means
that by grasping contingent opportunities, the militant intellectual acts
in such a way that reformulates the rules of the system game, reposi-
tioning the place of symbolic signification (Other) and the place of the
imaginary other (fellow neighbour), yet not knowing fully the destiny
of its intervention, because its effects are known by its becoming, better
stated in future perfect tense: "it will have been."

Lacan's proposal for a cure runs parallel to Freud's famous aspiration of psychoanalytical treatment "transforming your hysterical misery
into common unhappiness."[67] Progress towards a cure, for Lacan, is the
movement from *impotence* to *impossibility*. As it exceeds the limits of
this chapter, we won't engage in detail with Lacan's theory of discourse,
but suffice it to say that impotence emerges from a lack of correspond-
ence between the undisclosed truth of the political agent, who repeats
a Master signifier (s)he is not aware of, and the material effects of such
a signifier's embodied production. Impotence, then, is expecting that
only "punching a Nazi," policing intersectional signifiers, and so on, will
produce a political change. Impossibility, in contrast, corresponds to the
insufficiency of any truth to account and fully transform the Real. The
political act which acknowledges the (im)possibility of accounting for
the universal requires a "not-all" approach. The not-all in Lacan refers
to the feminine side of sexuation, as presented in *Seminar XX*, which
provides a know-how with regards to enjoyment of the field outside the
phallic order. The phallus in Lacanian theory refers to a "signifier that
is destined to designate meaning effects as a whole,"[68] whose singular
epitome is the Master signifier. The not-all is found on the feminine
side, not to be understood in its anatomic sense, but rather as a position
taken with regards to the incompleteness of the symbolic field. A not-all
approach is the left needed today: warm instead of cold, wet instead of
dry, flexible instead of rigid, addressing structure rather than appearance, open to the awareness of subjective division and on the side of the
impossibility, not of impotence.

The Gramscian idea of the organic intellectual or the individual legislator, as Vacca reads it, proposes that an intellectual is an "efficacious
instrument of hegemony" in civil society and an individual legislator
that would render the collective will effective.[69] I believe that this organic
intellectual/legislator/psychoanalyst should situate their hegemonic

efficacy in the immediate social cell of the subject among others, which is the field of the institution (family, workplace, university, political party etc.) being the collective will, an aspiration to the universal of what is precisely excluded. Or, as Arendt once proposed, we need to become "conscious pariahs."[70]

The responsibility of the intellectual from a psychoanalytic perspective consists, then, not in becoming the *caudillo* of a social totality, but a leader who reads possibilities and grasps decidability, with clear and audacious desire, to transform the dramas of the couple, family, workplace or social group, at the very site of their struggle.

The responsibility of the intellectual/analyst thus consists in an epistemological unsettling of their immediate world while accounting for their own unconscious through an act that creates possibilities in their social milieu. This is akin to the Kantian *Mündigkeit*, in the way Adorno discusses it as the maturity to speak for oneself in an intimate way or "live contact with the warmth of things";[71] yet in a Lacanian twist, it is about the ability to think for oneself with others in presence of the unconscious.

Pavón-Cuéllar pertinently draws from psychoanalytic theory the conclusion that the subject engages in an epistemological shift that questions the effects of ideology via a praxis of a method.[72] The intellectual/analyst needed is aware of the entwinement of individual and social history, and so is able to work against discourses that kill (the fascisms of the superego through guilt, hate, rigidity, bureaucracy, desubjectifying or dehumanizing practices) and in the interest of discourses that give life (lawful articulation of the ethics of the singular universal within a social link). Alemán states that the new man of neoliberalism lacks the symbolic legacy to decipher the history of what is proper of the subject: "the singular and incurable that resides in each of us ... abolished in the service of a certain productivity that goes beyond the symbolic possibilities with which men and women enter into the social bond."[73] If, as Gandesha and Hartle argue, the history of political struggles concerns "the possibility of the subject matter to, itself, become the content of history writing at all,"[74] the history that needs to be written is that of the excluded, the *universal singular* of the not-all.

CONCLUSION

Drawing from clinical insights, in this chapter I initially argue for a politics of inscription, which refers to the task of partial symbolization of the traumatic residues brought about by the Real, understood as the social bond structure that sustains the ontological crisis of late capitalism. In parallel to inscription, I argue that such politics also includes processes of re-inscription, which involves rewriting naturalized histories. Following this, I claim that the Master signifier is partially hindered by the reification of social relations and thus unable to sustain the subject symbolically, resorting to imaginary mechanisms, such as identarian politics. I argue that the Master signifier differs from universality and is approached divergently by the right and the left. While the far-right imposes the Master signifier as a false reified universal, corresponding to the particularity of a race or ethnic group, an effective left should be attentive to the traumatic residues that exceed any given actualization of the universal. Finally, I argue that in light of the circumstances we are just starting to face, such as the spectre of fascism in the climate change crisis, the intellectual must become a militant leader, a Gramscian analyst, on the side of the feminine logic of the not-all, with clarity of desire, aware of their subjective division, to grasp opportunities to transform conditions (inscribe and re-inscribe) in the immediate cell of the institutions in which they dwell.

NOTES

Unless otherwise stated, URLs were last accessed on 15 September 2019.

1. Immanuel Kant, *On History* (New York: Macmillan, 1963), 17.

2. Jacques Lacan, *The Seminar of Jacques Lacan Book XXIV: L'insu que sait*, trans. Cormac Gallagher, 24:113, accessed 26 March 2017, www.lacaninireland. com/web/wp-content/uploads/2010/06/insu-Seminar-XXIV-Final-Sessions-1-12-1976-1977.pdf.

3. Samir Gandesha, "Understanding Right and Left Populisms," in J. Morelock, ed., *Critical Theory and Authoritarian Populism* (London: University of Westminster Press, 2018), 63, doi.org/10.16997/book30.d, licensed under CC BY-NC-ND 4.0.

4. Sigmund Freud, "Beyond Pleasure Principle (1920)," in Strachey, ed., *Standard Edition*, 18:9.

5. Yannis Stavrakakis, *The Lacanian Left: Essays on Psychoanalysis and Politics* (Edinburgh: Edinburgh University Press, 2007), ebookcentral.proquest. com/lib/sfu-ebooks/detail.action?docID=334896. Stavrakakis refers to the works of Castoriadis, Laclau, Žižek and Badiou.

6. Jacques Lacan, *The Seminar of Jacques Lacan Book XX: Encore* (New York: Norton, 1998), trans. Bruce Fink, 20:59.

7. Jacques Lacan, *The Seminar of Jacques Lacan Book XVII: The Other Side of Psychoanalysis* (New York: Norton, 2007), trans. Russell Grigg, 17:13.

8. Chantal Bonneau, "Du 'réel contingent,'" UFORCA, 29 March 2016, www. lacan-universite.fr/du-reel-contingent/. Bonneau renders clearly Lacan's deployment of these modal logics and its relation to Aristotelian categories of repetition: necessity is linked to *automaton* (repetition of signifiers as a support of discourse) and contingency linked to *tuché* (the unpredictable and chance).

9. Lacan, *Seminar of Jacques Lacan Book XVIII: On A Discourse that Might Not Be of Semblance*, trans. Cormac Gallagher, accessed 9 September 2018, www.lacaninireland.com/web/wp-content/uploads/2010/06/Book-18-On-a-discourse-that-might-not-be-a-semblance.pdf.

10. Michael Friedman and Samo Tomšič, "Introduction," in *Psychoanalysis: Topological Perspectives* (Bielefeld: Verlag, 2016), 97. The Kantian transcendental aesthetics refer to the time and spatial dimension of human aesthetic perception; the *Undinge* refer to those aspects who are present but intractable through these given categories.

11. Theodor Adorno, *Negative Dialectics* (New York: Continuum, 1973), 5–6.

12. Lacan, *Seminar XX*, 86–7.

13. Walter Benjamin, "Theses on the Philosophy of History," in *Illuminations* (New York: Schocken, 1968), 8:257.

14. Lacan, *Seminar XX*, 59.

15. Sigmund Freud, "Instincts and Their Vicissitudes (1915)," in Strachey, ed., *Standard Edition*, 14:121–2.

16. Lacan, *The Seminar of Jacques Lacan Book VII: The Ethics of Psychoanalysis* (New York: Norton, 1992), trans. Dennis Porter, 7:112.

17. Slavoj Žižek, "From Desire to Drive: Why Lacan is not Lacaniano," in *Žižek Live Journal*, 19 April 2004, accessed 12 August 2019, zizek.livejournal.com/2266.html.

18. Jacques Lacan, *The Seminar of Jacques Lacan Book XI: The Four Fundamental Concepts of Psychoanalysis* (New York: Norton, 1998), trans. Alan Sheridan, 11:33.

19. Ibid.

20. Žižek, "From Desire to Drive."

21. Michael J. Chandler and Christopher Lalonde, "Cultural Continuity as a Hedge against Suicide in Canada's First Nations," *Transcultural Psychiatry* 35, No. 2 (1998): 191–219, doi.org/10.1177/136346159803500202.

22. Lacan, *Seminar VII*, 321–3.

23. Bruce Fink, *Lacan On Love* (Cambridge: Polity Press, 2016), 101.

24. Herbert Marcuse, *Eros and Civilization* (Boston, MA: Beacon, 1996), 12.

25. Lacan, *Seminar XVII*, 12.

26. For a thorough discussion of Lacan's theory of discourses, see Bracher et al., eds., *Lacanian Theory of Discourse* (New York: New York University Press, 1994); Paul Verhaeghe, *Beyond Gender: From Subject to Drive* (New York: Other Press, 2001); Slavoj Žižek, "Jacques Lacan's Four Discourses," lacan.com, 2006, www.lacan.com/zizfour.htm; Stjin Vanheule, "Capitalist Discourse, Subjectivity and Lacanian Psychoanalysis," *Frontiers in Psychology* 7 (2016), www.ncbi.nlm.nih.gov/pmc/articles/PMC5145885/.

27. Samo Tomšič, *The Capitalist Unconscious* (New York: Verso, 2015), 204.

28. Samir Gandesha and Johan F. Hartle, *The Spell of Capital: Reification and Spectacle* (Amsterdam: Amsterdam University Press, 2016), 12.

29. Nestor Braunstein, *El inconsciente, la técnica y el discurso capitalista* (Mexico: Siglo XXI, 2012), 148.

30. Lacan, "On Psychoanalytic Discourse: Milan Discourse, 1972," Scribd, trans. Jack W. Stone, accessed 20 November 2017, www.scribd.com/document/151026214/Milan-Discourse-Lacan, licensed under CC BY-NC 2.0.

31. Braunstein, *El inconsciente*, 164.

32. Freud, "The Future of an Illusion (1927)," in Strachey, ed., *Standard Edition*, 21:27.

33. Lacan, *Seminar XI*, 21.

34. Lacan, *Ecrits* (New York: Norton, 2006), 685.

35. Lacan, *Seminar XVII*, 120.

36. Jacques-Alain Miller, "Psychoanalysis in Close Touch with the Social," trans. Thelma Sowley, lacan.com, June/July 2007, www.lacan.com/jamsocial.html.

37. Lacan, *Seminar XX*, 94.

38. I developed this idea in: Hilda Fernandez, *Narci-capitalism* (Dublin: Lacunae, 2016).

39. Lacan, *Seminar XVII*, 207.

40. Lacan, *Seminar VII*, 183.

41. Jean-Michel Rabate, "Lacan's 'année érotique' (1968/1969)," in Samo Tomšič and Andreja Zevnik, eds., *Jacques Lacan: Between Psychoanalysis and Politics* (New York: Routledge, 2016). Rabate presents a thorough analysis of Lacan's engagement with the French student movement of May 1968.

42. Livio Boni, "Formalisation and Context: Some Elements of a Materialist Reading of Lacan's 'Four Discourses,'" in Ian Parker and David Pavón-Cuéllar, eds., *Lacan, Discourse, Event: New Psychoanalytic Approaches to Textual Indeterminacy* (London: Routledge, 2014), 136. Lacan's analysis is perhaps prophetic precisely because one of the leaders of 1968, Daniel Cohn-Bendit, is now an advisor to Emmanuel Macron who is widely regarded as the representative of financial capital.

43. Lacan, *Seminar VII*, 187.

44. Stephen Frosh, "Disintegrating Narrative Research with Lacan," in Parker and Pavón-Cuéllar, eds., *Lacan, Discourse, Event*, 19.

45. Mark Fisher, "Exiting the Vampire Castle," *openDemocracy*, 24 November 2013, www.opendemocracy.net/en/opendemocracyuk/exiting-vampire-castle/.

46. Uday Jain, "White Marxism: A Critique of Jacobin Magazine," *New Socialist*, 11 August 2017, newsocialist.org.uk/white-marxism-critique/.

47. Todd McGowan, "The Absent Universal: From the Master Signifier to the Missing Signifier," *Problemi International* 2, No. 2 (2018): 195–214.

48. Wendy Brown, "Neoliberalism's Frankenstein: Authoritarian Freedom in Twenty-First Century "Democracies," in Wendy Brown, Peter Gordon and Max Pensky, *Authoritarianism: Three Inquiries* (Chicago and London: University of Chicago Press, 2018).

49. Alain Badiou, "Eight Thesis on the Universal," lacan.com, 19 November 2004, www.lacan.com/badeight.htm.

50. Ibid.

51. McGowan, "The Absent Universal," 198–9.

52. Ibid., 214.

53. Jacques Rancière, *Dissensus: On Politics and Aesthetics*, ed. Steven Corcoran (London: Continuum International Publishing Group, 2010), 60.

54. Samir Gandesha, "Not Only the Difference Between Identities but the Differences Within Them," *openDemocracy*, 19 November 2019, www.opendemocracy.net/en/not-only-difference-between-identities-but-differences-within-them/.

55. Ian Parker, "Lacanian Discourse Analysis in Psychology," *Theory and Psychology* 15, No. 2 (2005): 164–82, doi.org/10.1177/0959354305051361.

56. Gregory Bistoen, *Trauma, Ethics and the Political Beyond PTSD* (New York: Palgrave Macmillan, 2016), 160.

57. Yannis Stavrakakis, *The Lacanian Left*, 59.

58. In "From the Letter to the Signifier: The Process of Residual Inscription" (Unpublished, *Ecrits Conference*, Ghent, Belgium, September 2018) I discuss a clinical case of psychosis and argue that the process of inscription is carried out in an interstitial way: "Both analyst and analysand hold a piece of these always surprising and tangible unnamables and share the task of carrying the materiality of the immaterial."

59. Lacan, *Ecrits* (New York: Norton, 2006), 677.

60. Rancière's critique of sublimation as a "pacifying procedure" of politics and Marcuse's own approach to this phenomenon invites us to discuss the problem of sublimation but it exceeds this chapter. For now, and to sustain this argument: an act needs to be sublimatory because the entropic nature of the drive – source of passions and affect – requires a pairing thought to successfully overcome its violence. "The action must be discharged in the words that articulate it." Lacan, *Seminar VII*, 244.

61. Badiou, "Eight Thesis on the Universal."

62. Lacan, *Seminar XX*, 145.

63. Noam Chomsky, "The Responsibility of Intellectuals, Redux," *Boston Review*, 11 September 2011, bostonreview.net/noam-chomsky-responsibility-of-intellectuals-redux.

64. Bracher et al., eds., *Lacanian Theory of Discourse*, 124.

65. Sigmund Freud, "Group Psychology and the Analysis of the Ego (1921)," in Strachey, ed., *Standard Edition*, 18:78.

66. Bistoen, *Trauma, Ethics and the Political Beyond PTSD*, 162.

67. Sigmund Freud, "Civilization and its Discontent (1930)," in Strachey, ed., *Standard Edition*, 21:305.

68. Lacan, *Ecrits*, 579.

69. Giuseppe Vacca, "The Crisis of the State in Europe in the Interwar Period: From New Order to the Prison Notebooks," *Antonio Gramsci: A Legacy for the Future* (SFU Conference, 20 October 2018). Vacca quotes Gramsci: "I extend considerably the notion of the intellectual and I am not

limiting it to the current notion that refers to the great intellectuals ... it is specially in civil society that intellectuals work ... a kind of lay pope and a very efficacious instrument of hegemony."

70. Hannah Arendt, "The Jew as Pariah: A Hidden Tradition," in *The Jewish Writings* (New York: Schocken Books, 2008): 275–97.

71. Iain Macdonald, "Cold, Cold, Warm: Autonomy, Intimacy and Maturity in Adorno," *Philosophy and Social Criticism* 37, No. 6 (2011): 671.

72. David Pavón-Cuéllar, "Del método crítico-teórico lacaniano a sus reconfiguraciones práctico-políticas en discursos concretos: cuestionamiento de la ideología, compromiso del investigador y subversión del sujeto," in *Miradas y prácticas de la investigación psicosocial* (Puebla: BUAP, 2014), 157.

73. Jorge Alemán, *Neoliberal Horizons in Subjectivity* (Excerpts), *Public Seminar*, 20 October 2017, www.publicseminar.org/2017/10/neoliberal-horizons-in-subjectivity/.

74. Samir Gandesha and Johan F. Hartle, "Introduction," in Samir Gandesha and Johan F. Hartle, eds., *Aesthetic Marx* (London: Bloomsbury, 2017), xxi.

10

Micro-Fascism in the Age of Trump

Gary Genosko

In developing a theory of fascism as a proliferating molecular phenomenon, Félix Guattari embedded in it black-hole effects as a principle that explained how the energy of mass desire is channelled into self-destruction. The decentring of this process (i.e. from around the gaze of *a* or *the* Führer)[1] clears the way for the emergence of a multiplicity of micro-fascist phenomena that resonate together. Resonance was a concept Guattari borrowed from physicist René Thom and adapted to the new end of explaining small-scale – that is, flexible, self-regulating, molecular – fascisms adequate to advanced forms of infocapital and how they seep into the pores of a society. This is the kind of society that elects Donald Trump as its president. Trump has been on Guattari's radar for years, at least since the late 1980s, and he devolves him into a species of algae for his reckless property development schemes: "In the field of social ecology, men like Donald Trump are permitted to proliferate freely, like another species of algae, taking over entire districts of New York and Atlantic City; he 'redevelops' by raising rents, thereby driving out tens of thousands of poor families, most of whom are condemned to homelessness, becoming the equivalent of the dead fish of environmental ecology."[2] The resonances of Trumpian politics are explored in this chapter through the proliferation of the "Sad Frog" meme, a potent and contested symbol of the alt-right, and the involutive, inspiralling forces of post-truth, alternative facts, hate, racism, sexism, the vagaries of the manosphere and the sputtering outrage machine, in the choked mental ecology of America today.[3] First, I will turn to Guattari's explanation of black-hole effects and his deployment of the concept of resonance to explain how molecular fascist intensities proliferate and vibrate together under a political banner.

BLACK HOLES AND RESONANCE

In Guattari's usage, black holes generate echoes. This lengthy quote explains echolalic relations based in the study of drug abuse:

> These black holes swarm and proliferate across the social field. The question is whether subjectivity is going to echo them in a way that an individual's entire life, all one's modes of semiotization, depend upon a central point of anguish and guilt. I propose this image of a black hole in order to illustrate the phenomenon of the complete inhibition of semiotic components of an individual or group which finds itself cut off from any possibility of an exterior life. By the expression 'echo of a black hole' I aim to establish resonances among several systems of blockages (i.e. you have a stomach cramp and you can no longer think about it; you 'embody' it; you invest an erogenous zone on your pain; you persecute your partner, your children, and all these domains begin to resonate).[4]

Systems of blockages resonate together – vibrate synchronically – under the influence of one or more general black holes, like addiction. On the one hand, the components of consciousness, reterritorialized in nosographic redundancies, create a subjective black hole by presenting subjectivity with the nothingness of the empty resonances that set it spinning; on the other hand, the black holes can manipulate these nuclei of nothingness by forcing them to a limit from which they can escape, *but only* in the form of strange a-signifying particles carrying "charges of nothingness" – subjectivity merely affirms their impotence by echoing them, or by giving them free reign. Super-empowered, deterritorializing sign particles are born in a place of grief and distress.[5] A highly intense nothingness is a force to be reckoned with if it can free itself.

Although he borrows much of his conceptual language regarding reso-nance from Thom,[6] there are limits clearly set out by Guattari. For Thom, the schema typical of all resonance involves the free interaction of two independent dynamical systems (tuning forks) that tend to degenerate towards a common, mixed regime of resonance.[7]

Resonating black holes have the strength to disempower and empty redundancies of meaning; at the same time, they are machinically super-empowered and grant them autonomy. The redundancies become more and more decentred, and less and less efficient, but extremely powerful. In this state, the redundancies of consciousness ensure that subjectivity turns in on itself. Resonance, in addition, is transferred to one or more of the redundancies of consciousness where it sets up a bastion from which it controls the others; these are named by Guattari following typical clinical syndromes. The important point is that the black hole has both disempowering and super-powerful effects; its energy may at some point release particles that escape from all systems of redundancies. It is both involutive and potentially creative. Thus, Guattari adapts Thom's terminology but in the process retains, in addition to the degenerative dimension of resonance (disempowerment) in the triggering of a black hole of subjectivity, the hypothetical "quanta of possibility" carried by the matters of expression (a-signifying part-signs) emitted from it. Black holes, in other words, can emit strange and chaosmic potentialities – like "hashtag activism," in which clicks, posts and tweets guide an entangled hopeful disempowerment and transversal striving to cut through the barrier of the digital and to remake the world.

Why are echoes of a black hole of subjectivity so dangerous? Echoes are reflective resonance phenomena that provide alibis for the false separation of all the components they hang on a single involutive process. The delayed reflection of an echo creates the illusion of separation – that is, independence – from its source. Moreover, as an echo path may move around, more and more of the affected components and their inter-componential relations may evoke the same denial, thereby expanding the stifling draw of the general black hole. Now, let's see how this works with fascism.

MICROPOLITICS OF FASCISM

Guattari's first approach to fascism is to develop a threefold typology of how its forms are typically analysed. He starts with a sociological category, based on analytical-formalist distinctions that identify species of fascism (national historical types), finds common traits among them, and then describes small differences between them. Differences are minimized the more commonness is elevated, and differences are magnified the more they help to isolate layers and kinds. He finds little of interest in this approach and moves through it quickly.

The second approach he notes is neo-Marxist thought grounded in a synthetic-dualist paradigm. The approach here is to appreciate how to both acknowledge the revolutionary desire of the masses and recognize the mediations from Marxism's theoretical vocabulary imposed upon them, "massifying" mass-desire: "restored to standardized formulations whose necessity is deemed to be justified in the name of the cohesion of the working class and party unity."[8] Overcoming the distinction between theoretical description and revolutionary praxis yields only the dualist trap of the code-wielding political caste and the obedient mass followers, which is played out reductively and its impotence multiplied along a series of "schematic oppositions" (i.e. molar dualisms like city/country; good and bad camps) and a unique third object (the power of the State) that gives meaning to them. He wishes to outflank such dualisms and their distancing mechanisms. Let's not make too much of this passage through a particularistic version of a massified desire that shows more of its molar rather than molecular face.

In the third approach, Guattari mounts what he calls an analytic-political approach that he makes his own. He does not abandon the question of what kind of state is built under fascism, but he reserves this investigation for elsewhere in *A Thousand Plateaus*, to which I will return momentarily. In the meantime, the third approach launches a series of provisos: "a micropolitics of desire would no longer present itself as representing the masses and as interpreting their struggles."[9] At the same time he doesn't entirely reject the need for a political analysis of party lines and actions, and underlines the importance of diversifying and pluralizing any already formed and centralizable wholes into social groupings beyond the working class and its set task of dissolving the contradiction it embodies, refusing to yoke it to dominant expressions of its character, whatever these might be, that allow it to carry out unique tasks according to stated objectives of its party in relation to the mediations of the transcendent object of the state. No more Leninist exhortations straight out of the "April Theses" of spring 1917 to make the masses see the true form of revolutionary government and to interpret their practical needs in this light[10] – instead, a conception of desire without an object, without a centre either in a person or in a body constituted as ideally pre-unified. Desire is multiple and different; it consists of singular intensities that combine with one another in incompatible ways, rather than in terms of identities that may be totalized by a party apparatus, that is, "by the totalitarian machine of a representative party."[11] Lenin, it may be said, tried to tap into the molecular revolutionary forces that expressed themselves in a unique moment of hope, and for this he was considered to have gone mad. This is the Lenin that Žižek admires and wants to regain; yet as I just pointed out, the contrary tendencies at play in the "April Theses" are just as strongly expressed through specific representations and interpretations – that is, direction and explanation of the non-spontaneous awakening of desire of a mass of proletarians as it is coaxed into existence and led to make the right choices by a mobilized party using the tools at its disposal.

Nevertheless, Guattari claims mediators must be bypassed in the relationship between social objectives and praxis. Desire tends to wander and to get off topic and away from ready-made encodings. A micropolitical analysis of desire doesn't represent what is already formed, but contributes to the formation and thus is "immediately political." What does Guattari mean when he claims that "when saying is doing" micropolitics is immediately political? No more specialists either of saying or of doing. Collective assemblages (rather than individual idiolects) within the mass find their own means of expression, perhaps combining fragments of archaic discourses, recontextualized images, slang and recycled codes. A rehearsal of the correct slogans is not required. It is theoretically messy to give permission to the masses to speak. There are no guarantees. The crystallization of situational collective desires in utterances and other semiotic materials always struggle with the influence of dominant overcodings, and are directly linked into machinic processes of all kinds, like mangling auto-correct functions, that underline the distorting a-signifying elements of contemporary communication. Theorists of digital disobedience, especially DDoS (Distributed Denial of Service) attacks, note that the a-signifying dimension of disabling and "disrupting" servers is closely tied to the imperative to communicate in contemporary capitalism, and with the focus on circulation over meaning, breaking the "reproducible signal value" of messages, acquires a powerful effect of redirecting attention away from the usual suspects of the sending and receiving estates in the name of new stakeholders engaged in searches for non-meaning.[12]

There are all kinds of fascisms: "A micro-politics of desire means that henceforth we will refuse to allow any fascist formula to slip by, on whatever scale it may manifest itself, including within the scale of the family or even within our own personal economy."[13] Fascism is irreducible to historical phenomena like National Socialism in Guattari's estimation. The study of fascism is neither the purview of professional historians nor of political theorists. No one should bury it in historical periodicity and feel relief that it is over, the good guys having triumphed in the end in the beautiful confluence of the Red Army and Allied forces at the River Elbe, and then in the meeting of the heads of state at Yalta. There wasn't only one Nazi party: Guattari wants to avoid simplifications that make us blind to how the elements of certain historical forms of fascism continue to exist. Fascism leaps or skips transhistorically between generations and adapts itself to new conditions along the way: "What fascism set in motion yesterday continues to proliferate in other forms, within the complex of contemporary social space."[14] Fascisms proliferate and never stop adapting.

SUBREDDIT POLITICS

Updating Guattari, the icons of Hitlerism may be combined with Donald Trump's name by those, for or against him, who have no need of any firm ideas about Nazism. To see a graffito like *swastika-r.u.m.p.* as a micro-crystallization of fascism adapted to our contemporary political landscape requires a reflection on the digital source materials for semiotic production. A good place to begin is Dale Beran's attempt to formulate an interpretation of Trump's appeal through the mutations of 4chan – the "opprobrious" image board and sprawling forums/chat site launched in 2003 and known for its incivility and creativity as incubator of Anonymous, trolling, rickrolling, memes and just doing it for the lulz.[15] The Guattarian theory of desire both decentres the individual person as source and the object as lack instead positing an assemblage of mutable heterogeneous components as a process that is auto-organizing but also influenced by dominant historical trends, such as the mutual imbrications of humans and machines in the time of immaterial labour and production. But Guattari is a kind of Arendt in full reverse. If humans are cogs, and they are machinically enslaved, there is potential there, because they no longer have the kinds of social identities that are easily alienated. Disindividuation is not subjugating (socially subjecting), but machinically combinatory. On 4chan, anonymity is the goal but not always the rule, but based on a local ethic, individuation is strongly denied to persons and persona, until games of status erupt and offline events intervene to manufacture celebrity. These are still largely anathema. The fusion of the post and the subjectless subject, or Anon, releases intense flashes of desiring production, which can only be described as a "cesspool." For Beran, Trump is the alpha and beta, the fantasy of winning and the despair of losing, both at once rolled into the loser who won. He builds an analogy based on Charles Bukowski's novel *Factotum* in which two underpaid warehouse workers devise a scheme to accept money from their coworkers to bet on horse races, but only insofar as all the horses selected never win, because the bets are never placed. In the words of Manny and Henry:

"Hank, we take their bets."

"Those guys don't have any money – all they have is the coffee and chewing gum money their wives give them and we don't have time to mess around with the two dollar windows."

"We don't bet their money, we keep their money."

"Suppose they win?"

"They won't win. They always pick the wrong horse. They have a way of always picking the wrong horse."

"Suppose they bet on our horse?"

"Then we know we've got the wrong horse."[16]

This is the pathetic reality of the Trumpians, according to Beran: "younger Trump supporters know they are handing their money to someone who will never place their bets – only his own – because, after all, it's plain as day there was never any other option."[17] Further, Beran concludes: "Support for Trump is an acknowledgement that the promise is empty."[18] Trump will only place his own bets with the money of others. There is nothing really discordant about how this works. This is the Guattarian theory of machines (some highly abstract, others highly technical) that constantly seek out dis/connections (breaks and flows and residualities) with other machines for which they are flows. It's not exactly a Goldberg machine, but a 4chan contraption in which anonymous processes of subjectivation subsist in the bowels of unfettered digital desire: where semiological powerlessness meets machinic superpower, with strange results. The more the machine goes off the rails, the better it works, the more collectively enunciative 4chan becomes as its denizens take new formations, much to their own surprise: unstructured, ad hoc, short-lived assemblages, some of which are offline! The foundation of Trumpian politics might very well be the cesspool in which micro-fascist forces connive and collide. This cesspool attracts and holds the attention spans and affects of many. This is what Guattari called a black-hole effect: a phenomenon of subjective collapse that is attached to empty promises, and spectacularized policy, like Trump's televised executive orders that are reproduced widely in the post-mediasphere and invite participatory meme manufacture. The memefication of Trump as Pepe the Frog (Sad Frog Meme), the spectre of this prank invoked by Hillary Clinton as a white supremacist figure, and unleashed into the wild by alt-right appropriators and anti-defamation league critics alike, demonstrated the semiotic potentiality of comic strip characters to interact with wildly diverse components from across the political spectrum.[19] Trumpism spews forth empty promises and groundless pronouncements, racist, xenophobic and paranoid POTUS tweets, and spits out newly charged semiotic components that liberate the desire immanent to the political landscape and make it not only resonate across the alt-right mediascape, but into the mainstream and alternative media as well – all against the backdrop of the laments of the frog's creator Matt Furie.

Intense attachment fosters belonging and forgetting, and echoes them in public reproductions of the signifiers of rampant misogyny and raging xenophobia. As Bruce Bennett put it, Trump's body is a "semiotic salad"[20] that fails to cohere; and this is part of the appeal as every effort to discredit him at once builds his legitimacy among astonished believers and detractors. Processes of subjectivation open them to the option of aligning with the resonances of undelivered wagers and belligerently confirming their impotence, with hateful affects. This is how Deleuze and Guattari define micro-fascism: it occupies micro-black holes and resonates among them acting on the masses through millions of catastrophes.[21] Black holes are not exactly empty, and this where Guattari helps us to refine Beran's efforts; they absorb the energy of empty promises, the unplaced bets, as it were, and trap subjectivity in their resonances across the social field, interacting with a range of resonant political beliefs: 1950s nostalgists; emptiness is good for business yahoos; and maybe, for the millennials, a vote for a defiant emptiness. The InCels (Involuntary Celibates: a movement of violently misogynistic, predominantly white, men who can't get laid) can get in tune with Women for Trump Facebookers because both possess molar certainty crammed within their molecular machinic assemblages that resonates across social media groupings.

The analysis of desire's micro-fascism sounds a bit science-fictional, Guattari admits, but he is not deterred, because fascism is for him a dangerous, cancerous molecular phenomenon: "What makes fascism dangerous is its molecular or micro-political power, for it is a mass movement: a cancerous body rather than a totalitarian organism."[22] It is not a question of going small for the sake of minutiae, or for that of a Pascalian view of how different things would have been if Cleopatra's nose had been a bit longer.[23] Adopting the language of mutation, proliferation and molecularity allows Guattari to think through the capacity of fascism to spread throughout the social body. And, eventually, one party did try to overwhelm it, or "win" it electorally. This "potentially" gives to desire a fascist inclination since desire is not undifferentiated and instinctual, but results from highly complex and supple micro-formations and refined interactions (like the so-called Great Meme War of 2015–16), the kind we see on IRC (Internet Relay Chat), on 4chan, but just as well on Breitbart News. In discussing resonance and molecular fascism, Deleuze scholar Brent Adkins has recourse to viral videos as a prime example: "The potential for fascism arises when the black holes of several subjectivities begin to resonate with one another. The most straightforward way to think about resonance is to think about viral videos on YouTube."[24] Resonance phenomena ask us to work in the plural, in a proliferating and multiplex array of uploads – in Adkins' example, visual materials with notoriously negative comment postings.

For Deleuze and Guattari in *A Thousand Plateaus*, what makes fascism so frighteningly catastrophic for capitalism is that, unlike totalitarianism (especially of the Stalinist type), it liberates the desire of the masses for their own deaths, in spite of themselves. They are neither tricked nor desirous of their own masochistic repression. They are not driven internally to suicide by a death drive. Rather, fascism constructs a totalitarian state that is suicidal. National Socialism was focused on destruction, of everyone, including all Germans, as a project that would resonate throughout Europe and beyond the continent. Suicide of the state and the end of its own people would be a "crowning glory."[25] When there were no means to subdue mass desire to fulfil its own destruction, no deals could be brokered. The only option was an alliance for the United States and United Kingdom with Stalinism, because its brand of terror was acceptable, a more stable and efficient system for controlling mass turbulence (by the working class, colonials and minorities), and it too was threatened by National Socialism. For Guattari, "The last World War will thus have been the opportunity to select the most efficient totalitarian machines, those best adapted to the period."[26] Yet micro-fascisms have managed to seep into capitalism as Stalinism failed to molecularize its economy and labour force. Capitalism searches for new models of totalitarianism inside itself, and finds all kinds of "new forms of molecular fascism."[27] These find an environment conducive to infestation in infocapitalism's forms of affective and communicational labour that are directly productive of value.

New micro-fascisms find fertile ground in the fast-circulating redundancies of Internet memes and other post-media artefacts like the use of echo quotations as antisemitic signifiers. Extremely involutive black holes draw processes of subjectivation into themselves as their power increases with every iteration (repost) of them. Caught up in the pleasures of empty promises, Pepe memes, 4chan rants and actions, combover and spray tan jokes, comedic mimesis and alt-right outrage, and staging policy by spectacle, with so many supercharges of nothingness to go around, desire cannot extract itself from the echo chamber of emptiness that modulates its existence, making it lose its bearings, finding solace in distress that travels surprisingly well along the molecular bubbling of social media. For Guattari, "Fascism, like desire, is scattered everywhere, in separate bits and pieces, within the whole social realm; it crystallizes in one place or another, depending on the relationships of force."[28] The Trump presidency is a kind of general black hole into which the swirling phenomena of emptiness is drawn, simultaneously providing an attachment that allows belonging and forgetting to co-exist, as it emits forged lines of alterity: alternative facts, policy formation by Tweet, and bottomless post-truths that deflect and distract sober investigation and confound analysis.

Guattari reminds us that it is incumbent upon theorists of micro-fascism to search in the most "'incomprehensible' revolutionary transformations"[29] for investments of desire. In the transition from classical types of fascism to molecularized micro-fascisms, desire is at once liberated and subjected to repressive attributions tailored to new modes of production. This is why the Trump and 4chan hypothesis is so compelling, as it directs us to epic fails, perhaps beginning with the inauguration: the more it breaks down the better it works, which is the credo of Deleuze and Guattari with regard not only to capitalism, but to America as well. Trumpism seeks to install into every black hole the superior affect of hate attached to wired subjectivation, yet even in the most niche assemblages lines of flight escape that refuse the denigration of the office of the president, self-interested fortune seeking and the pathos of the deal.

The recent work on "Trumpology," by Christian Fuchs, successfully typologizes the capitalist and state relationship under Trump as direct through the figure of a billionaire president whose form of authoritarianism has the following attributes: greed is a brand (possessive hyper-individualism); the value of hard work is that it generates luck (ideology of hard labour); winning-ness (leadership skills); and self-interest transferred to domestic and foreign policy (social Darwinism).[30] What is interesting is that Fuchs begins with a more Guattari-friendly approach regarding the affective social ecology of fascism; rather than mass movement regression, Guattari points us toward echolalic degeneration as a form of contagious empty spinning. Although Fuchs rather abruptly abandons or, perhaps more kindly, converts this approach into economic factors, in isolating the black-hole effect of collective anxiety the media of its echoes are exposed: anxiety finds an institutional base in the Republican Party and gains hundreds of thousands of followers across social media. In ego surrender to a leader with whom one identifies, the resonance of multiple kinds of alienation is captured in a highly sharable scapegoating of enemies (leakers, labour leaders, broadcast media fakers, illegal immigrants and turncoats). The machinic conjugation of anxieties and reactionary racist formations closes the political assemblage in as much as it traps or, at least, delays the release of promising vectors of resistance and dismantlement as the terrible voids continue to stare out from a white-washed wall of right-wing nationalism, like Charlottesville. It is the snowballing of Trump's mangled syntax, his inarticulacy, the about-faces and the incoherence that dance on the rim of a black hole and spin into it. Nonetheless, Guattari was optimistic about what could emerge once these empty resonant redundancies shoot out of the black hole and finally escape it; he thought he could not be said to have put everything in the same bag, reactionary forces and their proto-revolutionary enemies, on the micro-fascist level![31] What is required is an analytical interpretation of interventions that minimize and perhaps prevent echo effects, and new social assemblages that contain the circulation of paranoiac and repressive contaminants.

NOTES

1. Pierre-Félix Guattari, *Lines of Flight: For Another World of Possibilities*, trans. Andrew. Goffey (London: Bloomsbury, 2016), 89.
2. Pierre-Félix Guattari, *The Three Ecologies*, trans. Ian Pindar and Paul Sutton (London: The Athlone Press, 2000), 43.
3. I first developed this material on micro-fascism for a public presentation, "The Proliferation of Micropolitical Fascisms," in the Spectres of Fascism Free School at Simon Fraser University in March 2017. This revised and

expanded version was presented at the Cultural Typhoon Conference at Ryukoku University in Kyoto in 2018.

4. Pierre-Félix Guattari, "Socially Significant Drugs," in Anna Alexander and Mark S. Roberts, eds., *High Culture: Reflections on Addiction and Modernity* (Albany, NY: SUNY Press, 2003), 201.

5. Pierre-Félix Guattari, *La revolution moléculaire* (Fontenay-sous-Bois: Encres/Editions Recherches, 1977), 331.

6. Janell Watson, *Guattari's Diagrammatic Thought: Writing Between Lacan and Deleuze* (London: Continuum, 2009), 84.

7. René Thom, *Mathematical Models of Morphogenesis (Mathematics and its Applications)*, trans. William M. Brookes and Dave Rand (Chichester: Ellis Horwood, 1983), 170; quoted partially in Watson, *Guattari's Diagrammatic Thought*, 194, No. 23.

8. Pierre-Félix Guattari, "Everybody Wants to Be a Fascist," in Sylvère Lotringer, ed., *Chaosophy* (New York: Semiotext(e), 1995), 29.

9. Ibid., 230.

10. Vladimir Lenin, "The Tasks of the Proletariat in the Present Revolution ('April Theses'), Chapter 2," in Slavoj Žižek, *Revolution at the Gates: Zizek on Lenin: The 1917 Writings* (London: Verso, 2002), 58.

11. Guattari, "Everybody Wants to Be a Fascist," 231.

12. Molly Sauter, *The Coming Swarm: DDOS Actions, Hacktivism, and Civil Disobedience on the Internet* (New York: Bloomsbury, 2014), 28–31.

13. Guattari, "Everybody Wants to Be a Fascist," 239.

14. Ibid., 236.

15. Dale Beran, "4chan: The Skeleton Key to the Rise of Trump," *Medium*, 14 February 2017, medium.com/@DaleBeran/4chan-the-skeleton-key-to-the-rise-of-trump-624e7cb798cb#.g6bubp3lq; Gabriella Coleman, *Hacker, Hoaxer, Whistleblower, Spy: The Many Faces of Anonymous* (New York: Verso, 2014), 41.

16. Charles Bukowski, *Factotum* (New York: Ecco, 2002), 106–7.

17. Dale Beran, "4chan."

18. Ibid.

19. See Elizabeth Chan, "Donald Trump, Pepe the Frog, and White Supremacists: An Explainer," The Office of Hilary Rodham Clinton, 12 September 2016, accessed 23 April 2019, Wayback Machine: web.archive.org/web/20170210051311/https://www.hillaryclinton.com/feed/donald-trump-pepe-the-frog-and-white-supremacists-an-explainer/; see WarriorTang, "Nazi Pepe Controversy," Know Your Meme, last modified 19 May 2018 (02:03PM EDT), accessed 23 April 2019, knowyourmeme.com/memes/events/nazi-pepe-controversy.

20. Bruce Bennett, "Trump's Body," *The Sociological Review* (blog), 18 November 2016, www.thesociologicalreview.com/blog/trump-s-body.html.

21. Félix Guattari and Gilles Deleuze, *A Thousand Plateaus*, trans. Brian Massumi (Minneapolis: University of Minnesota Press, 1987), 214.

22. Guattari and Deleuze, *A Thousand Plateaus*, 215.

23. Guattari, "Everybody Wants to Be a Fascist," 237.

24. Brent Atkins, *Deleuze and Guattari's A Thousand Plateaus: A Critical Introduction and Guide* (Edinburgh: Edinburgh University Press, 2015), 132.

25. Guattari and Deleuze, *A Thousand Plateaus*, 231.

26. Guattari, "Everybody Wants to Be a Fascist," 242.

27. Ibid., 244.

28. Ibid., 245.

29. Ibid., 248.

30. See Christian Fuchs, "Donald Trump: A Critical Theory Perspective on Authoritarian Capitalism," *tripleC* 15, No. 1 (2017): 1–72.

31. Guattari, *Lines of Flight*, 92.

PART III

The Contemporary Horizon

11

Fascist Neoliberalism and Preventive Counter-Revolution: The Second Round of the Latin American Laboratory

Vladimir Safatle

> *... a stable democracy and liberty, clean of impurities.*
>
> Friedrich Hayek[1]

In 1980, economist Paul Samuelson was invited to exercise his speculative imagination and describe capitalism in the year 2000. In his response he insisted that we should turn our eyes to Latin America, for there would be a model that would certainly be a paradigm in the near future. Samuelson then describes his understanding of such a paradigmatic situation:

> Generals and admirals seize power. They exterminate their left-wing predecessors, exile opponents, imprison dissident intellectuals, stifle unions, control the press, and paralyze all political activity. But, in this variant of market fascism, military leaders distance themselves from economic decisions. They do not plan the economy or accept bribery. They entrust the whole economy to religious fanatics – fanatics whose religion is the laissez-faire of the market ... So the clock of history walks backwards. The market is liberated and the money supply is strictly controlled. The social assistance credits are cut, the workers must accept anything or starve ... Low inflation is reduced to almost nothing ... Political freedom being out of circulation, income inequalities, consumption and wealth tend to grow.[2]

It is clear that the concrete case which so inspired Samuelson was the Chile of Augusto Pinochet and his "Chicago boys." Samuelson had realized that something paradigmatic was taking place in Chile, with its combination of political brutality and economic ultra-neoliberalism.[3] At the same time that neoliberalism appeared as a model of social management in the United Kingdom of Margaret Thatcher and the United States of Ronald Reagan, Chile showed the true regulatory horizon to guide this new phase of world capitalism. This was a horizon that had to be realized in an intensive manner because the social conflicts could no longer be solved within the dynamics proper to parliamentary democracy.

If Chile could appear as a paradigm, it was because Milton Friedman's statement about such a synthesis of authoritarianism and neoliberalism, "Chile is the exception, not the rule," was false. The Chilean experience was not the exception, but the true model. We know, for example, the statement of Friedrich Hayek: "I prefer to sacrifice democracy temporarily, I repeat, temporarily, rather than have to do without liberty, even if only for a while."[4] What claims such as these revealed was the true nature of the system.

This singular way of claiming that freedom could exist in the absence of democracy should not surprise us, as it came from someone who was faced with the task of denouncing the risks of a "totalitarian democracy" or defending the possibility of an "authoritarian liberalism."[5] Hayek was not saying that the democracy we have is merely formal and, therefore, should be surpassed in the direction of models of self-management and immanent deliberation of citizens. This criticism can be found in the traditions that insist that political life should be the space of continuous exercise of the constituent and destituent force of popular sovereignty.[6] Rather, in Hayek's view, the real risk of political life was the limitation or destruction of what would be the only truly concrete dimension of the notion of freedom, namely economic freedom, free disposition of property and the logic of accumulation – in short, the act of reducing objects and the world as a whole to the general form of private property and the rationality of entrepreneurialism. Hayek claimed that the only *totalitarian* regime that South America had known until the 1980s was not the Brazil of the generals, not Pinochet's Chile, nor Videla's Argentina, but Allende's Chile.[7] Hayek was able to make such a claim because, rather than collective self-determination, what C.B. Macpherson called "possessive individualism" appeared as the true form of "freedom."[8] Any attempt to create forms of life in which property no longer had this central and structuring role was the *very* expression of totalitarianism.

This horizon did not simply appear as a fact of nature – it would have to be deliberately constructed. Citizens do not naturally accept the reduction of their experience of freedom to the mere freedom to be an entrepreneur. The historical experience of struggles for freedom consists of the desire to negate the compulsive subsumption of activity beneath the category of labour, the desire for a form of radical equality that eliminates the putative naturalness of exploitation, the desire for the liberation of the world of things from determinations of property and possession. Therefore, social engineering was imperative to negate such experiences, to create a social monophony that could only be done, paradoxically for neoliberalism, through *more* state rather than *less* state: It was a question of subjecting our forms of life to a profound "depoliticization of society." After all, within the neoliberal world, it is the opposition produced by vulnerable sectors of society toward the unregulated market mechanism that produces the real risk to "freedom." Only a depoliticized society, radically limited in its ability to intervene in the economic rationality of market dynamics, insensitive to the pressures of regulation from unions, associations, activists, impoverished regions and vulnerable classes, could realize this unique "freedom." But, paradoxically, a society of this nature demands a strong and continuously active state. Such an imperative can explain statements such as this from Hayek:

> I would say that, as long-term institutions, I am totally against dicta-torships. But a dictatorship may be a necessary system for a transi-tional period. At times it is necessary for a country to have, for a time, some form or other of dictatorial power. As you will understand, it is possible for a dictator to govern in a liberal way. And it is also possible for a democracy to govern with a total lack of liberalism. Personally I prefer a liberal dictator to democratic government lacking liberalism.[9]

It is in phrases that have the rhetorical model of "I know very well, but still ..." that we find the true core of the regulatory horizon of social rationalization models: I know very well that we must be against dicta-torships, but still they are necessary. They are necessary long enough for social antagonisms to be destroyed, immanent contradictions stifled, and the last opponents tortured, exiled or liquidated.

Unsurprisingly, this model of a dictatorship that governs in a liberal way comes from the experience of Nazism. In this sense, a fascist horizon has always been the axis of the social organization of neoliberalism. Once again, Latin America is the privileged space for such an experiment.

Let us turn our attention to Carl Schmitt: Schmitt is the original author of this idea that parliamentary democracy with its trading systems tends to create a *total state*.[10] Having to deal with multiple demands from various organized social sectors, democracy would eventually allow the state to intervene in all areas of life, regulating all dimensions of social conflict, transforming itself into mere emulation of the antagonisms present in social life. Against this, one would not need *less state*, but to think of another form of *total state*. In this case, a state capable of depoliticizing society, having sufficient strength to intervene politically in the class struggle, to eliminate the forces of sedition in order to liberate the economy from its alleged social obstacles:[11] "It is a strong-weak state, strong with some, weak with others, against democratic demands and social redistribution, but weak in its relations with the market."[12]

But for that, it would require the continuous mobilization of actions and discourses aimed at the radical transformation of the processes of sensibility, affection and visibility. The social body must cease to be affected by the awareness of the violence produced against historically vulnerable groups, it should no longer see the logic of spoliation at work, and it must be insensitive to the immanent inequality of social relations in capitalism, its construction of racism as the tacit justification of economic submission and social subjection. At this point, the function of the state as a war machine for cultural hegemony becomes explicit; for it is only in this way that the body politic's sensibility becomes atrophied.

It is not possible to understand what is happening in Latin America today, and in Brazil in particular, without understanding the emergence of new laboratories in which this fascist matrix of neoliberalism can be re-introduced. Such a matrix will again be implemented because it was the only possible response to a situation of social disidentification, frustration, and demands for an end to the politics of representation that could lead to a revolutionary moment. This situation is systematically spread throughout the world. That is, one can say that this intersection of neoliberalism and a militarism with fascist traits was the realization of what we could call a preventive counter-revolution. In this sense, while the Brazil case is already significant given its substantial regional economic influence, its significance extends to the broader regional and global context. It can provide a magnifying glass for trends immanent to the challenges present in core sites of global capitalism. What is happening in Brazil today exemplifies to a greater or lesser extent a logic that can be seen globally.

We must discuss a preventive counter-revolution; answering such a spectral fascism cannot be done by attempting to resuscitate our democratic experience up to this point. The greatest of all errors lies in thinking we are simply dealing with a "social regression" in which the supposedly primal instincts of isolation, fear and hatred permeate the field of politics. The regression model seeks to naturalize an evolutionary view of social life, a view that is present in a certain notion of historical progress in which liberal democracies would play the final stage of social maturity. This is a lesson the first generation of the Frankfurt School has taught us: that the emergence, or return, of fascism is based on real discontent with the unfulfilled promises of liberal democracy (see Chapter 8).[13] If fascism posits itself as "counter-revolution," the emphasis is on the second of the two terms, *revolution*. The true content of fascism lies in the mobilization of the experience of structural rupture, in the critique of the "theatrical" character of parliamentary politics, and in the insistence on the distance between the structure of socioeconomic and political power, on the one hand, and popular sovereignty, on the other. Against that, a revolutionary response is imperative. It is the absence of precisely such a response, however, that marks the impotence of the contemporary forces of transformation.

NEOLIBERALISM WITH AN INHUMAN FACE

In Brazil, significant sectors of the society tacitly defended the military dictatorship, evinced a lack of social solidarity with vulnerable groups, and, in addition, were invested in a cult of violence as a response to the generalized fear of a country that constituted itself through oppression and war against Indians, Blacks and the poor. Nonetheless, the New Republic prevented such sectors from becoming efficacious political actors. A combination of international and national factors allowed the awakening of these dormant elements of society.

A comparison between the European and Brazilian extreme right can help us understand what is happening at this moment. Two dates are fundamental to the consolidation of the far-right on the Europe–United States axis: 2001 and 2008.[14]

After the attacks of 9/11, it became clear that the legitimacy of the sovereign power of the state in advanced capitalist societies would regress to its original ground, namely, the use of insecurity and fear as central political affects. Several analysts insisted that actions aimed at the "war on terror" were not, to a large extent, ruled precisely by the calculation of the actions needed against the real causes of terrorism, neither by a global consolidation of alliances.[15] The disproportionate nature of actions such as the invasion of Afghanistan and Iraq, and the actual results concerning the security of the citizens of the First World's liberal democracies became obvious. But this was necessary, since such actions were closely related to the logics of production of social adhesion from the impact of the generalization of fear.[16]

However, it was clear that, on this horizon, the far-right would be the great political beneficiary of the new situation. Its ideas had always been the result of a paranoid notion of nation-state, in which the themes of the border, boundary, invasion, necessary immunization and contagion were the central elements (see Chapter 7 in this volume). Now its rhetoric was moving toward the centre of the political debate. It was enough to force associations between immigrants and terrorists, a relatively simple operation if we take into account how the signifiers "Arab" and "Turk" (the most relevant groups of immigrants in Europe) were linked in the European imagination to colonial wars and their primordial stereotypes.

There was one more element to consolidate the European far-right wing and it came with 2008. The economic crisis demonstrated the inanity of hegemonic politics based on the balance between social democracy and liberalism. The same "austerity" policies were applied by both putatively "left-" and right-wing governments. From the point of view of their economic policies, Schroeder and Merkel in Germany, Sarkozy and Hollande in France, Zapatero and Aznar in Spain, and Tony Blair and David Cameron in the United Kingdom did not mean any substantial change and this became clear to the impoverished citizens of these states, submitted as they were to increasingly brutal regimes of social insecurity. The far-right understood this and positioned itself with an anti-liberal discourse marked by the rejection of free trade, the return to protectionist practices, the critique of the global financial market, and with proposals of security and social guarantee shared with the left. The difference was that their proposals were articulated with a national and xenophobic vocabulary and grammar. The theme of international solidarity and indifference to the nation in the name of a concrete universality, so dear to the left, was deliberately omitted.

This anti-liberalism of the European far-right showed what it could produce with Brexit and with the threat of the return of national currencies and customs controls. This has forced European neoliberalism to adapt, creating a "neoliberalism with a human face" whose laboratory is Emmanuel Macron's France: a government that applies the most brutal policies to dismantle social rights, the most explicit application of police violence against all forms of protests while cultivating speeches based on tolerance, cosmopolitanism and citations of Paul Ricoeur's philosophy. Yet, today, one can note this form of neoliberalism's lack of stamina. Sunk in a general crisis of governability, the Macron government faces a social uprising not seen since 1968.

However, it is clear that this model cannot be applied to Brazil. Neither the fight against terrorism in a country completely outside the colonial axis, nor the 2008 financial crisis as a space for the implementation of "austerity" policies in the European way, affected Brazilian society. Initially, the horizon that allowed the rise of the far-right in Europe seemed far away.

Thus, all attempts to win presidential elections in Brazil with neoliberal policies were shipwrecked and would continue to fail. This impossibility was guaranteed. Polls conducted by Ipsos showed that 68 per cent of the Brazilian population were against privatizations, 71 per cent were against pension reform, and 85 per cent were against labour reform.[17] This was not the result of some form of "Iberian heritage," rather, it was grounded in a simple pragmatic realization: labour relations in Brazil are marked by brutal dispossession, given the wage differences between the richest and the poorest. According to IBGE (Brazilian Geographical and Statistical Institute) data, the richest part of the Brazilian population earns wages (not counting bonuses and stock options) 36 times higher than the poorest part.[18] In this context, the poorer section sees the state as some form of shield against particularly oppressive production relations.[19]

In Brazil, the neoliberal agenda could only be applied under conditions of authoritarian rule and/or through undermining the electoral process. To do so, it would initially be necessary to recreate an alliance around political actors outside the New Republic's governance axis, namely the PT (Worker Party) and the PSDB (Brazilian Social Democratic Party). For both parties have committed themselves, each in its own way and following different inflections, to a certain regime of consensus proper to the post-dictatorship period. Applying the neoliberal model, then, would entail deploying a model that was initially tested in Pinochet's Chile by an alliance between neoliberalism, on the one hand, and extreme-right authoritarianism, on the other.

In Brazil, the deployment of the neoliberal model meant leaning on dormant cells intact since the end of the military dictatorship. A country that had produced an infinite, never-ending democratic transition, which never applied elementary principles of transitional justice and the imperative of "working through the past," was particularly ripe for precisely such a deployment of neoliberalism. Brazil is the only Latin American country that failed to bring torturers from the military regime to justice.[20] Unlike other Latin American countries like Argentina, Chile and Uruguay, Brazil was chosen as the world laboratory for the new version of fascist neoliberalism because it stood out on this continent for its inability to put torturers in jail, its inability to remove politicians and businessmen compromised by their links to the dictatorship, and its ineffectual demands for the dismantling of the police state. Even the years of the left in power did not change that. On the contrary, state apparatuses such as anti-terrorist legislation were passed under governments supposedly of the "left" (Dilma Rousseff's government).

It would not be possible to directly present the true matrix of the economic agenda with its pledges of "privatizing everything" for the payment of public debt, its sacred respect to the ceiling of investments of the Brazilian state with the consequent final dismantling of public services and the autonomy from the Central Bank. It would be necessary for such discussions to give way to rhetoric in which "disorder," "corruption" and "violence" were the major elements of political contestation. And, at this point, the popular demonstrations of 2013 in Brazil were decisive. In a way, for the far-right, 2013 was our 2001, because it was the moment at which fear consolidated itself as a central political affect.

POPULAR MOBILIZATIONS WITHOUT CONSTITUTED HEGEMONY

Since 2008, the world has witnessed almost uninterrupted sequences of popular uprisings, from the Irish anti-austerity protests, to the 2009 Iranian elections, through the 2010–11 Arab Spring and Occupy movement. These uprisings have one central characteristic: they are produced without constituting new hegemonic blocs. Usually they are like an explosion and a contagion. A punctual moment produces a revolt and restless sectors of civil society are impelled to take to the streets; symbols of power are destroyed, police orders are put in question. Within

Figure 11.1   Fire in the Brazilian Foreign Affairs Office during the demonstrations of 2013

these insurrections emerges the figure of an "ungovernable" society in which subjects are no longer willing to submit to the injunctions of the economic order with its alleged "rationality." For here we see evidence of a dizzying level of social disidentification, of revolt against political invisibility, of a refusal to join work. These are potentially revolutionary moments and from their emergence we always also see the dynamics of preventive counter-revolution.

Brazil is still dealing with the consequences of a situation like this from 2013 (the biggest mass movement of Brazilian history, made first against bus fare increases but quickly transformed into a strong confrontation with the government). It must be remembered that the paradigmatic image of 2013 was the destruction of a symbol of the state and its order. This image shows a mass of demonstrators in Brasilia setting fire to the Itamaraty Palace (Ministry of Foreign Relations), since it had been prevented by police from doing the same to the National Congress. Never before in Brazilian history was the expression of the *disidentification* between the population, on the one hand, and the institutions of the state order, on the other, so manifest. Along with this, the Brazilian population saw, over a period of several months, an uninterrupted series of demonstrations in which the "visibility of the invisible" became clear and took concrete shape. Vulnerable groups (such as women, LGBTQ, Blacks etc.) demanded legal guarantees, showing how the profile of patterns of existence within Brazilian society tended to change; add to this an explicit rebellion in the world of work. In the single year of 2013, Brazil saw some 2,050 strikes, more than half of which were in the private sector. There has never been a year with so much labour unrest in Brazil since the beginning of the historical series that was brought to an end with the advent of the military dictatorship.[21] Several of these strikes were wildcat strikes, strikes made against the union leadership itself. Clearly, these were workers who no longer recognized themselves in their "representatives," creating a dynamic of ungovernable conflicts, of uncontrollable antagonisms.

The possibility of creating structures of resonance between the uprising against the exploitation of labour, the revolt against the limits of liberal democracy and the resizing of social visibility regimes could have, in fact, led us to an effectively revolutionary situation. That is, the protests of 2013 demonstrated the existence of something that we could call the *revolutionary plasticity* of Brazilian society. But for such plasticity to produce the figure of a social body to come, it should have been assumed without fear. Primarily, what we might call "strategies of creating hegemony in motion" would be necessary. Since such revolts are not the fruit of a previously created hegemony, that is, without a clearly constituted political subject, they must give way to the creation, *in medias res*, of a political subject. This means operating by lateral joints constituted through generic implications, by collective nomination.

In the absence of this, whatever emerges from popular uprisings such as these are *reactive* subjects, namely, subjects who seek to translate social disidentification into a desire for a return to the past, in general, and to the time of the dictatorship, in particular.[22] It is on such reactive subjects that preventive counter-revolutions rely. This has been the norm since at least the emergence of the *Lumpenproletariat* in the French revolution of 1848 and the subsequent installation of the Second French Empire under Napoleon III; remembering Marx's lesson in *The 18th Brumaire of Louis Bonaparte* is imperative today.[23] It is not by chance that it was from 2013 in Brazil that discourses demanding "order" gained increasing momentum. Every real movement of social revolt always has as its counterpoint the production of reactive subjects who will try to deny the emancipatory force of events. Faced with a burning Brasilia, it is not surprising that several voices began loudly demanding "their country back," wrapped in the national flag and dreaming of "military intervention."

The signifiers "violence" and "corruption" could have been the basis for the hegemony of a leftist discourse in Brazil. For the left, "violence" was associated with the obscene, structural inequality of Brazilian society and "corruption" with a political system that was completely disconnected from popular deliberation and direct participation. But, at the same time, the moment of 2013 produced another hegemonic discourse in which the lack of a strong military government appeared as the cause of the degradation of the republic, even though tyranny was the fundamental form of corruption, given the corrupt history of the dictatorship, itself Brazilian. In fact, allied to neoliberal anti-statism, the fight against "corruption" was only the password for the middle and upper classes to legitimize their unconfessed desire to eliminate all forms of social solidarity through taxation systems. It was in this way that the Brazilian extreme right was created, with its neoliberalism with an inhuman face.

NOTES

Unless otherwise stated, URLs were last accessed on 30 April 2019.

1. Cited in Robert Leeson, *Hayek: A Collaborative Biography Part X: Eugenics, Cultural Evolution, and the Factual Conceit* (Cham, Switzerland: Palgrave Macmillan, 2017), 203.

2. Paul Samuelson, "The World Economy at Century's End," in Shigeto Tsuru, ed., *Human Resources, Employment and Development* (London: Macmillan, 1983), 1:75.

3. In these first pages, I follow here a structure of arguments and examples presented first in Grégoire Chamayou, *La société ingouvernable: une généalogie du libéralisme autoritaire* (Paris: La fabrique, 2018).

4. See Andrew Farrant, Edward McPhall and Sebastian Berger, "Preventing the 'Abuses' of Democracy: Hayek, the Military Usurper and Transitional Dictatorship in Chile," *American Journal of Economics and Sociology* 71, No. 13 (2012): 513–38.

5. Friedrich Hayek, *Studies in Philosophy, Politics and Economics* (New York: Touchstone, 1969), 161.

6. According to Agamben, while destituent power outlines a force that in its very constitution "deactivates the governmental machine." See Giorgio Agamben, "What Is a Destituent Power?" *Environment and Planning D: Society and Space* 32, No. 1 (February 2014): 65–74, doi.org/10.1068/d3201tra.

7. Let us remember statements such as: "I have not been able to find a single person even in much maligned Chile who did not agree that personal freedom was much greater under Pinochet than it had been under Allende." (Friedrich Hayek, Letter to *The Times*, 3 August 1978.)

8. See C.B. MacPherson, *The Political Theory of Possessive Individualism: Hobbes to Locke* (Oxford: Oxford University Press, 2011).

9. Friedrich Hayek, Interview to *El Mercurio*, 12 April 1981.

10. See Carl Schmitt, "Starker Staat und gesunde Wirtschaft. Ein Vortrag für Wirtschaftsführern," in *Volk und Reich: Politische Monatshefte für das junge Deutschland* 2, No. 1 (1933): 81–94. About the similitudes between Hayek

and Schmitt, see: Renato Cristi, "Hayek, Schmitt y el estado de derecho," *Revista Chilena de Derecho* 18, No. 2 (1991): 189–201.

11. Hayek recognizes the cleverness of the "extraordinary German student of politics, Carl Schmitt" in this topic. See Friedrich Hayek, *Law, Legislation and Liberty* (New York: Routledge, 1998), 3:194–5.

12. Wolfgang Streek, "Heller, Schmitt and the Euro," *European Law Journal* 21, No. 3 (May 2015): 364.

13. See Max Horkheimer, "The Revolt of Nature," in *Eclipse of Reason* (London: Continuum Press, 2002).

14. See "The Brazilian Matrix: Between Fascism and Neoliberalism, Vladimir Safatle and Samir Gandesha in Conversation," *Krisis* (forthcoming).

15. See, for example: Bernard Harcourt, *The Counterrevolution: How Our Government Went to War Against Its Own Citizens* (New York: Basic Books, 2018). About the new paradigm of war and peace, see also Giorgio Agamben, *State of Exception* (Chicago: University of Chicago Press, 2005).

16. A good work about this new affective structure of contemporary politics is: Judith Butler, *Precarious Life: The Power of Mourning and Violence* (New York: Verso, 2004).

17. Respectively: Ipsos, August 2018; Datafolha, May 2017; Vox Populi, May of 2017.

18. Nielmar de Oliveria, "IBGE: ricos receberam 36 vezes acima do que ganharam os pobres em 2017," Agência Brasil, 11 April 2018, agenciabrasil. ebc.com.br/economia/noticia/2018-04/ibge-1-mais-rico-recebeu-em-2017-36-vezes-mais-do-que-metade-da-populacao.

19. About the Brazilian labour market, see Ruy Braga, *The Politics of the Precariat: From Populism to Lulista Hegemony* (New York: Brill, 2018).

20. For the consequences of the dictatorship in the Brazilian New Republic, see Vladimir Safatle and Edson Telles, *O que resta da ditadura: a exceção brasileira* (São Paulo: Boitempo, 2010).

21. See Paula Marcelino, "Sindicalismo e neodesenvolvimentismo: analisando as greves entre 2003 e 2013," *Tempo Social* 29, No. 3 (2018): 201–27.

22. For the concept of reactive subject, see Alain Badiou, *Logiques des mondes* (Paris: Seuil, 2014).

23. This implies a refusal of some interpretations of the *Lumpenproletariat* as a real revolutionary subject, as we can see in: Peter Stallybrass, "Marx and Heterogeneity: Thinking the Lumpenproletariat," *Representations*, No. 21 (1990): 69–95, doi.org/10.2307/2928400. See also: Ernesto Laclau, *La razón populista* (Buenos Aires: Fondo de Cultura Económica, 2011).

12

Decolonizing the "Contemporary Left"?: An Indigenous Reflection on Justice in the New World Order[1]

Patricia M. Barkaskas

I am a Métis person who lives and works on the traditional, ancestral and unceded territories of the xʷməθkʷəy̓əm (Musqueam), Sḵwx̱wú7mesh (Squamish) and səl̓ílwətaʔɬ (Tsleil-Waututh) in Vancouver, British Columbia. I acknowledge that I am an uninvited guest on the territories of these sovereign nations. I write these words because they have meaning, particularly as forms of politics and protocol. These words allow me to engage in the work I do with truth and humility. They remind me who I am and how that makes me accountable in a colonial world, outside of the myth of "post-settler" society in Canada.[2] These words also disrupt the post-settler comfort that feeds into what Eva Mackey has observed is an "angry sense of ongoing entitlement," on the part of settlers, when faced with the realities of ongoing Indigenous existence and jurisdiction, as in the case of land claim disputes.[3]

My approach in this chapter is partially self-reflective. I initially attempted to write about the links between fascism and colonialism in a more typical academic style by taking a position and defending it through expository argumentation. However, this approach and the rhetorical tools within it were not working for me. Perhaps it is because this is an ongoing conversation, observation and situation; that is, as an Indigenous person I think about and live – through my work and daily existence – the reality of colonialism's impact on Indigenous peoples in Canada every day. This might sound like an exaggeration, but it is not. To write about the lived experiences of the impacts of colonialism as an intellectual exercise or experiment – using the standard tools of argumentative critique – seemed stilted and less genuine than the approach I have set out in this chapter.

My methodological approach relies upon personal narrative, in part, with reflections about justice in a largely unjust world from my perspective as an Indigenous person. I work from the foundational truth that a new world order came into Indigenous peoples' lives in what is now called Canada hundreds of years ago.[4] It could even be said that the rise of a totalitarian power arrived on these shores with the coming of European settlers and the eventual imposition of Canadian state authority on Indigenous nations (see also Chapter 11 in this volume).[5] I hope to illuminate links between the normalized violence of settler colonialism and the laws, policies and practices of the Canadian state as something potentially akin to the totalitarian rule of fascist regimes. And, recently, scholarship has confirmed the importance of the colonial imaginary for fascism itself (see Introduction of this volume). It is no surprise that people often conceive of colonialism as an obvious fact of Canada's past and present. However, cognitive dissonance exists when considering the lived reality for Indigenous peoples under the current colonial state compared to its abstracted obviousness.

From the start, I struggled with what I would write about, other than observing how colonialism and fascism are not so different. I do recognize the historical specificity of fascist and neofascist regimes. However, with the extant dangers of *fascism* looming once more, and the daily examples that continue to emerge not only in Canada but also around the world, I must admit that I see more connections between colonialism and fascism than differences. We must also not fail to recognize that *spectres of fascism* directly invoke traces of twentieth-century fascist dictators and their macabre antecedents.

For Indigenous peoples in Canada, the historic and ongoing imposition of the imperial state apparatus and the ongoing nightmare of colonialism express themselves not so much as shadowy prospects in the present (simultaneously referencing the past and alluding to a horrific future), but, rather, as simply the *fact* of everyday reality. Though, let us not fool ourselves that, if sustained, the colonial project does not also lead to horrific futures; the record of history is clear – the end game of colonialism includes genocide. In other words, for Indigenous peoples this means the very cancellation of the future as such. This has become especially evident and urgent with the recent election of Jair Bolsonaro in Brazil and his attacks on the Indigenous inhabitants of the Amazon rainforest[6] as well as the Indian state's ongoing oppression of the Adivasi or "tribal" peoples in India.[7]

Today, this truth is especially poignant. I write these words only one day after the release of "Reclaiming Power and Place: The Final Report of the National Inquiry into Missing and Murdered Indigenous Women and Girls."[8] As the Executive Summary of the National Inquiry's Final Report makes clear, the truth of Indigenous peoples' existence in Canada has been one of resisting purpose-built policies and practices that are the tools of genocide:

> The truths shared in these National Inquiry hearings tell the story – or, more accurately, thousands of stories – of acts of genocide against First Nations, Inuit and Métis women, girls, and 2SLGBTQQIA people.
>
> This violence amounts to a race-based genocide of Indigenous Peoples, including First Nations, Inuit, and Métis, which especially targets women, girls, and 2SLGBTQQIA people. This genocide has been empowered by colonial structures, evidenced notably by the Indian Act, the Sixties Scoop, residential schools, and breaches of human and Inuit, Métis and First Nations rights, leading directly to the current increased rates of violence, death, and suicide in Indigenous populations.[9]

As Métis writer Cherie Dimaline aptly points out about the experiences of Indigenous peoples in Canada, "We have survived our apocalypse. I thought of the worst thing I could write about and it was stuff that had already happened."[10]

This apocalypse or genocide includes the various and multiple policies and practices of the Canadian state described in the National Inquiry's Final Report with respect to attempts to eliminate Indigenous peoples, communities and nations. As the report provides, these actions have targeted Indigenous women, girls and 2SLGBTQQIA (two-spirit, lesbian, gay, bisexual, transgender, queer, questioning, intersex and asexual) peoples in specific ways with the resulting impact of multiple and various intergenerational injustices.[11]

The realities of Canada's residential school system and its horrors are just one way that genocide has been enacted in Canada. At least 150,000 Indigenous children were forcibly removed from their families and communities,[12] and provided with numbers and/or European names in place of their actual names.[13] These children were forced to live in unsanitary conditions,[14] without access to proper medical treatment in many cases,[15] and used as subjects in nutritional deprivation experiments in some schools.[16] Many children died and, to this day, their families do not know where they are buried.[17] Despite an apology from then prime minister Stephen Harper on 11 June 2008, and a national class action to provide survivors and their families with compensation for the mental, psychological and spiritual anguish, and the emotional, physical and sexual abuse suffered by Indigenous children at the schools, the impact of residential schools on Indigenous families, communities and nations is still fresh.[18] The last schools closed in 1996.[19]

The residential schools were just one aspect of Canada's protracted and purposeful strategy to eliminate Indigenous peoples, communities and nations. This policy of genocide still exists; for example, the provincial child welfare programmes notoriously apprehend Indigenous children from their families in far greater percentages than other children.[20] Ominously, the fascism re-appears when considering the direct aim of the residential schools was "to kill the Indian in the child."[21]

The Truth and Reconciliation Commission of Canada released its Final Reports and its Calls to Action on 23 July 2015,[22] and now the National Inquiry's findings and 231 recommendations framed, significantly, as "Calls for Justice," remind us that we truly have not entered an "Age of Reconciliation."[23] Current Canadian prime minister Justin Trudeau has made many claims about his personal and professional commitment to reconciliation, but the actions of his Liberal government do not necessary align with this rhetoric. For example, his government sent an armed militia, the Royal Canadian Mounted Police (RCMP), to remove the Wet'suwet'en Unist'ot'en Land Protectors on 7 January 2019, for exercising their inherent jurisdiction on their traditional, unceded and ancestral territory.[24] Not surprisingly, Indigenous peoples might wonder with some scepticism what difference it will make that the Prime Minister has also publicly acknowledged, although not at the actual ceremony for the release of the National Inquiry's Final Report,[25] that Canada did commit genocide against Indigenous peoples.[26] One wonders whether it also matters that the RCMP action took place under the first Indigenous minister of justice and attorney general in Canadian history.[27]

The power of propaganda comes in many forms, especially with an election on the horizon. I know this may inspire refrains from the left, on which I also firmly situate myself, about the lack of viable political choices available to us despite our pseudo-democratic system. I am just as terrified as anyone else about the very real concern that alt-right-influenced political parties or leaders with quasi-fascist visions could successfully gain power in Canada as they have elsewhere in the world. Regardless, I remain sceptical about any possibility of significant change for Indigenous peoples in Canada no matter who is in power. Unless, that is, we can move closer to *decolonizing* Canada.

Few non-Indigenous activists, academics, artists, politicians and scholars engage with, and talk about, the connections between the rise of the alt-right, the inhumane brutality of neoliberalism as an economic and social system, and the violence of settler colonialism's past, present and future. In the panic about the return of fascism, there is a seeming dearth of dialogue coming from the left about the obvious links to an ongoing colonial project throughout history, a project with significant ties to fascism as a way to reinforce monolithic culture based upon the imperial image of itself (an important exception is Vladimir Safatle; see Chapter 11, his contribution to this volume).[28] The Canadian state is, at its core, an imposed imperial power that relies in the present on the fiction of itself as a naturalized post-settler society;[29] the genocide against Indigenous peoples is either removed from the average Canadian's mind or, more horribly, justified through the naturalization of settler-colonial racism.

The Canadian nationalist project is grounded in the authoritarian violence of settler colonialism. There is no way to separate the Canadian state from the history, and ongoing project, of colonialism. My discussion here addresses the violence of the contemporary period by focusing on justice.[30] As the Final Report of the National Inquiry indicates about the 231 Calls for Justice in response to genocide, these are "not simply moral principles: they are legal imperatives."[31] Canada prides itself on being a just nation; a nation that upholds the liberal values of freedom and equality. Globally, it is still upheld as a model multicultural state that can be constructively emulated by other nations. Justice is a fundamental notion to the concept of law. If we are going to intervene against the normative violence of settler colonialism – primarily premised on this notion of justice – we have to begin with unlearning what we think justice is and understand that there is little to be found for Indigenous peoples in the Canadian justice system. Given the significance of the Truth and Reconciliation Commission's findings and the focus on implementing the 94 Calls to Action,[32] most of which are about justice, along with the 231 Calls for Justice, we also need to acknowledge a fundamental truth about justice and Indigenous peoples in Canada.

Indigenous resistance theory, grounded in Indigenous ontology and epistemology, challenges dominant discourses about the power and purpose of law and shifts the very notion of how justice is defined, perceived and enacted. Such approaches in both the academic and practical aspects of legal understanding in Canada intervene in violent normative legal ideology and challenge the colonial hegemony under-pinning the Canadian legal system. Indigenous scholars who examine law and justice, such as Natalie Clark, Darlene Johnston and Sarah Hunt, frame decolonial resistance grounded in Indigenous methodologies as a way to disrupt how people have been, and are being, taught to think about Canada. As Clark indicates in her discussion of grounding Indigenous methodology in our experiences and expressions, "if context is primary, then the words we use to describe our methodologies must flow from the ontologies and languages from which they are born."[33] Thus, these scholars examine from their location as Indigenous women how Canadian laws, policies and practices are responsible for the injustices experienced by Indigenous peoples by contributing their knowledge of how colonialism is entrenched in and replicated through the Canadian legal system and the policies and practices that are justified by colonial law. The Canadian justice system perpetuates settler-colonial perspec-tives where the law is used as a tool of dispossession and oppression. This reflection contemplates the place of critical decolonial and Indigenous methodologies in interrupting hegemonic legal knowledge production by engaging with approaches that resist dominant discourses about the power and purpose of law. Perhaps this is not so dissimilar to histor-ical and present attempts in other places around the world where people have confronted or are confronting the violent truths of the past to build generative societies. I do not suggest that attempts to address colonialism and its ongoing consequences in Canada are the same as other examples which exist, but rather there may be examples that serve as reference points for accepting historical traumas involving genocide in the present. For example, the South African post-apartheid Truth and Reconciliation process, on which to some extent the Canadian Truth and Reconcilia-tion process was based as part of the legal settlement agreement between Canada and survivors of the Indian residential school system, included the creation of the Institute for Justice and Reconciliation to continue the work of the reconciliation process, including ensuring the horrors of apartheid are not forgotten.[34] Germany serves as another example of a society that has attempted to embed in its collective sociocultural memory the horrors of its past. This active remembrance of the Holocaust attempts to acknowledge the truth of the genocide while also looking to the future to ensure such heinous crimes against humanity never occur again.[35] And, indeed, the fact that in Brazil there was no coming to terms with the bloody years of the military dictatorship has allowed the far-right to seize the opportunity in the context of a struggle to democratize the state, to re-assert itself in the figure of Bolsonaro (see Chapter 11).

However, a more fulsome discussion or comparative analyses of genocide in Canada versus other contexts is not the point of my exploration here. I am intentionally focusing on the Canadian context in order to draw out the specific circumstances of this historical and present situation, especially as it relates to the uncanny return of *fascism*.

Using Johnston's concept of "situated relatedness," I have a responsibility to situate myself as an Indigenous person within the context of my community and relations, so that people understand my approach to the work I do is informed by my experiences as a Métis woman. For example, I situated myself relationally as an Indigenous person within the context of my relationships to the people and lands around me at the opening of this chapter. In so doing, I want people to understand that my experience as a Métis woman informs the work I do as a lawyer and an educator. I often situate myself further: I tell perfect strangers what it means for me to be Métis and what my relational history is to my family's Indigenous genealogy and identity. My story, the story of my family, includes numerous intergenerational injustices, such as my great-grandfather's experience of residential school and how that led him to not allow his children to speak Cree and to not teach any of them to fiddle, despite his being an accomplished Métis fiddler. I talk to people about how even just these two examples have meant I did not have access to this knowledge as a Métis person. This was not knowledge that was lost; it was destroyed. The abuses my great-grandfather suffered at residential school resulted in intergenerational trauma, including the loss of vital cultural knowledge. Contending with that loss in the present remains a struggle.

I want to help expand people's understanding of intergenerational injustice and to demonstrate an embodied concept of Indigenous justice. By performing an act of justice, I assert jurisdiction over my personhood as it relates to my historic and present-day Indigeneity. This act denies the Canadian state power to rob me of my personhood through the inevitable consequences of Canada's historical policies and legal actions meant to erase not just Indigenous sovereignty, but also the very existence of Indigenous people, including our families, communities and nations. By telling people my own story, I hope to crystallize, if only to some degree, the abstracted obviousness of colonialism. Colonialism's objectives anticipate fascism's desire to eradicate the existence of many peoples' truths. And, in some cases, the aim is to remove actual existence in favour of a monolithic mythology of white supremacist dominance, oppression and terror, grounded in a distorted phantasmal world built on the fantasy of those who are driven to dominate.

We are often asked to "position" ourselves and that is important. Johnston's situated relatedness also asks people to think beyond positionality – to consider the relationships they have to the lands they occupy and spend their time upon, the people with whom they have relations, and their personal histories. Ultimately, this work asks people to think about the ways in which who we are and how we are situated change the ways we define justice. It is important for people to consider what it means to live on unceded Indigenous lands and also what it means to live on treaty lands and then also to reflect on the acknowledgement that the existence of treaties does not imply the cessation of Indigenous jurisdiction, despite Canada's legal perspective on this point.[36] According to Indigenous legal principles, treaties were not about ceding Indigenous jurisdiction over lands or self-determination. Treaties were nation-to-nation agreements confirming relationships between sovereign nations to live and exist together – each with existing and recognized responsibilities, along with rights, that flowed from the relationship conferred by the treaty promises. Certainly, the notion of land use and resource extraction were not unfamiliar to Indigenous nations. However, the unsustainable economic model of industrial capitalism (and now neoliberal capital), the driving force of empire, imperialism and colonization over the past 250 years, did not resemble Indigenous nations' resource use and extraction practices, which were based on their various ethical relationships with and stewardship of the lands and non-human living beings around them.

Returning to Indigenous methodologies, I want to consider how justice either perpetuates the acceptance of settler-colonial violence as normal or allows us entry points into disrupting this concept (e.g. through deliberate interventions such as situated relationality). As Hunt observes, the inundation of sensationalized accounts of violence against Indigenous peoples in Canada – violence enacted against Indigenous nations, communities and bodies, especially the bodies of Indigenous children, women and 2SLGBTQQIA folks – normalizes this violence to such an extent that it leads to a sense of apathy or indifference in the general public about such violence. Moreover, the violence comes to be read as a part of the Indigenous experience and, therefore, a pathology of Indigenous existence, rather than being seen for what it truly is – the ongoing violence of settler colonialism and the result of colonial dehumanization of Indigenous peoples over centuries.[37] "Reclaiming Power and Place" documents the ways in which the Canadian state has often attempted to dismiss genocide targeting women, girls and 2SLGBTQQIA folks as "domestic violence."[38] Colonial state-sanctioned violence is often framed through an idea that somehow Indigeneity comes with inherent and inevitable violence.[39]

Clark calls this "the doctrine of shock and awe," where the violence of injustice as it plays out in Indigenous peoples' lives is overemphasized and naturalized while nothing is done about the systemic factors that lead to these injustices.[40] When speaking about injustice and its intimate connection to the violence of colonialism, it is important to do it through an intersectional lens grounded in Indigenous knowledge. Thus, as Clark states, Indigenous, trauma-informed approaches call for the development of "models for addressing violence that are aligned with Indigenous values, Indigenous paradigms and epistemologies and that are based in strengths, resistance and survivance."[41] She suggests "that we should move beyond decolonizing Western models of trauma, and instead attend to the centering of 'wise practices' and specific Indigenous Nations approaches ... within a network of relational accountability."[42]

Clark's "Red intersectionality," or what can be called an Indigenous intersectional approach, includes five principles:

1) Respecting sovereignty and self-determination;
2) Local and global land-based knowledge;
3) Holistic health within a framework that recognizes the diversity of Indigenous health;
4) Agency and resistance;
5) Approaches that are rooted within specific Indigenous nations relationships, language, land, and ceremony.[43]

We must apply these approaches to justice in order to acknowledge the links of present-day colonialism to its imperial foundations. We can then recognize the purposeful and violent imposition of the Canadian state's rule over Indigenous peoples, communities and nations as necessary for the Canadian state to maintain its dominance, enacted through historical and present-day acts of colonial violence perpetrated against Indigenous peoples in order to justify Canadian state control over Indigenous lands and sovereignty.

Applying Clark's "Red intersectionality" to the notion of the naturalized "post-settler society" allows us to reveal the deep complicity of settler innocence in denying genocide against Indigenous peoples. The collective erasure of the atrocities of Canada's campaign to eradicate Indigenous pasts, presents and futures is a kind of collective "settler move to innocence."[44] This process forfeits truths for a blissful ignorance and acceptance of the lie of Canadian colonial justice.[45] The everyday politics of resisting and refusing the accepted notion of "justice" through Indigenous approaches considers how this discussion is largely framed through colonial values and politics, including the acceptance of common law and civil law systems in Canada as normal and right. I would like us to consider how we unpack and unsettle the foundational neoliberal notions of individualism and liberty when reframing discussions about justice to include Indigenous perspectives and decolonial approaches.

Thinking about justice through theory and practice grounds legal work with Indigenous peoples who encounter the Canadian colonial injustice system as a barrier to justice every day. I focus on teaching law students how to listen to Indigenous clients based on the premise that they, the clients, are experts on their own lives. These Indigenous clients may require assistance with a legal issue, but they are best placed to tell us what they need from us in order to assist them. In attempting to teach students how to work from a framework of decolonial understanding, they need to consider how Indigenous peoples are impacted by what Hunt has referred to as the "carcereality of everyday life."[46] Such historical colonial carceral strategies, from which twentieth-century fascisms learned a great deal,[47] such as reserves, established as open-air prisons, and residential schools or the child welfare system, continue for Indigenous peoples today. The rising numbers of Indigenous peoples overrepresented in Canada's criminal justice system and prison industrial complex are testament to this truth. While non-Indigenous activists and scholars may recognize that Indigenous peoples and bodies are criminalized, marginalized, pathologized and surveilled, and may even agree on how this looks or what the consequences of it are for Indigenous peoples, there is still a tension about the assumed value of state interference and intervention in the everyday lives of Indigenous peoples for their own protection.[48]

Hunt points out, as part of a productive critique commenting on Glen Coulthard's *Red Skin, White Masks*,[49] how the tendency to focus on *scaling up* Indigenous resurgence against the Canadian state often takes place alongside an erasure of the everyday circumstances of Indigenous peoples in our encounters with it.[50] She directly addresses the impact on Indigenous women:

> Indigenous women have instead had little choice but to appeal to police, the government and the Canadian public to recognize that we are being slaughtered. In doing so, we knowingly call on people who may be racist or indifferent, who may blame us, further victimize us, criminalize us, take away our kids and deepen state surveillance of our daily lives.[51]

The notion that colonial state systems, no matter how well meaning the policies or people behind them, should be used to effect change for Indigenous peoples simply does not reconcile with Indigenous ideas about national and personal jurisdiction or justice.

Hunt also provides a concrete example of one instance of what Indigenous justice might look like, reframing Coulthard's call for direct action in the lives of Indigenous women:

> So what would happen if every time an Indigenous woman had her personal boundaries crossed without consent, we were moved to act in the same way as we've seen to the threat of a pipeline in our territories – the Chiefs and elders, the language speakers, children and networks of kin, all in our regalia, our allies and neighbors all across the generations show up outside the house of a woman who had been hurt to drum and sing her healing songs. What if we looked to the land for berries and to the ocean for fish and herring eggs and seaweed to help her body to heal? What if we put her within a circle of honor and respect to show her that we will not stand for this violence any longer. We would bring her food and song and story, we would truly protect her self-determination and to defend the boundaries of her body which had been trespassed and violated.[52]

Justice looks quite different through Indigenous lenses when the power of the Canadian state is entirely diminished. In this dynamic, there exists the possibility of only the living law of sovereign Indigenous nations enacting resurgent practice through self-determination in the face of prescribed annihilation.[53] Resistance grounded in Indigenous justice, decolonized regarding each nation's legal orders, as Hunt's warning reminds us, gives the insidious nature of colonial power. It has been replicated through Indian Act policies and politics that have undermined and, in some cases, entirely distorted Indigenous laws.

As a possible antidote to colonialism, and as well as the global trend of neofascism, it is my hope that by challenging colonial notions of justice and focusing on Indigenous concepts of justice, non-Indigenous Canadians can transform the ways they think about their role in Canada's colonial state policies and practices as they impact Indigenous peoples.

I come to this reflection from a personal place as an Indigenous person. Being Métis has shaped the way colonial justice has impacted my family and our lived realities in particular ways. We need to think about the truth of what has been lost and also what survives. We need to recognize the resilience of Indigenous peoples and the resurgence of Indigenous laws. We need to acknowledge what still needs to be addressed when it comes to the relationship between Indigenous and non-Indigenous peoples in Canada and what this has to do with how we understand justice. Even the National Inquiry into Missing and Murdered Indigenous Women and Girls, for all the 231 Calls for Justice demand and may invite real change, came only after many decades of Indigenous women and families of the disappeared and murdered (acknowledging that these two groups are not mutually exclusive) fought to bring local, regional and state awareness to this genocide. For example, Clark and Hunt, referenced throughout this chapter, have both been working for decades with survivors, families and communities in order to work for Indigenous-led actions and on-the-ground capacity building within Indigenous communities to address the genocide against Indigenous women, girls and 2SLGBTQQIA individuals.

Each of us can assist in revealing future possibilities for justice to be transformed by making and holding space for Indigenous truths, creating practices of engagement with Indigenous perspectives about colonial injustices and our strength and resilience, and acknowledging, recognizing, hearing and believing Indigenous experiences. By creating space for conversations that imagine transformative justice – as complex, messy and difficult as those discussions might be – we combat one-dimensional, authoritarian and even fascist ideologies.

Bringing this discussion full circle, I invite engagement in critical self-reflection about ideas of justice, settler colonialism, the history of Indigenous–settler relations in Canada, the veracity of the Canadian legal system and the current conversation about reconciliation. I challenge us all to consider what historical and present truths must be acknowledged and understood before a meaningful conversation about justice for Indigenous peoples in Canada can begin.

NOTES

Unless otherwise stated, URLs were last accessed on 10 October 2019.

1. As a Métis person, I make no claims to Indigenous experience or knowledge outside of my own. I do not speak for anyone else and acknowledge wherever possible the specific individuals whom I am grateful to for mentorship, guidance, and, of course, for the use of their intellectual material as specifically cited.
2. See Catherine Dauvergne, *The New Politics of Immigration and the End of Settler Societies* (Cambridge: Cambridge University Press, 2016). Dauvergne discusses a disturbing trend toward reframing Canada as a "post-settler" society. Within this paradigm, what we might also call neocolonialism, the colonial past and present are erased and those who come here from elsewhere are all cast in the same light – people who relocated or are relocating by choice to a society that has always existed, despite its imperial and colonial past, and any notion of pre-colonial societies dealt with accordingly. The land has been "settled," removing traces of Indigenous peoples, communities and nations that may have existed pre-settlement or who continue to exist.
3. Eva Mackey, *Unsettled Expectations: Uncertainty, Land, and Settler Decolonization* (Nova Scotia: Fernwood Press, 2016), 8.
4. The project of colonialism and its effects depends on geographic location and historical context.
5. This also brought the ethnogenesis of the Métis people and the rise of the Métis nation.
6. See, for example: theintercept.com/2019/02/16/brazil-bolsonaro-indigenous-land/.
7. See, for example: www.counterpunch.org/2019/05/31/modis-escalating-war-against-indias-forests-and-tribal-people/.
8. "Reclaiming Power and Place: The Final Report of the National Inquiry into Missing and Murdered Indigenous Women and Girls," Executive Summary of the Final Report, National Inquiry into Missing and Murdered Indigenous Women and Girls, 3 June 2019.

9. Ibid., 1.

10. Adela Talbot, "Dimaline Refuses to Settle for Soundbites," Interview, *Western News*, 15 November 2018.

11. Hadley Friedland, "Indigenous Law Can Help Confront Intergenerational Injustice," *Policy Options*, 5 October 2018, policyoptions.irpp.org/magazines/october-2018/indigenous-law-can-help-confront-intergenerational-injustice/.

12. "Honouring the Truth, Reconciling for the Future," Executive Summary of the Final Report of the Truth and Reconciliation Commission of Canada, 23 July 2015, 3.

13. Ibid., 40, 145 and 280.

14. Ibid., 43 and 158.

15. Ibid., 90–9 and 158.

16. See Ian Mosby, "Administering Colonial Science: Nutrition Research and Human Biomedical Experimentation in Aboriginal Communities and Residential Schools, 1942–1952," *Social History* 46, No. 91 (2013): 145–72; and Clint Burnham, "'We were very lonely without those berries': Gastronomic Colonialism in Canada's Indian Residential Schools," in Derek Gladwin, ed., *Gastro-Modernism: Food, Literature, Culture* (Clemson and Liverpool: Clemson University Press and Liverpool University Press, 2019), 153–64.

17. "Honouring the Truth," Preface VI, 43, 90–101, 258–63, 315, 333, 370, 372, 375 and 377.

18. I have previously discussed the colonial violence of the legal process of the Indian Residential Schools Settlement Agreement. See, for example: "Truth Before Reconciliation: Reframing/Resisting/Refusing Reconciliation," Public Lecture, Simon Fraser University Institute for the Humanities' Public Lecture Series, 10 March 2017, www.youtube.com/watch?v=mB_7odACIpI.

19. Ibid., Appendix 2: 357–60.

20. "Reclaiming Power and Place," 23; Cindy Blackstock, "Residential Schools: Did They Really Close or Just Morph into Child Welfare?" *Indigenous Law Journal* 6, No. 1 (2007): 71–8.

21. Ibid., 130, 369 and Appendix 4: 376.

22. "Honouring the Truth"; "Truth and Reconciliation Commission of Canada: Calls to Action," 23 July 2015.

23. Sarah Hunt and I have previously discussed the tendency to focus on reconciliation as a turn away from the truth of settler-colonial violence, intergenerational injustice and the ongoing impacts of the colonial project specifically in Canada. "Truth Before Reconciliation: Reframing/Resisting/Refusing Reconciliation," Public Lecture, Simon Fraser University Institute for the Humanities' Public Lecture Series, 10 March 2017, www.youtube.com/watch?v=mB_7odACIpI.

24. Unist'ot'en: Heal the People, Heal the Land, "Timeline of the Campaign: A Timeline," unistoten.camp/timeline/timeline-of-the-campaign/.

25. Justin Brake, "Trudeau silent on genocide after accepting MMIWG Inquiry final report," APTN National News, 3 June 2019, https://aptnnews.ca/2019/06/03/trudeau-silent-on-genocide-after-accepting-mmiwg-inquiry-final-report/.

26. Catharine Tunney, "Trudeau says deaths and disappearances of Indigenous women and girls amount to 'genocide," CBC News, 4 June 2019, https://www.cbc.ca/news/politics/trudeau-mmiwg-genocide-1.5161681.

27. Significantly, the Honourable Jody Wilson-Raybould, whose Kwakwa-ka'wakw name is Puglass ("woman born to noble people"), was appointed Minister of Veterans Affairs in January 2019, after refusing to become the Minister of Indigenous Services, and before resigning from the Liberal cabinet on 12 February 2019. She has remained an independent Member of Parliament and has spoken publicly about the challenges she experienced as an Indigenous person acting in her role as the first Indigenous Minister of Justice and Attorney General of Canada. See, for example: Canada, Parliament, House of Commons, Standing Committee on Justice and Human Rights, Evidence, Meeting Number 132, 1st Session, 42nd Parliament, Thursday, 21 February 2019, https://www.ourcommons.ca/DocumentViewer/en/42-1/JUST/meeting-132/evidence; Canada, Parliament, House of Commons, Standing Committee on Justice and Human Rights, Evidence, Meeting Number 135, 1st Session, 42nd Parliament, Wednesday, 27 February 2019, https://www.ourcommons.ca/DocumentViewer/en/42-1/JUST/meeting-135/evidence; and Brian J. Barth, "What Jody Wilson-Raybould Really Thinks," *The Walrus*, 9 October 2019, https://thewalrus.ca/what-jody-wilson-raybould-really-thinks/.

28. There are also many other exceptions to this claim; however, the point here is to highlight that largely this is not analysis that is engaged with frequency.

29. See Dauvergne, *The New Politics of Immigration and the End of Settler Societies*.

30. I acknowledge and am indebted to the many Indigenous activists, academics, artists, politicians and scholars who continually address the violence of settler colonialism here in what is now called Canada and elsewhere across the globe.

31. "Reclaiming Power and Place," 54.

32. "Truth Before Reconciliation," www.youtube.com/watch?v=mB_70dACIpI.

33. Natalie Clark, "Red Intersectionality and the Violence-Informed Witnessing Praxis with Indigenous Girls," *Girlhood Studies* 9, No. 2 (Summer 2016): 46–64, 48.

34. See, for example: Institute for Justice and Reconciliation, www.ijr.org.za/about-us/.

35. See, for example: "Holocaust Remembrance in Germany: A Changing Culture," Deutsche Welle, 27 January 2019, www.dw.com/en/holocaust-remembrance-in-germany-a-changing-culture/a-47203540.

36. Constitution Act of Canada, 1982, Part II Rights of Aboriginal People of Canada, Section 35, Recognition of existing aboriginal and treaty rights.

37. Sarah Hunt, *Witnessing the Colonialscape: Lighting the Intimate Fires of Indigenous Legal Pluralism*, PhD Dissertation, Simon Fraser University, 2014, 1, 37 and 85.

38. "Reclaiming Power and Place," 310, 330–1 and 435.

39. Natalie Clark, "Red Intersectionality" and "Shock and Awe: Trauma as the New Colonial Frontier," *Humanities* 5, No. 14 (2016): 11.
40. Ibid.
41. Ibid.
42. Ibid. Sarah Hunt and I have previously discussed the necessity of utilizing this approach when considering the experiences of Indigenous peoples' encounter with the justice system in a report written for the Canadian Department of Justice. Patricia Barkaskas and Sarah Hunt, "Access to Justice for Indigenous Adult Victims of Sexual Assault," Report for the Department of Justice, October 2017.
43. Ibid.
44. Eve Tuck and K. Wayne Yang, "Decolonization is Not a Metaphor," *Decolonization: Indigeneity, Education & Society* 1, No. 1 (2012): 1–40.
45. Ibid.
46. Sarah Hunt, "Violence, Law and the Everyday Politics of Recognition," Comments on Glen Coulthard's *Red Skin, White Masks*, Presented at Native American and Indigenous Studies Association (NAISA), Washington DC, 6 June 2015, 4.
47. See Enzo Traverso, *The Origins of Nazi Violence* (New York: New Press, 2003).
48. Hunt, "Violence, Law and the Everyday Politics of Recognition," 4.
49. Glen Coulthard, *Red Skin, White Masks: Rejecting the Colonial Politics of Recognition* (Minneapolis: University of Minnesota Press, 2014).
50. Hunt, "Violence, Law and the Everyday Politics of Recognition," 8.
51. Ibid., 7.
52. Ibid., 9.
53. This is not to suggest that all Indigenous interpretations of justice would look the same or that there is a pan-Indigenous approach to the matter of injustice.

13

The Outsider as Insider: Steve Bannon, Fourth Turnings, and the Neofascist Threat

Joan Braune

Steve Bannon – millionaire, international political wheeler-dealer – wants you to know that he is a hardscrabble outsider like you, and a natural ally of the "working class," the "deplorables," and the "hobbits."[1] This chapter takes its title from Peter Gay's book *Weimar Culture: The Outsider as Insider*.[2] Although I do not engage Gay's work directly here, I operate on the thesis that the fascist cultural "outsider" is also an elite and an "insider," who plays on populist rhetoric while simultaneously upholding a hierarchical, anti-egalitarian worldview.

From working-class origins, Steve Bannon worked his way up through a series of channels (the Navy, the Pentagon, Goldman Sachs, Silicon Valley, Hollywood, right-wing media and the Tea Party) to the helm of Donald Trump's presidential campaign, where he helped to shape Trump's xenophobic, nationalistic rhetoric. Bannon followed Trump into the White House, serving as White House chief strategist, until he left the Trump administration in August 2017 following the violent torch-lit racist march in Charlottesville, Virginia.

Bannon subsequently declared a "season of war" on the Republican Party "establishment," accusing it of disloyalty to Trump's nationalist agenda.[3] Employing populist rhetoric, Bannon stumped for "outsider" candidates while appropriating rhetoric from the left for his far-right aims. After the failure of some of his political campaigns, most notably his support for bigoted fundamentalist and alleged child molester Roy Moore in Alabama, Bannon focused his attention on Europe, making connections with the European far-right. He has toyed with creating a "*Breitbart* for the left" and has called the Republican Party a "workers party."[4] Now he is building a network called "The Movement," headed by Belgian People's Party leader Mischaël Modrikamen and including far-right Italian politician Matteo Salvini, and Bannon recently attempted to establish a school in Rome for right-wing populists.

Although styling himself a "populist economic nationalist," Bannon's political agenda is fuelled by a reactionary gnostic elitism with racist and fascist influences, and is constructed according to an apocalyptic political vision. As noted by the two main biographies of Steve Bannon (one critical and one favourable), Bannon was influenced by the "Traditionalist School,"[5] in which Italian fascist esotericist Julius Evola was a major figure. Anti-Enlightenment and suspicious of the masses, "Traditionalists" believe that great religions share a secret, ancient content, known only to select initiates. They believe in a natural social hierarchy, which it is the duty of the spiritual elite to preserve (or restore), and that history moves in cycles of death and rebirth. They believe that the current time is one of decline, preceding the restoration of a past golden age. Bannon's embrace of Jean Raspail's racist propaganda novel *The Camp of the Saints* (1973), his promotion of 1990s bestseller *The Fourth Turning*, his propaganda films and his affinities with Vichy France's Charles Maurras, among other elements, combine to show that Bannon envisions a coming conflict, led by reactionary millennials, entailing racist violence.

"FOURTH TURNINGS": BANNON'S CATASTROPHISM

Following the violent fascist rally in Charlottesville, Virginia in August 2017, Trump appeared to be having a bad week. He was being met with calls for impeachment, increasingly bipartisan critiques, mass resignations, and condemnations around the globe for his unprincipled response ("very fine people on both sides")[6] to the deadly torch-lit march. Almost a third of Americans, it was reported, now believed Trump was a white nationalist.[7]

Weirdly, though, Bannon seemed to think everything was going great: "Tear down more statues. Say the revolution is coming. I can't get enough of it," he chortled to *The New York Times*.[8] Bannon's seemingly incongruous glee – "say the revolution is coming; I can't get enough" – is explainable through his views on war, "generations" and "tradition."

Bannon never wanted Trump to be universally beloved or a peacemaker, and hardly anticipated Trump's presidency to go smoothly. In Bannon's view, it is always darkest before dawn, and it needs to get a whole lot darker in the United States and the world before history can reset itself back to the traditional, hierarchical, romanticized past that he envisions.

Vatican Jesuit newspaper *La Civiltà Cattolica* harshly criticized Bannon's "apocalyptic geopolitics," describing Bannon's "Manichaean" vision of politics as the site of a cosmic, metaphysical battle between the forces of good and evil.[9] They were correct. Bannon's political film documentaries, for example, consistently strive to achieve a sense of heightened conflict and impending war. Although he is ostensibly a non-practising,[10] right-wing Catholic, Bannon is also influenced by an apocalyptic school of thought, that is, as noted previously, by the eclectic Traditionalist school, which has occultist and neo-pagan influences as well as some historical and contemporary ties to fascism.[11]

As previously suggested, Traditionalism is a reactionary, anti-Enlightenment school of thought that includes among its founding figures René Guénon, Frithjof Schuon, Mircea Eliade and, most notably, Italian fascist and race theorist Julius Evola.[12] Some Traditionalists, especially Evola, have been very influential on the thinking of today's far-right, including the neofascist US "alt-right."[13]

Although they disagree in various ways, Traditionalists tend to share the belief that all great religions have a secret content known only to small numbers of elite initiates, not the ordinary pious rubes in the pews. This "secret content" pre-dates Judaism and Christianity, and is rooted in the ancient past. All great religious traditions, according to Traditionalists, contain the *same* secret content. However, this content can only be accessed through practising an individual tradition, they believe, not through a synthesis of religions. Consequently, each member of the spiritual elite must choose one Tradition (such as Hinduism, Christianity or Germanic paganism) in order to access its secret content. From the standpoint of Catholicism, Traditionalism would probably be most properly understood as a variant of the Gnostic heresy, as Jacques Maritain argued, who attempted to place Guénon's works on the Catholic Church's Index of Prohibited Books.[14]

"Traditions," as understood by thinkers like Guénon, do not evolve – their hidden content is unchanging, rooted deep in the mythical and primordial past of human history.[15] History is thus an eternal recurrence of the same, a continual return to static, buried truths, a cycle of remembering and forgetting the ancient truth. Only a small spiritual elite can preserve the proper social hierarchies that lie at the core of Tradition, they believe, and can thus ensure that each individual is properly placed in her social role. Traditionalists see social hierarchy as fundamental to a sense of meaning and purpose, favour the idea of social "castes," are anti-Enlightenment, and are highly sceptical of democracy.

According to Traditionalism's cyclic view of human history, the collapse of Enlightenment and democratic ideals is coming soon, inaugurating a new Golden Age of hierarchy and obedience. But things have to get maximally bad before they can get maximally "better." Appropriating the terminology of a four-part Hindu cosmology, Traditionalists like Guénon and Evola believed that a present dark age known in Hinduism as the *Kali Yuga* (The Age of Kali) would be ending soon, returning human history to a thousands-of-years-long Golden Age. The *Kali Yuga* is characterized by all the sorts of things one would expect in an age of decline: natural disasters, poor health and immorality. But a crucial sign that the *Kali Yuga* is nearing its end is a reversal of social roles: those who should be priestly Brahmins act like servants, and servants act like Brahmins, that is, a reversal of social roles and of the hierarchy of values, a phenomenon that leading scholar of Traditionalism Mark Sedgwick calls "inversion."[16] No doubt defenders of hierarchies of class, race and sex are attracted to the idea of a coming Golden Age that reverses equality, returning the oppressed who have won small or large gains back to their subservient "place" in the social hierarchy.

The final end of the *Kali Yuga* arrives with the return of a mythical leader, known in Hindu cosmology as Kalki, an avatar of Vishnu. Following World War II, neo-Nazi Hitler-cult founder Savitri Devi took the Traditionalists' theories further, arguing that Hitler was Kalki and the herald of the end of the *Kali Yuga*. Her ideas have continued to influence parts of the far-right.[17] Fascist Richard Spencer even suggested (probably jokingly, but who knows?) that Donald Trump might be Kalki.[18]

As will become clear, it seems quite unlikely that Bannon believes Trump is Kalki. It seems more likely that Bannon sees Trump mainly as a bumbling opportunist and not as a mystical warrior – he even called Trump "a blunt instrument for us" in an interview with *Vanity Fair* in the summer of 2016, saying, "I don't know whether he really gets it or not."[19] Rather, as we shall see, it seems more likely that Trump's role is to escalate the current crisis, and that it will fall to a generation of reactionary millennials, in his view, to end the crisis and restore order.[20]

Bannon's time frame for the ending of the era of crisis can be uncovered through his ardent enthusiasm over a 1997 book called *The Fourth Turning: What the Cycles of History Tell Us About America's Next*

Rendezvous with Destiny, by William Strauss and Neil Howe, a book somewhat influenced by Traditionalism and similar thinkers. (Oswald Spengler, Mircea Eliade and Martin Heidegger are cited.[21] The *Kali Yuga* is briefly mentioned.[22]) Bannon even made a film, *Generation Zero*, about how Strauss and Howe's book could be used to analyse the 2008 financial crisis. The film's thesis was that the millennials, "Generation Zero," were sold out by the hippie generation because the hippies failed to recognize that history cannot be changed radically (so his argument goes); that real utopia is impossible and that history always proceeds in a predetermined cycle of rises and declines; and they unleashed the mood of frenetic economic speculation that led to the subprime mortgage crisis.[23] It also follows from this view that rage by millennials against boomer elders is at least in some sense rational – and, in Bannon's view, reactionary youth have a significant role to play in this historical drama.

On Bannon's imagined timeline, the current era of crisis, or the *Kali Yuga* in some loose and casual sense of the term, is probably not scheduled to end for another ten to 20 years, since it began with the 2008 financial crisis, and according to Strauss and Howe, each historical crisis lasts roughly 25 years. Thus, the Trump administration is probably not poised to direct the country out of the Crisis but to lead it further into it. Since the last three Crises in US history according to Strauss and Howe were the American Revolution, the Civil War and World War II, the coming Crisis would have to be similarly dramatic in scale and impact.[24] According to Bannon's *Generation Zero*, as well as Strauss and Howe's *Fourth Turning*, this sort of thing happens approximately every 80–100 years: a generation of hippies ("prophet generation") comes along and disrupts peaceful periods of stability, tradition and economic success.[25] This brings decades of decline in social order that can only be reinstated by a new "hero generation," which wages a bloody conflict to restore what was lost by the utopians that preceded them; this period, known as "Crisis," analogous to the *Kali Yuga*, should last approximately 20–25 years.[26] And according to Neil Howe, the current Crisis started around 2010,[27] suggesting about 15 years of the Crisis before a return to a new "High." Because Bannon swears by Strauss and Howe's work so fervently, it is likely that on Bannon's timeline as well, we must go much deeper into the dark age of chaos and collapse before we can re-emerge into a new 1950s and, as the slogan goes, "Make America Great Again."

Although Strauss and Howe believe history is determined – they believe the cycle is unavoidable – they do suggest that Crises can end either with the reinstitution of Golden Ages or with a final, apocalyptic breakdown of history.[28] How well the cycle of regeneration goes depends upon the skill of generations in directing the Crisis.[29] The coming Crisis, according to Strauss and Howe, might simply lead to a rebirth of the United States on a firmer footing, but it could lead to more sweeping transformation, including the end of modernity: "There could be a total collapse of science, culture, politics, and society," they write in the concluding chapter of their book.[30] "The Western civilization of Toynbee and the Faustian culture of Spengler would come to the inexorable close their prophesiers foresaw. A New Dark Ages would settle in, until some new civilization could be cobbled together from the ruins."[31]

Does Bannon take this Fourth Turning stuff seriously? Definitely: "I'm a big believer in generational theory," he told Joshua Green.[32] Green's book confirmed what many had already suspected since Bannon's 2014 speech to right-wing Catholic think tank the Human Dignity Institute,[33] in which Bannon praised Traditionalism: Bannon not only knows what Traditionalism is, but he undertook a serious study of it, especially through the works of Guénon.[34] Bannon's 2014 speech included references to Julius Evola and current Traditionalist writer and Russian fascist Aleksandr Dugin.[35]

According to Howe, writing in the *Washington Post*, Bannon worked with him on "several film projects."[36] Under Bannon's editorship, the far-right website *Breitbart* ran dozens of articles drawing on Strauss and Howe's theories of generations, reprinting headlines dozens of times from the blog *Generational Dynamics: Forecasting America's Destiny ... And the World's*,[37] which is devoted to applying Strauss and Howe's theories to geopolitics. Strauss and Howe, for their part, are political operators as well: they have consulted with dozens of powerful corporations, including weapons manufacturers, and designed a strategic manual for the US Army on recruiting millennials that was distributed to thousands of US Army recruiters.[38]

Breitbart, under Bannon's editorship, actively promoted the neo-fascist, anti-immigrant European Identitarian Movement, which Richard Spencer's "white identitarianism" and the US-based fascist group Identity Evropa (recently rebranded as "American Identity Movement") seek to adapt for a US context.[39] European Identitarians polemicize against the baby boomers or the "generation of '68,"[40] blaming them for a host of cultural and economic ills, as do Bannon's film, *Generation Zero*, Milo Yiannopoulos (whom Bannon discovered and recruited to *Breitbart*) and other leading alt-right figures in the United States today, for whom "boomer" is a frequent internet insult. The European Identitarians present themselves as the hip new shock troops of the reaction. Together with a range of young reactionaries, some of whom Bannon had a penchant for collecting around *Breitbart* and the Trump administration, and disaffected males online enraged at society, this may be the "hero generation" that Bannon probably expects to lead the way into battle to restore what was lost before humanistic and emancipatory utopian visions undermined hierarchies and obedience to tradition.

What will that coming battle look like, in Bannon's opinion? Bannon has been remarkably effective in dodging charges of racism in his interviews, but his nationalism is plainly not unmoored from questions of ethnicity. Although Bannon has said that he is an "economic nationalist," not an "ethno-nationalist,"[41] his vision of a "nation" is rooted deeply in notions of cultural identity, not simply the prioritization of the economic needs of one's country over those of others. Bannon has favourably cited French Nazi sympathizer Charles Maurras,[42] who distinguished between a mere "legal" country and the "real" country (like Bannon's hero Sarah Palin's "Real America")[43] tied together by a common cultural identity. In a famous interview with Donald Trump, before Bannon signed on to his campaign, Bannon resisted Trump's expression of support for the presence of highly skilled immigrants, saying: "When two-thirds or three-quarters of the CEOs in Silicon Valley are from South Asia or from Asia, I think … a country is more than an economy. We're a civic society."[44] Further, if Bannon's interest in the genocidal French novel *The Camp of the Saints* is any indication, perhaps Bannon foresees that as the Crisis deepens, nearing the Traditionalists' return of Kalki or Strauss and Howe's hero generation of reactionary millennials, racist violence will become a central component of that deepening Crisis.

Jean Raspail's *The Camp of the Saints*, which Bannon and *Breitbart* have praised,[45] takes its title from a passage in the apocalyptic biblical Book of Revelation, quoted at the opening of Raspail's book. The passage describes the "camp of the saints" of redeemed Christians at the end of the world encircled by the invading armies of "Gog and Magog."[46] The same biblical passage fascinated the Traditionalist René Guénon: in *The Reign of Quantity and The Signs of the Times*, Guénon invokes the armies of Gog and Magog, entering to lay waste to the world.[47] When history is at the height of its cycle, during its recurring Golden Ages, the cosmos is spiritually encircled by a "Great Wall," Guénon writes, that protects it from the forces of evil and is open at the top, allowing communion with the transcendent.[48] But in the dark age of decline that he calls the *Kali Yuga*, the cosmos is enclosed in a giant "egg,"[49] and the connection of humanity to the transcendent is broken. As the giant "Egg of the World" begins to crack, preparing for a rebirth of history, it cracks first at the base, not the top, allowing the forces of evil, which Guénon calls "Gog and Magog," to enter.[50]

Whether Raspail had Guénon in mind is not certain, although it would not be surprising. Raspail has remained unapologetic for his 1973 novel and lives in nostalgia for the past. His novel's title takes up his book's theme of encircled battlements falling at last, in the absence of walls to keep races separate. Raspail envisions white Christian Europe and the United States as surrounded by subhuman darker menacing hordes. Following Raspail's typically racist description of a Black and Puerto Rican neighbourhood in New York ("the wail of police cars; the savage, less-than-human howls"), one of Raspail's characters muses, "Black would be black, and white would be white. There was no changing either, except by a total mix, a blend into tan. They were enemies on sight, and their hatred and scorn only grew as they came to know each other better."[51] A "blend into tan" might not sound like something to worry about, but Raspail is mightily worried.

At the beginning of the novel, a retired professor casually murders a young hippie before going back into his house for a glass of wine. In his private monologue before the murder, he fantasizes about being a medieval crusader, a Christian soldier at the Battle of Lepanto, a Confederate soldier, a KKK member, a French soldier killing members of the Algerian uprising, and a cop murdering a Black Panther in a police van.[52] As the professor meditates on his murder of the hippie, he considers:

> That scorn of a people for other races, the knowledge that one's own is best, the triumphant joy at feeling oneself to be part of humanity's finest – none of that had ever filled these youngsters' addled brains, or at least so little that the monstrous cancer implanted in the Western conscience had quashed it in no time at all.[53]

That "monstrous cancer" is compassion for people not of one's own race. "Man never has really loved humanity all of a piece – all its races, its peoples, its religions – but only those creatures he feels are his kin, a part of his clan, no matter how vast," Raspail writes. "As far as the rest are concerned, he forces himself, and lets the world force him. And then, when he does, when the damage is done, he himself falls apart. In this curious war taking shape, those who loved themselves best were the ones who would triumph."[54]

As the novel concludes, the dark invading hordes initiate a second "fall of Constantinople" and an end to civilization.[55] All told, the novel is one of the most blatant pieces of racist propaganda imaginable. It meshes well with *Breitbart*'s reporting (articles tagged under a "Black crime" category,[56] reminiscent of Nazi-era *Der Stürmer*'s reporting on Jewish crime) and Bannon's incomplete script for a version of Shakespeare's *Coriolanus* set in Los Angeles during the 1992 riots,[57] which relies on racist caricatures. The novel also meshes well with Bannon's *Corialanus* in another way: each unite a populist rhetoric with an elitism or a defence of powerful hierarchies and control.[58] The coming chaos that Bannon appears to envision implies two things simultaneously: the need for rabble-rousing defenders of tradition, but also the need for authoritarian management to shepherd the world out of a crisis and into a new reality.

Racist violence, as it is often conceived in the US imagination, probably only partly covers the coming conflict that Bannon envisions. While race war tends to be conceived of in the US imaginary as a conflict between Whites and Blacks, part of the coming conflict envisioned by Bannon should be understood through Bannon's clash of civilizations worldview, envisioning not only a sort of "race war" in the US city, as seen in *The Camp of the Saints* or Bannon's *Coriolanus*, but also civilizational conflict between the "Judeo-Christian West," China and Islam.[59] Furthermore, as women emerge as a contending force in the Trump era, Bannon sees something "primal" at work, stating that the "Time's Up movement" seeks to undo thousands of years of history.[60] Bannon is profoundly interested in women, and in their strength, which he plainly views in essentialist terms but whom he does not discount as a tool for his own far-right agenda if appropriately harnessed. Bannon made two films, for example, about right-wing women: his film on women in the Tea Party movement, *Fire From the Heartland* (2010), and his film on Sarah Palin, *The Undefeated* (2011).[61] He also recruited young women like Julia Hahn to *Breitbart*, allegedly dubbing them "Valkyries."[62]

As heightened violence by armed fascists and proto-fascist authoritarians continues in the United States, Bannon's anticipated deepening of crisis appears to be occurring, though a return to "Tradition" by millennials seems comically absurd as an overriding cultural trend. Perhaps Trump's apparent sympathies for white nationalism will mean that street battles and acts of terror by the far-right will be allowed to continue unchecked. However, Schmittian "states of emergency" and increasing militarization of the police in the wake of racist far-right violence[63] – supposedly in the interest of restoring order – could also help to deepen the crisis that far-right ideologues like Bannon envision. (Trump is, after all, the same leader who wants a military parade in his honour,[64] thinks protesters who interrupt his speeches should be "dragged out on a stretcher,"[65] and has expressed a desire to occupy Chicago with "the feds."[66])

A final note on theory and praxis: as the left seeks to respond to the growing threat of fascism in numerous contexts globally, it seems that Frankfurt School critical theory has played a remarkably small role in the discussion – "remarkably," given how formative critical theory has been for understanding fascism and authoritarianism (although for exceptions to this see Chapters 2 and 8). Although it is not possible to go into depth on critical theory's contributions here, it is worth noting that Frankfurt School thinker Erich Fromm is uniquely poised to offer a radical left rejoinder to Bannon's reactionary apocalypticism. Fromm was a persistent critic of "catastrophic or apocalyptic messianism," which views the fulfilment of historical hopes as dependent on a catastrophic destruction and remaking of the world through the intervention of transcendent forces (such as totalitarian leaders, rather than mass social movements).[67] The tendency to submit to superhuman historical forces as a way of ceding agency was already critiqued in Fromm's early 1941 *Escape from Freedom*, the central thesis of which was that the United States was vulnerable to becoming a fascist state – it could truly "happen here."[68] Throughout his later works in the 1960s and 1970s, Fromm expressed continuing concern about the destructive impulse of catastrophic messianism. By the time of his final magnum opus *The Anatomy of Human Destructiveness*, Fromm had a fully fledged theory about how the "necrophilous" desire to destroy all that is living, growing and changing, and to render it controllable and dead, undergirded fascist ideology and posed a continuing threat in the present.

More recently Naomi Klein, whose writings on the "shock doctrine" mirror Fromm's concern about catastrophic messianism,[69] warned that the Trump administration is likely to exploit a coming catastrophe in order to implement shock doctrine-style economic and political changes and attain totalitarian control.[70] Klein warned that the left needs to get organized and be ready to refuse to comply en masse if the Trump administration declares a state of emergency and outlaws protest, pouring into the streets and defying any curfews or similar restrictions. However, mere resistance to stop the machine may not be enough: we need a positive alternative vision, one that reclaims human beings and the international working class as the agent of history, transcending nationalistic determinisms.

In light of Bannon's ideological moorings, it is plain that his down-home Americanisms, his attempts at "aw-shucks" populist rhetoric, are not based on any egalitarian or progressive impulses. Any attempt to see Bannon as "complicated," rather than simply far-right, is a dangerous misnomer. Fascism has always appropriated ideas and rhetoric from the left, and to the extent that some fascist ideology is influential on Bannon, it is no surprise that he does the same. But fundamental to his worldview is his commitment to the vision of the Traditionalists: a coming apocalypse that will remake history, and, he hopes, restore past social hierarchies.

NOTES

Unless otherwise stated, URLs were last accessed on 1 May 2019.

1. David Martosko, "Steve Bannon Says Right-Wing 'Hobbits' and 'Deplorables' Should 'Hold ALL of Us Accountable—Including Me' As Trump White House Takes Shape," *Daily Mail*, 30 December 2016, www.dailymail.co.uk/news/article-4076570/Steve-Bannon-says-right-wing-Hobbits-Deplorables-hold-accountable-including-Trump-White-House-takes-shape.html; Nolan D. McCaskill, "Bannon Tells Breitbart: 'Hobbits' and 'Deplorables' Were Key to Trump's Success," *Politico*, 30 December 2016, www.politico.com/story/2016/12/steve-bannon-breitbart-hobbits-deplorables-donald-trump-233074.

2. Peter Gay, *Weimar Culture: The Outsider as Insider* (New York: W.W. Norton & Company, 2001).

3. Garrett Haake and Daniel Arkin, "Bannon Declares 'Season of War' Against GOP Establishment," NBC News, 14 October 2017, www.nbcnews.com/politics/politics-news/steve-bannon-declares-season-war-against-gop-establishment-n810731.

4. Michael Wolff, *Fire and Fury: Inside the Trump White House* (New York: Henry Holt and Company, 2018), 59; ABC News (Australia), "Steve Bannon on how the strategy that elected Trump is going global | Four Corners," YouTube, 3 September 2018, www.youtube.com/watch?v=q8BGvG3pPfo.

5. Joshua Green, *Devil's Bargain: Steve Bannon, Donald Trump, and the Storming of the Presidency* (New York: Penguin, 2017), 204–8; Keith Koffler, *Bannon: Always the Rebel* (Washington, DC: Regnery Publishing, 2017), 113–15.

6. Politico Staff, "Full Text: Trump's Comments on White Suprema-cists 'Alt-Left' in Charlottesville," *Politico*, last modified 15 August 2017, www.politico.com/story/2017/08/15/full-text-trump-comments-white-supremacists-alt-left-transcript-241662.

7. Ariel Edwards-Levy, "More Americans Think Donald Trump Supports White Nationalism Than Think He Opposes It," *Huffington Post*, last modi-fied 16 August 2017, www.huffingtonpost.com/entry/americans-trump-white-nationalism-poll_us_59941e9ee4b04b193361c305.

8. Jeremy W. Peters, Jonathan Martin and Jack Healy, "Trump's Embrace of Racially Charged Past Puts Republicans in Crisis," *The New York Times*, 16 August 2017, www.nytimes.com/2017/08/16/us/politics/trump-republicans-race.html?smid=tw-share&referer=https://t.co/izyDjh9vUZ%3famp=1.

9. Antonio Spadaro and Marcelo Figueroa, "Evangelical Fundamentalism and Catholic Integralism: A Surprising Ecumenism," *La Civiltà Cattolica*, 13 July 2017, www.laciviltacattolica.it/articolo/evangelical-fundamentalism-and-catholic-integralism-in-the-usa-a-surprising-ecumenism/.

10. Austin Ruse, "A Bannon Apologia," *Crisis Magazine*, 3 February 2017, www.crisismagazine.com/2017/a-bannon-apologia.

11. Green, *Devil's Bargain*, 115–16; Koffler, *Bannon: Always the Rebel*, 113–15.

12. Mark Sedgwick, *Against the Modern World: Traditionalism and the Secret History of the Twentieth Century* (Oxford: Oxford University Press, 2004), 24.

13. Prominent fascist and alt-right publishing house Arktos has released numerous translations of Evola's works, and the alt-right website associ-ated with Richard Spencer, AltRight.com, has dozens of article entries on Evola (accessed 6 June 2019). Evola was also an influence on Russian fascist Aleksandr Dugin and figurehead of the fascist French New Right Alain de Benoist, among others.

14. Sedgwick, *Against the Modern World*, 30.

15. Luis Gonzalez-Reimann, "The Yugas: Their Importance in India and Their Use by Western Intellectuals and Esoteric and New Age Writers," *Religion Compass* 8, No. 12 (2014): 363.

16. Sedgwick, *Against the Modern World*, 24–5.

17. On Savitri Devi, see Alexander Reid Ross, *Against the Fascist Creep* (Chico, CA: AK Press, 2017), 76, 79–80, 85.

18. David Lawrence, "Hindu Mysticism and the Alt-Right," Hope Not Hate, 23 March 2018, hopenothate.com/2018/03/23/hindu-mysticism-alt-right/.

19. Emily Jane Fox, "Is Donald Trump Just a Pawn in Steve Bannon's Game?" *Vanity Fair*, 26 January 2017, www.vanityfair.com/news/2017/01/is-donald-trump-a-pawn-in-steve-bannons-game.

20. Ken Stern, "Exclusive: Stephen Bannon, Trump's New C.E.O., Hints at His Master Plan," *Vanity Fair*, 17 August 2016, www.vanityfair.com/news/2016/08/breitbart-stephen-bannon-donald-trump-master-plan.

21. William Strauss and Neil Howe, *The Fourth Turning: An American Prophecy—What the Cycles of History Tell Us About America's Next Rendezvous with Destiny* (New York: Broadway Books, 1997), 9, 32, 68–9, 330. (Eliade belongs to the Traditionalist School. Heidegger has been important to the European far-right, including playing a major role for current Russian Traditionalist fascist Aleksandr Dugin. Spengler's racism and cyclical vision of history were influential on the ideas of the far-right, including Evola.)

22. Strauss and Howe, *The Fourth Turning*, 29.

23. *Generation Zero*, directed and written by Stephen K. Bannon, starring Michael Barone, Bruce Bartlett and John Bolton (Washington, DC: Citizens United, 2010).

24. Strauss and Howe, *The Fourth Turning*, 50.

25. *Generation Zero*; Strauss and Howe, *The Fourth Turning*, 84.

26. Strauss and Howe, *The Fourth Turning*, 3, 19, 38–9.

27. McAlvany Financial, "Neil Howe Interview: 'We Are 8 Years Into the Fourth Turning' What's Next? | MWC 2017," YouTube, 4 July 2017, www.youtube.com/watch?v=FohiCeA2paM.

28. Strauss and Howe, *The Fourth Turning*, 330–1.

29. Ibid., 332.

30. Ibid., 330.

31. Ibid., 330.

32. Green, *Devil's Bargain*, 150–1.

33. J. Lester Feder, "This is How Steve Bannon Sees the Entire World," Buzz-Feed, last updated 16 November 2016, www.buzzfeednews.com/article/lesterfeder/this-is-how-steve-bannon-sees-the-entire-world.

34. Green, *Devil's Bargain*, 206–7.

35. Feder, "This is How Steve Bannon Sees the Entire World."

36. Neil Howe, "Where Did Steve Bannon Get His Worldview? From My Book," *Washington Post*, 24 February 2017, www.washingtonpost.com/entertainment/books/where-did-steve-bannon-get-his-worldview-from-my-book/2017/02/24/16937f38-f84a-11e6-9845-576c69081518_story.html?utm_term=.dbf0785d70f3. While affirming his ties to Bannon, Howe also stated in his *Washington Post* article that he does not identify with the views of *Breitbart*. Strauss passed away some years ago.

37. "Generational Dynamics: Forecasting America's Destiny … and the World's," Generational Dynamics, accessed 9 June 2019, www.generationaldynamics.com/ww2010.htm.

38. "Life Course Associates: Military," accessed 3 October 2018, www.lifecourse.com/practice/military.html.

39. See, for example, Chris Tomlinson, "WATCH: The Future of Europe—Hipster Right Wingers Slam Merkel's Migration Catastrophe," *Breitbart*, 23 January 2016, www.breitbart.com/london/2016/01/23/hipster-right-wingers-slam-merkels-migration-catastrophe/; for another example: Oliver Lane and Chris Tomlinson, "WATCH: Anti-Mass Migration Campaigners Stage Protest on Roof of World Famous Imperial Theatre," *Breitbart*, 30 April 2016, www.breitbart.com/london/2016/04/30/identitarians-protest-viennas-famous-theatre/.

40. See, for example, Markus Willinger's *Generation Identity: A Declaration of War Against the '68ers* (London: Arktos, 2013).

41. Robert Kuttner, "Steve Bannon: Unrepentant," *American Prospect*, 16 August 2017, prospect.org/article/steve-bannon-unrepentant.

42. Emma-Kate Symons, "Steve Bannon Loves France," *Politico*, 23 March 2017, www.politico.eu/article/steve-bannons-french-marine-le-pen-front-national-donald-trump-far-right-populism-inspiration/.

43. Sam Stein, "Sarah Palin Explains What Parts of the Country Not 'Pro-America'" *HuffPost*, updated 25 May 2011, www.huffpost.com/entry/palin-clarifies-what-part_n_135641.

44. David A. Fahrenthold and Frances Stead Sellers, "How Bannon Flattered and Coaxed Trump on Policies Key to the Alt-Right," *Washington Post*, 15 November 2016, www.washingtonpost.com/politics/how-bannon-flattered-and-coaxed-trump-on-policies-key-to-the-alt-right/2016/11/15/53c66362-ab69-11e6-a31b-4b6397e625d0_story.html?utm_term=.f42e570803f8.

45. Paul Blumenthal and J.M. Rieger, "This Stunningly Racist French Novel is How Steve Bannon Explains the World," *Huffington Post*, updated 6 March 2017, www.huffingtonpost.com/entry/steve-bannon-camp-of-the-saints-immigration_us_58b75206e4b0284854b3dc03; Virgil, "Decline and Fall: The Grim Message of *The Camp of the Saints*," *Breitbart*, 24 November 2014, www.breitbart.com/politics/2014/11/24/decline-and-fall-the-grim-message-of-the-camp-of-the-saints/; Julia Hahn, "'Camp of the Saints' Seen Mirrored in Pope's Message," *Breitbart*, 24 September 2015, www.breitbart.com/politics/2015/09/24/camp-saints-seen-mirrored-popes-message/; "Camp of the Saints: Europe Braces for Unabated Wave of Migrants After 1M+ in 2015," *Breitbart*, 1 January 2016, www.breitbart.com/national-security/2016/01/01/camp-of-the-saints-europe-braces-for-unabated-wave-of-migrants-after-1m-in-2015/.

46. Jean Raspail, *The Camp of the Saints*, trans. Norman Shapiro, accessed 9 June 2019, www.jrbooksonline.com/pdfs/camp_of_the_saints.pdf.

47. René Guénon, *The Reign of Quantity and The Signs of the Times*, trans. Lord Northbourne (Hillsdale, NY: Sophia Perennis, 2004), 172–3.

48. Ibid., 172–3.

49. Ibid., 137.

50. Ibid., 172–3.

51. Raspail, *The Camp of the Saints*, 7.

52. Ibid., 6.

53. Ibid., 4.

54. Ibid., 4.

55. Ibid., 103.

56. The "Black Crime" tag is no longer used on *Breitbart*. A link to an archived format of this *Breitbart* section, accessed 8 June 2019: web.archive.org/web/20170203142814/https://www.breitbart.com/tag/black-crime.

57. "*The Thing I Am*: The Table Read," Now This, accessed 8 June 2019, nowthis-news.com/steve-bannon-hip-hop-rap-musical.

58. Bannon's *Coriolanus* is interesting for other reasons as well; Daniel Pollack-Pelzner points out in *The New York Times* that, "In the last century, two interpretations [of *Coriolanus*] held particular force: one that glorifies the Roman general as the heroic strongman his country needs (a view so popular in Hitler's Third Reich that the American occupation banned the play in Germany after World War II), and another that sees the Roman mob as a necessary corrective to the greedy excesses of the ruling elite (a view common in Soviet-era adaptations). [Bannon's *Coriolanus*] brazenly combined these two perspectives to fashion the radical populism of the Tea Party in service of Mr. Trump as a national savior." Daniel Pollack-Pelzner, "Behold, Steve Bannon's Hip-Hop Shakespeare Rewrite: Coriolanus," *The New York Times*, 17 December 2016, www.nytimes.com/2016/12/17/opinion/sunday/steve-bannon-hip-hop-shakespeare-rewrite-coriolanus.html. Here, again, we see that Bannon's populist rhetoric is united with his elitism.

59. When asked, "Was the late Samuel Huntington right when he argued that geopolitics in the 21st century will be defined by a clash of civilizations?" Bannon answered, "Absolutely. What we're seeing today is China, Persia, and Turkey—three ancient civilizations—coming together to form a new axis. It's confronting the Christian West and also a big part of Islam that is tied to the West." Ben Schreckinger, "Steve Bannon is Hatching His Comeback," *GQ*, 28 February 2018, www.gq.com/story/steve-bannon-february-2018-interview. Strauss and Howe also reference Huntington's four-part historical cycle theory (Strauss and Howe, *The Fourth Turning*, 89).

60. Isobel Thompson, "Steve Bannon is Obsessed With the Fall of the Patriarchy," *Vanity Fair*, 28 February 2018, www.vanityfair.com/news/2018/02/steve-bannon-is-obsessed-with-the-patriarchy.

61. *Fire From the Heartland: The Awakening of the Conservative Woman*, directed and written by Stephen K. Bannon, starring Michele Bachmann, Deneen Borelli and Ann Coulter (Washington, DC: Citizens United, 2010); *The Undefeated*, directed by Stephen K. Bannon and written by Stephen K. Bannon and Sarah Palin, starring Andrew Breitart, Mark Levin and Kurt Gibson (Stephen K. Bannon, 2011).

62. Green, *Devil's Bargain*, 149; Peter Maas, "Birth of a Radical: White Fear in the White House," *Intercept*, 7 May 2017, theintercept.com/2017/05/07/white-fear-in-the-white-house-young-bannon-disciple-julia-hahn-is-a-case-study-in-extremism/.

63. The threat of "states of emergency" calls to mind Nazi legal theorist Carl Schmitt, cited by alt-right fascists Richard Spencer and Augustus Sol

Invictus, among others, as a leading influence. Schmitt was less interested in *which* minority group – Jews, immigrants, etc. – would be scapegoated by those in power, than he was in the role of the political leader in naming an enemy and establishing a situation in which rule of law can thus be suspended.

64. Eileen Sullivan et al., "Citing Costs, Trump Retreats From Massive Military Parade in Capital," *The New York Times*, 17 August 2018, www.nytimes.com/2018/08/17/us/politics/trump-military-parade.html.

65. Michael E. Miller, "Donald Trump on a Protestor: 'I'd Like to Punch Him in the Face,'" *Washington Post*, 23 February 2016, www.washingtonpost.com/news/morning-mix/wp/2016/02/23/donald-trump-on-protester-id-like-to-punch-him-in-the-face/?noredirect=on&utm_term=.5f6e98e470ed.

66. Rebecca Hersher, "Trump Threatens to 'Send in the Feds' Over Chicago's Violent Crime," NPR, 25 January 2017, www.npr.org/sections/thetwo-way/2017/01/25/511582874/trump-threatens-to-send-in-the-feds-over-chicago-s-violent-crime; J. Weston Phippin, "Trump Says He's Sending the Feds Into Chicago," *Atlantic*, 30 June 2017, www.theatlantic.com/news/archive/2017/06/trump-chicago-gun-task-force/532410/.

67. Erich Fromm, *On Being Human* (New York: Continuum, 1994), 114; Erich Fromm, *You Shall Be As Gods: A Radical Interpretation of the Old Testament* (New York: Holt, Rinehart and Winston, 1966), 133. See also my book on Fromm's distinction between prophetic and catastrophic messianism: Joan Braune, *Erich Fromm's Radical Hope: Prophetic Messianism as a Critical Theory of the Future* (Rotterdam: Sense Publishers, 2014).

68. Erich Fromm, *Escape from Freedom* (New York: Avon Books, 1969).

69. For her writings on the "shock doctrine," see Naomi Klein, *The Shock Doctrine: The Rise of Disaster Capitalism* (Toronto: Random House of Canada, 2007).

70. Naomi Klein, *No is Not Enough: Resisting Trump's Shock Politics and Winning the World We Need* (Chicago: Haymarket, 2017), 134–52.

14

Populism, Fascism, Neoliberalism: Theorizing Contemporary India[1]

Ajay Gudavarthy and Vijay Gudavarthy

Analyses of fascism have rather unnecessarily been polarized with Marxist accounts overemphasizing economic causality, on the one hand, and non-Marxist approaches overemphasizing ideology, politics, organizational aspects and social psychology, on the other.[2] It is important to demarcate the difference in the historical condition and context in which the analysis of the current regime in India is being made. Gramsci defined fascism on an international scale as "an attempt to resolve problems of production and exchange with machine-guns and pistol shots."[3] The condition in which we find the rise of the authoritarian regime with fascist tendencies in India, however, is certainly not a result of the nation being caught up in an international war. What is perhaps more significant is the social base that tends to lend consent to an authoritarian model of politics and governance and the forms in which it surfaces exhibiting fascist tendencies.[4] The fascist regimes of the inter-war period and during World War II were different from the post-war period and specifically with reference to the analysis of the experience of the developing nations like India. In this context, the distinction between fascist *movements* and *regimes* is an important one and there seems to have been a right-wing extremist movement pushing for the rise of such a regime in the Indian context.[5] While Narendra Modi's regime cannot be characterized, strictly speaking, as fascist, it certainly can be characterized as an *authoritarian regime with fascist tendencies*. What needs to be explained is how such a regime manages to manufacture popular consent. This chapter attempts at providing such an explanation by, in the first section, exploring the underlying developmental processes which contextualize the relevance of right-wing populism; the second section analyses the modes through which right-wing populism has managed to usher in a regime with fascist tendencies by mustering popular consent.

NEOLIBERAL DEVELOPMENT, SOCIAL CRISIS
AND RIGHT-WING POPULISM

In India the rise of an authoritarian state precedes the manifestation of its fascist tendencies. The ideal liberal constitutional state has been displaced by a pragmatic authoritarianism associated with the use of force to address imperatives of capital accumulation as part of the neoliberal development model.[6] In many ways, the current condition is diametrically opposed to the assessment made by Michał Kalecki with reference to the functional role that Nazism served in the economic development of Germany.[7] In the neoliberal model, the role of force lies in compelling citizens to accept the denials and deprivations following the withdrawal of the state. The challenge for analysis, however, is to explain the manufacture of consent to such force.[8] The authoritarian state associated with the neoliberal development process in the Indian context has acquired a new political legitimacy given by the Sangh Parivar forces in the name of clean governance,[9] which attempts at reconciling the neoliberal development project with the cultural nationalist Hindutva agenda addressing the deepening social crisis neoliberalism has produced.

The rural agrarian crisis resulting from the neoliberal development project, in the context of an extremely skewed land ownership structure, has resulted in the specific contradiction arising out of the fact that absentee landlords seek to perpetuate their social hegemony without playing a role in the rural economy. This, then, forces aspirational groups to rely on patronage relations for tenancy as a means of coping with mounting and intensifying social and economic risks and uncertainties. Consequently, this, in turn, opens an important space for cultural revivalism as the basis for social unity.[10] It is these aspirational groups that are exposed to the enormous risks associated with the agrarian crisis. The nature of the transition from self-cultivating farmers to tenants is an important change in this development process associated with the social origins of authoritarian regimes.[11] It is a well-recognized phenomenon that the reinforcement of traditional customary hegemonies and consent to domination has a significant role in societies experiencing "uneven and combined development" in the context of recovering, through an appeal to the glorious past and cultural social nationalist mobilizations, the nation-state and its sovereignty that are rendered vulnerable on account of neoliberal globalization.[12]

Those social groups and classes that fail to cope with the crisis of the rural economy in India end up experiencing distress and displacement. Such social groups and classes end up joining the ranks of the millions of temporary, seasonal and circular migrants in search of employment in other rural, semi-urban and urban areas engaging predominantly in interstate mobility.[13] The uncertainty about the future experienced by such workers is a direct result of insecure, unstable, precarious and unwritten contracts and conditions of employment, wherein workers lack the proof of being employees, are denied minimum legal social protections, and are exposed to super-exploitation in the sweatshops that employ them. Such informal labour is disorganized, that is, lacks trade union representation, and, as a result, is rendered voiceless as it is displaced from its places of origin only to surface in the form of outsiders and migrants in the place of work; here they are disenfranchised and disconnected from local communities.[14] These workers are, as it were, internal exiles.

Right-wing populist majoritarian identity, on the one hand, provides assimilation into the "imagined" "Hindu community" and an "emancipation" of migrants who are rendered outsiders by development through the definition or projection of the cultural-nationalist idea of the outsider or "enemy." *The outsiders of development are thus transformed into the insiders of a powerful cultural-national narrative.* On the other hand, such workers who see employment as a survival strategy face abuse and physical violence which is normalized as so many neoliberal modes of management and control of the labour process through everyday practices. The nature of labour relations in such informal employment has been characterized severally as "un-free," "neo-bondage" and "modern slavery."[15] It is this sphere of labour relations that has been tremendously exacerbated by neoliberal policy – policy that produces a social condition and a space which supplies all micro-elements and manipulations that contribute to the building of a social psyche which could easily lend legitimacy to the rise of an authoritarian regime (compare with Genosko's account of "micro-fascism" in Chapter 10 of this volume).[16]

Far from generating solidarity amongst those experiencing poverty and deprivation, vulnerability and insecurity generate predatory modes of social relations between competing networks for survival. These social relations and coping strategies hardly enable such marginalized workers to distinguish a *democratic* from an *authoritarian* regime in their lived experience. To the contrary, the institutions and norms of liberal democracy, from the vantage point of these workers, are elite privileges constitutively denied to them. While these workers operate on the basis of the norms of their own "common sense," that generate trust and co-operation within their narrowly restricted networks, for such a society of workers to convincingly cast its normative frames in universal liberal political values of natural rights and modern social rationalities would be a far-fetched expectation.[17]

The micro, small and medium enterprises, whether reliant on wage labour or as self-employed enterprises, play a significant role in the economy, but are threatened by the rise of big capital.[18] To cope with this challenge, this segment of the economy also depends on social networks embedded in traditional social identities based on caste, community, regional and linguistic identities, both to derive protections against legal regulations as well as in order to be able to simply carry on their economic activities. Social closures and social exclusions are innately built into these networks. These networks typically rely on institutional-ized cultural idioms, customs and rituals – practices easily appropriated by the right-wing political institutions.[19] The neoliberal development process involving withdrawal of state regulation did not consequentially lead to an unambivalent "modernization" through unbridled competi-tion, but has generated socially mediated markets and market-driven patronage.[20]

The social transformation resulting from interventions by the welfare state has failed (an experience which has many similarities with the failure of the Weimar Republic).[21] The failure of several policy inter-ventions needs to be understood on the backdrop of their inability to address the rising expectations raised through the promises made in land reforms, *Garibi Hatao* ("Abolish Poverty"!), modernization, rights-based approaches etc., which has led to a condition of social impatience amongst the aspiring social groups and classes seeking substantive mobility, who find that their political representatives seem to be engaged in the subversion of development.[22] The risk of democratic institutions being abandoned by the vulnerable social constituencies under such conditions and their inclination to support authoritarian regimes has long been recognized within the Marxian tradition, from Marx's *18th Brumaire* to Georg Lukàcs and the Frankfurt School just prior to the rise of European fascism.[23] The second dimension of the development process underway is the threat faced by petty capital in facing up to the challenges posed by the neoliberal reforms and competitive pressures from the penetration of big capital.[24] At the same time, it is possible to discern the impatience of big capital,[25] which characterizes constitutional rights and legal protections as dispensable constraints on growth and development. Both petty capital and big capital welcome the employment of the rhetoric of nationalism in the service of widespread violations of civil and political rights, as well as the dismantling of liberal and social democratic institutions.

Yet another important structural contributor to the rise of the current authoritarian regime in India has been the systematic subversion of institutions by financial capital. Financial capital, long operating in the "black economy," has played a major role in several economic activities, notably the resource-extraction sector, real estate and credit markets. Despite the fact that there is a significantly large proportion of value in it, this economy is largely characterized by illegal mining, "encroachments," "settlements," as well as the use of organized crime as the means by which contracts are enforced. While lack of law enforcement was a common phenomenon with respect to the informal economy, the actual use of illegal means such as organized crime became the hallmark of the rise of financial capital and its influence on the state machinery. This phenomenon has been analysed as marking the rise of the business of private protection when the state fails.[26] This massive state failure and normalization of illegality and criminality as part of economic transactions has become accepted as a dimension of hegemonic "common sense," and is yet another important source legitimizing the role of the "strongman" and authoritarianism, more generally.

It is against the backdrop of these socioeconomic conditions propelled by neoliberal development that the production of consent for the authoritarian populist regime with fascist tendencies needs to be understood. The following sections will present more concretely the various modes through which right-wing populism has managed to expand itself.

FROM MORAL REJECTION TO "POLITICAL INTERVENTION"

Contemporary populism in India has changed the nature of public and political discourse by inaugurating new meanings and effects through an overdetermination of significations that has foregrounded the limits of what we have generally understood as "progressive" politics.

The old distinctions between left and right are being replaced by a new kind of meta-narrative of "us" versus "them." The process of creating *the other* is achieved not merely through physical violence, coercion and intimidation. It is also executed through a sustained process of gaining consent to a moral discourse that combines old narratives, and given or prevalent moral and normative structures, with new aspirations, anxieties and social imaginaries.

Contemporary populism carefully sutures the *old* and the *new*, and shifts between both ends of the spectrum, sometimes synthesizing what we had earlier perceived as mutually exclusive practices. It fuses the polar opposites and produces new kinds of "de-binarized" discourses. It replaces ideas of antagonism and contradiction with continuity and social harmony; it replaces the emphasis on "rights" and "liberty" with "fraternity" and "community." It is therefore imperative to decode what is old and what is new in this discourse, what is populist and what is authoritarian, and what the social narrative is behind the more visible modes of exclusion, violence and criminalization of politics.

Chantal Mouffe has warned against a moral rejection or refutation of right-wing populism, suggesting that:

> The response of traditional parties to the rise of right-wing populism has clearly contributed to exacerbating the problem … This is why moral condemnation and the setting up of a "cordon sanitaire" have so often constituted the answer to the rise of right-wing populist movements.[27]

Instead, we need to analyse "its specificity and its causes." "Moral condemnation" of the right has to be replaced by an analysis of the "moral structure" on which it builds its politics. As Jan-Werner Müller puts it:

> Populism … is a particular moralistic imagination of politics, a way of perceiving the political world which places in opposition a morally pure and fully unified people against small minorities, elites in particular, who are placed outside the authentic people.[28]

This idea of a "fully unified people" in the Indian context refers to a unified Hindu community. While it excludes the minorities in the first instance, it must also create a palpable unity within a diversified, contradictory majority. The diversity internal to such a majority needs to be recast into a unity. Differences of social location, conflict of interests, and structural contradictions have to be constituted in terms of social harmony, community, fraternity and continuity with change: a glorious past with a compelling future. It aims for a change that is non-disruptive.

Much of the analysis of populism has focused on the larger narrative of "us" versus "them," largely ignoring how right-wing populism attempts to maintain the unity of "us," and how it produces an authentic majority which is essentially divided, in the Indian context across caste, region, language, culture and lifestyles. It is here that right-wing populism has introduced a new set of political discourses and practices, the tenability of which can help to inform us of the future of right-wing populism in India.

INDIAN RIGHT-WING POPULISM: WHAT IS MAKING IT THRIVE?

We will attempt to map these new sets of practices in order to produce a *political*, rather than a *moral*, critique of right-wing populism in India. Right-wing populism has managed to turn traditional progressive political practices on their head. Critique is absorbed or resignified, often in opposition to its original meaning. For instance, the reason for the defeat of the INC (Indian Congress Party), as is typically argued, has been its shoddy implementation of welfare policies such as the NREGRA (National Rural Employment Guarantee Act).[29] The BJP (Bharatiya Janata Party) began with a critique of such poor implementation through a discourse on "corruption," but gradually turned it into a critique of such welfare schemes per se. The BJP was able to place anger against growing economic inequalities, paradoxically, in the service of its own pro-corporate politics.

Similarly, a critique of institutional crises, and the non-responsive character of institutions, leads to the adoption of strategies that *further undermine* institutions. It does not lead in a progressive and linear manner to a demand for more transparency and accountability, but to further obscurity and inscrutability. For instance, a critique of a sluggish judiciary and a corrupt police force in India has led to the legitimization of a strategy or, rather, a policy of extra-judicial killings or "encounters," as recently announced by Uttar Pradesh's chief minister Yogi Adityanath. Here, it is instructive to observe how the left-liberal critique of the class character of democratic institutions is appropriated and legitimizes an aggressive state that, in fact, makes institutions further dysfunctional to the peril of the socially and economically weak and in targeting India's numerous religious and tribal minorities. Furthermore, the right-wing critique of Pakistan being a "dysfunctional democracy" – because it targets its minorities and is ruled by the army – is used to build exactly the same kind of governance model in India. (This is especially the case after the revocation by executive decree of Article 370, a constitutional provision granting special status to Kashmir.) Moral critique reverses itself into a moral justification of the very same set of practices it condemns.

The old structure of politics is stitched into a new imaginary, while its substance remains the same. The rise of right-wing populism also emerged as a critique of technocratic liberalism and governance based on experts. The reasoning behind such a critique was the dominance of small elite that blocks mass participation and thereby undermines the very essence of democracy. However, the rule of technocrats is replaced by demagoguery and the strongman phenomenon, only further undermining the democratic ethos and its institutionalization. As Mouffe observes: "Liberal theorists looked for other explanations to fit their rationalist approach, insisting for instance on the role of uneducated, lower-class voters, susceptible to being attracted by demagogues."[30] However, this susceptibility is prevalent in other sections of society too, including the middle class. It justifies the strongman phenomenon as a response to the rule of the elites, that is, the dynastic rule of the Congress Party, which will pave a way for the opening up of opportunities for mass participation. The strongman becomes a symbol of a kind of "resistance" against "consensus elites" and, therefore, ushers in extra-institutional forms of mobilization. The strongman phenomenon therefore co-exists with extra-institutional street violence. One justifies the other and one cannot continue to exist without the other.

Demagoguery produces street violence, that is, mass rioting and public lynching become modes of mass participation that are perfectly consistent with the inscrutability of authoritarian rule. In such scenarios, demagoguery symbolizes order, discipline and control of the old elites and religious minorities and it implies public sanction, patronage and impunity for the authentic majority constructed as a morally "pure" people. It also fuses the supposed polar opposites – authoritarian rulers and extra-institutional mobilizations – together.

In such a fusion the old structure of patronage politics, the rule of a few elites, is resignified without changing its substance by not meaningfully opening any new avenues for genuine, that is, expansive and inclusive democratic participation. Here, it articulates the critique established by left-liberal discourses to new kinds of extra-institutional mobilization. It builds on the fact that, in India, the discourse of formal equality has spread *without commensurate change* in the social and material conditions of various social groups. This inaugurates a different kind of social psychology.

Right-wing populists mobilize culture and passions or affect, and have a grasp on the social psychology of many social groups that are aspirational about the legitimacy of equal treatment, but are engaged in a concrete struggle against routine incivility and disrespect. Furthermore, right-wing populists also sympathize with the declining social power of dominant social groups. The outbursts by Jats, Patidars, Marathas, Kapus, Kshatriyas and other dominant castes is symptomatic of the anxieties that dominant castes experience during social transformation.[31]

Left-liberals offer no alternative political agenda for any of these groups. Moreover, among the dominant castes, there are those who experience economic decline and precarity. The conflicting interests between these caste groups are increasingly being replaced by mobility and unity. Reservations or quotas on the basis of economic criteria, instead of caste, are a case in point. It allows for mobility without the stigma of caste. Right-wing populism offers alternative ideas of social harmony, fraternity and community fellow-feeling that ostensibly allow mobility for the subordinate groups and also empathy with the dominant groups and their declining social power.

This is, yet again, an instance of attempting to fuse polar opposites into unity. It partly recognizes that the economically poor among the dominant castes are also socially stigmatized. For instance, the poor among the Brahmins are not elites in the traditional sense of the term. The right sees a possibility of forging a unity between the poor among the caste Hindus and the poor among the so-called lower castes, based on a shared experience of poverty. Cultural subalterns are, therefore, pitted against economic elites.

How these differences at one level are going to play out against a certain kind of commonality at another level is a continuing challenge for right-wing populism in India. It must stitch the "hurt pride" of the dominant castes together with the social stigma of the subaltern castes. The difficulty of such a mode or the socially conservative aspect of such an experiment is visible in the recent conflicts between Dalits and Marathas in Bhima Koregaon.[32]

At another level, this seems to be a feasible experiment with the emergence of new cultural subalterns across caste, class and region. They are marked by a common opposition to modernity, liberal institutionalism, the role of experts and technocrats, the shared difficulty of coping with global cosmopolitanism and its secular ethos, and the dominance of the English language and its accompanying cultural valuation, among other things. Right-wing populism articulates this common nodal point, at times successfully overcoming the sharp divisions between the various social groups. Despite very different sociological contexts, the Indian case demonstrates notable similarities with that of the United Kingdom. For example, David Goodhart notes, "The old distinctions of class and economic interest have not disappeared but are increasingly overlaid by a larger and looser one, between the people who see the world from Anywhere and the people who see it from Somewhere."[33]

NEW POLITICAL FAULT LINES

The new political fault line is between "Open" versus "Somewheres." The "Open" are people who are "portable," and have "achieved" identities based on educational and career successes which make them generally comfortable and confident with new places and people.[34] The "Somewheres," in contrast, are more rooted and usually have "ascribed" identities, which is why they often find rapid change more unsettling.[35] Finally, Goodhart observes that even in an advanced capitalist country like Britain education remains the "gold standard" that has introduced this dual process of generating an aspirational class alongside social groups that perceive their declining social status. Goodhart argues:

> The helter-skelter expansion of higher education in the past twenty-five years – and the elevation of educational success into the gold standard of social esteem – has been one of the most important, and least understood, developments in British society. It has been a liberation for many and for others a symptom of their declining status.[36]

This partly explains the unrest among the dominant castes in India, previously mentioned, who perceive their decline and feel a sense of anxiety as to how castes lower than them are moving ahead through affirmative action policies. For example, Marathas arguing against reservations for

Dalits and wanting to move out of the agrarian sector and into the formal job market is a clear point highlighting this tension.[37] Further, the carefully choreographed controversy around the educational qualifications of Narendra Modi, who claims to belong to a lesser-privileged class and caste status, and of Smriti Irani, a female public representative, play out precisely this tension. Any critique or suspicion around their academic degrees and qualifications becomes taken to be symbolic of the elites' denial of mobility to newly asserting social groups such as the lower castes and women.[38]

Similarly, the crisis in various institutions of higher education, including JNU (Jawaharlal Nehru University), UoH (the University of Hyderabad), IIT (the Indian Institutes of Technology), FTII (Film and Television Institute of India), among others, is representative of breaking the hold of the social elite and their grip on public institutions. The controversy surrounding JNU, under the current political regime, again represents a palpable critique of the supposedly "privileged spaces" occupied by an elite and marked by the life of the mind and the aspiration to question everything instead of expressing solidarity and loyalty. This is then linked to the discourse of nationalism and its *bête noire* in India, "anti-nationalism."[39]

Nationalism, in other words, is a political mode of representing those left out of this process, those suffering anxiety due to the spread of higher education. In spite of having a progressive admission policy, JNU becomes a so-called "elite" space, while the current regime's mode of changing the policy frame of admission, in spite of excluding the majority, becomes a step that is against divisive politics and symbolic of nationalist assertions.

"POLITICAL EMOTIONS" AND PROTO-FASCISM

In all of this, subaltern castes remain torn between cultural identification against elite/open spaces, where they perceive a commonality with the nationalist discourse, on the one hand, and the need for a more inclusive policy frame, on the other. Dalit and OBC (Other Backward Classes) politics, in its back-and-forth movement between identifying with the right and also generating a counter-narrative to it, has been a visible trend under the current populist regime. While the dominant castes suffer from the anxiety of decline, subaltern castes suffer the insecurity of losing hard-earned benefits; both need different modes of coping with the situation that cannot be strictly realistic but require a gloss of self-valorization.

The slogans of "New India" or "*acche din*" are more of what one desires than what is real. As de Sousa and Morton note, the place and role of emotions beyond the limits of "rational human agency". Emotions represent a person's situation, whether or not they are true depictions of the situation, they are invariably accurate in depicting it. Emotional intelligence needs to find its place in understanding how agency shapes itself.[40]

Instincts, gut feelings and perceptions allow for an articulation of what may not be otherwise considered legitimate in a hierarchal context such as that of India. The emergence of the new cultural subalterns has, in effect, recast the old "Bharat versus India" conundrum, with the old kind of class orientation around issues of economic inequality being refashioned around a conflict between economic elites and cultural subalterns.[41] This undoubtedly tunes into the fact that caste groups are unevenly placed across economic, political and social planes. For instance, Brahmins could be socially higher in the ritualistic order but economically weak, and politically not very influential. Similarly, certain sections of the OBCs could be landed, politically influential but socially – educationally – backward. While the rhetoric against the high-end and invisible economic elites creates one kind of commonality, common social stigma creates another kind of possibility.

The current round of populism has emerged in India since 2014. Indian democracy experienced a populist turn from the days of Indira Gandhi with her slogan of "*Garibi Hatao!*" ("Abolish Poverty!"). However, what is distinct about the current mode of populism is that it is not restricted merely to electoral practices, but has also begun to dictate the policy frame. Demonetization is a clear instance of this.[42]

The drama around demonetization pitched it against economic elites, while the combination of nationalism and a mounting crisis in institutions of higher education strives for a commonality of cultural subalterns. This allows for a discourse that is paradoxically pro-corporate but anti-modern; it helps to push for high-end capitalist growth symbolized by bullet trains and urbanization and also address the community anxieties that capitalist modernity introduces; it makes possible the synthesis of a claim to a legacy of the pure past with claims for a radically altered future; it promises the preservation of community identities, including control of their women and property, yet it can lay claim to a politics that is beyond caste and religious considerations. It is in such combinatory formulations that right-wing populism strikes and mobilizes a new kind of a common sense.

Indian democracy has moved beyond the "Congress system" and is entering a post-Bahujan phase. In other words, in the 1980s Indian politics was dominated by issues of "social justice" by mobilizing Dalits (Scheduled Castes) and the Backwards Castes. However, in the post-Bahujan phase large categories such as Dalit and OBCs are giving way to smaller subcategories articulating and claiming independent identities and moving between various political parties. This has allowed the BJP to draw up a new strategic coalition between the dominant castes, on one side, and Dalits and OBCs, on the other. They are fragmenting the polity, on the one hand, and reconstructing these very fragments with a unified Hindutva narrative, on the other. In doing this, a populist narrative works as a glue in creating a new kind of discourse of "us" and "them," in some instances vis-à-vis the economic elites, while in others it could be the Muslims. As Prashant Jha notes in his study of the BJP's electoral strategy:

> It was meant to make the Hindu bitter at what he was not getting; it was meant to make him feel resentful of the Muslim for being pampered; it was meant to bracket all other parties as pandering to specific interests based on religion. In the name of a common citizenry and an unbiased state, it was meant to divide communities.[43]

The development processes in the post-reforms scenario, as executed by the right-wing regime, seem to have found the neoliberal imperative of state withdrawal reconciled through the narrative of a nationalist project of clean governance. As the state withdraws, distressed or marginalized communities have to cope with vulnerabilities and insecurities as they increasingly get entrenched into a condition of a consequent ethical relativism displacing natural rights and constitutional morality. The right-wing regime then proceeds to pitch itself amidst intensifying social rivalry as the political agency which intervenes to generate majoritarian solidarity. And in this it was extremely successful in the 2019 general election in which Hindu majoritarianism and the exclusion of minorities was a key theme.

Populism has foregrounded what Carl Schmitt refers to as the "irreducibility of multiplicity."[44] While in the immediate context it seems to have undermined democratic institutions and ethos, it also carries with it the possibility of further democratizing the polity by highlighting the multiple voices that inhabit it. This, however, remains one possibility, while the continued assertion of the populist mode may also permanently alter the contours of democracy, providing new justifications for extra-institutional discourses.

NOTES

Unless otherwise stated, URLs were last accessed on 1 June 2019.

1. A shorter version of this chapter has been previously published: Ajay Gudavarthy, "How BJP Appropriated the Idea of Equality to Create a Divided India," *Economic and Political Weekly* 53, No. 17 (28 April 2018), www.epw.in/journal/2018/17.

2. Dimitrov's definition of fascism is the *open terrorist dictatorship of the most reactionary, most chauvinistic and most imperialist elements of finance capital.* Others held that fascism need not represent the interests of finance capital alone but could be understood as a process wherein financial capital plays the dominant role within combinations of various sections of the ruling classes ... fascism could therefore be seen also as representing the general interests of monopoly capital rather than specific sections of financial capital. Some scholars have held that the terrorist dictatorship of the general interests of monopoly capital must come in the form of a mass movement to qualify as a fascist regime; others have held that irrespective of mass movement and the underlying social composition, terrorist dictatorships must be seen as variant forms of fascist regimes. Margit Koves and Shaswati Masumdar, ed., *Resistible Rise: A Fascism Reader* (New Delhi: New Word Books, 2005).

3. Antonio Gramsci, "On Fascism," in David Beetham, ed., *Marxists in Face of Fascism: Writings by Marxists on Fascism from the Inter-War Period* (Totowa, NJ: Barnes and Noble, 1984), 82.

4. Gramsci is arguing that the normalization of brutality in the civil society is the source that manufactures the hegemony for decomposed consent to the fascist state. "To understand the full force of these assertions, it is enough to recall; that Italy holds first place for murders and bloodshed; that Italy is the country where mothers educated their infant children by hitting them on the head with clogs – it is the country where the younger generations are least respected and protected; that in certain Italian regions it seemed natural until a few years ago to put muzzles on grape pickers, so that they could not eat the grapes; and that in certain regions the landowners locked their labourers up in sheds when the working was over, to prevent meetings or attendance at evening classes." Gramsci, "On Fascism," 82–7.

5. "Secularists of every hue keep proclaiming the RSS [Rashtriya Swayam-sevak Sangh] to be a radical militant Hindu organization. But conscious perceptive Hindus cannot but see that RSS has proved to be a paper tiger ... On issue after issue RSS starts with a roar, then shrinks into a whisper, then grovels and gives up, defeated but careful to save its face by inventing excuses." (Views of the founding members of VoI (Voice of India), a Hindu extremist organization.) Meera Nanda, "Hindu Triumphalism and the Clash of Civilisations," *Economic and Political Weekly* 52, No. 31 (5 August 2009): 106–14; Georgi Dimitrov, "The Working Class Against Fascism," in Beetham, ed., *Marxists in Face of Fascism*, 381; Wilhelm Reich, *The Mass Psychology of Fascism* (New York: Orgone Institute Press, 1980), 432; Koves and Mazumdar, *Resistable Rise*, 325.

6. Jens Lerche, "A Global Alliance against Forced Labour? Unfree Labour, Neoliberal Globalization and the International Labour Organization," *Journal of Agrarian Change* 7, No. 4 (October 2007): 425–52; Michael Levien, "Special Economic Zones and Accumulation by Dispossession in India," *Journal of Agrarian Change* 11, No. 4 (October 2007): 454–83.

7. Michał Kalecki, "Fascism in Our Times," in *The Last Phase in the Transformation of Capitalism* (New York: Monthly Review Press, 1972), 99–104.

8. "One of the basic functions of Nazism was to overcome the reluctance of big business to large scale government economic intervention. German big business agreed to a deviation from the principles of laissez-faire and to a radical increase of the role of the government in the national economy – on conditions that the government machine would submit to direct control in their partnership with the Nazi leaders." Kalecki, "Fascism in Our Times," 100.

9. The Rashtriya Swayamsevak Sangh and its allied organizations, such as the Vishwa Hindu Parishad, Bajrang Dal etc., are together described as Sangh Parivar, literally implying the *parivar* (a large family) of the Sangh.

10. R. Vijay, "Structure Retrogression and Rise of 'New Landlords' in Indian Agriculture: An Empirical Exercise," *Economic and Political Weekly* 47, No. 5 (February 2012): 37–45; D.A. Murali and R. Vijay, "Revival of Agriculture Sector and Increasing Tenancy in India," *Economic and Political Week* 52, No. 31 (5 August 2017): 18–21.

11. Barrington Moore Jr. insists that fascism protected the interests of big agri-culture in Italy at the expense of agricultural labourers and small peasants. The number of owner-operators dropped by 500,000 between 1921 and 1931 while the number of "cash-and-share" tenants rose by 400,000. In Germany, says Moore, Nazism in power junked its psuedo-radical agrarian populism since building a strong war economy could only occur on the basis of industry. Barrington Moore Jr., *Social Origins of Dictatorship and Democracy: Lord and Peasant in the Making of the Modern World* (Boston, MA: Beacon Press, 1993), 592; Achin Vanaik, "Situation Threat of Hindu Nationalism," *Economic and Political Weekly* 29, No. 28 (July 1994): 1729–48; Barrett L. McCormick, "Modernization, Democracy, and Morality: The

Work of Barrington Moore, Jr.," *International Journal of Politics, Culutre and Society* 13, No. 4 (Summer 2000): 591–606.

12. Aijaz Ahmed, "Fascism and National Culture: Reading Gramsci in the days of Hindutva," *Social Scientist* 21, No. 3–4 (March–April 1993): 32–68; Adam David Morton, *Hegemony and Passive Revolution: Unraveling Gramsci* (London: Pluto Press, 2007), 272.

13. Jonathan P. Perry, Jan Breman and Karin Kapadia, eds., *The Worlds of Indian Industrial Labour* (New Delhi: Sage Publications, 1999), 480.

14. Jan Breman, *The Labouring Poor in India* (New Delhi: Oxford University Press, 2003), 364.

15. Jan Breman, *The Jan Breman Omnibus* (New Delhi: Oxford University Press, 2008), 351; Lakshmidhar Mishra, *Human Bondage: Tracing its Roots in India* (New Delhi: Sage Publications, 2011), 512.

16. G. Vijay, "Migration, Vulnerability and Insecurity in New Industrial Labour Market," *Economic and Political Weekly* 40, No. 23 (May 2003): 2304–12; G. Vijay, "De-Fragmenting 'Disintegration of Value Creation': From Value Chains to Value Cycles," *Economic and Political Weekly* 44, No. 22 (May 2009): 85–94.

17. Tathagata Sengupta and Vijay Gudavarthy, "The Uncivil and De-Institutionalizing Labor Relations of Accumulation Through Disuse: The Case of the Brick Kiln Industry in Tenangana," in D. Narasinha Reddy and Kailash Sarap, eds., *Rural Labour Mobility in Times of Structural Transformation* (Singapore: Springer Publications, 2017), 327–45.

18. Swapna Banarjee-Guha, *Accumulation by Dispossession: Transformative Cities in the New Global* (New Delhi: Sage Publications, 2010), 248.

19. Pieter Gorter, *Small Industrialists, Big Ambitions: Economic and Political Networks on a Large Industrial Estate in West India* (New Delhi: Oxford University Press, 1996), 204.

20. Barbara Harriss-White, "The Workforce and its Social Structures," in *India Working Essays on Society and Economy* (New York: Cambridge University Press, 2003), 316; Sukhdeo Thorat and Katherine S. Newman, *Blocked by Caste* (New Delhi: Oxford University Press, 2010), 377.

21. Young-Sun Hong, *Welfare, Modernity and the Weimar State 1919–1933* (Princeton, NJ: Princeton University Press, 1955), 304; Theo Balderston, *Economics and Politics in the Weimar Republic* (Cambridge: Cambridge University Press, 2002), 138.

22. Vijay Gudavarthy, "Subsistence Economy in a Subverted Development: Re-Thinking Development Concretely," in K.B. Saxena and G. Haragopal, eds., *Marginalisation, Development and Resistance: Essays in Tribute to S.R. Sankaran* (New Delhi: Aakar Publishers, 2016), 2:429.

23. "The situation today however is such that this exposure of the betrayal of democratic reforms, the democratic disguise of the fascistoid state machinery – based on the consent of all bourgeois parties, including social democracy – is becoming evident to the broad masses … the nihilism among the workers about bourgeois democracy as a result of disillusionment with

the politics of the Social Democratic Party has to be combated." Georg Lukács, "Blum-Theses, 1971," in Koves and Mazumdar, *Resistable Rise*, 226–40.

24. One of the approaches analyses fascism as a movement of the petit bourgeoisie. Fascism according to this approach represents the rebellion of the middle classes, who see their economic security and social status threatened alike by big business and organized working-class movements, expressing opposition to capitalism and socialism – identifying with assertions about reviving the glorious past. Koves and Mazumdar, *Resistible Rise*, 325.

25. "In its new guise, the state is openly partisan to the interests of monopoly capital, of big business, which is today busily engaged with state support in carrying on 'fusions' and 'mergers' and rapidly advancing the process of centralization of capital. This shift to a state that is blatantly partisan to big business has brought in its trail increasing privatizations for the working people everywhere." Prabhat Patnaik, "A Note on the Political Economy of the 'Retreat of the State,'" in *Whatever Happened to Imperialism and Other Essays* (New Delhi: Tulika Books, 1997), 194–210.

26. Diego Gambetta, *The Sicilian Mafia: The Business of Private Protection* (Cambridge, MA: Harvard University Press, 1993), 325.

27. Chantall Mouffe, *On the Political* (London: Verso, 2005), 72.

28. Jan-Werner Müller, *What is Populism?* (Philadelphia, PA: University of Pennsylvania Press, 2016), 83.

29. K.P. Kannan and Jan Breman, *The Long Road to Social Security: Assessing the Implementation of National Social Security Initiatives for the Working Poor in India* (New Delhi: Oxford University Press, 2013), 552.

30. Mouffe, *On the Political*, 65.

31. The castes mentioned here are landed intermediary castes who are politically and economically powerful but socially consider themselves to be backward and in the *varna* order belong to the last tier known as the *Shudras*.

32. The Battle of Koregaon (also called the Battle of Koregaon Bhima, after the river Bhima that flows close to it) was fought on 1 January 1818 between the British East India Company and the Peshwa faction of the Maratha Confederacy, at Koregaon Bhima. The commemoration of this battle in 2018 by the Dalits led to a clash between the Dalits and the Marathas in Maharashtra.

33. David Goodhart, *A Road to Somewhere: The Populist Revolt and the Future of Politics* (London: C. Hurst & Co., 2017), 3.

34. Ibid.

35. Ibid.

36. Ibid.

37. Please refer to: Shikha Trivedy, "Marathas vs The Dalits: The Seething Caste War in Maharashtra," NDTV, updated 27 September 2016, www.ndtv.com/india-news/maharashtras-seething-caste-war-marathas-vs-the-dalits-1467017.

38. Please refer to: Ashok Swain, "Controversy over PM Modi's Degree Damages Reputation of India's Education System," *DailyO*, 2 March 2018, www.dailyo.in/politics/narendra-modi-delhi-university-fake-degree-bjp-education-in-india/story/1/22636.html; The Wire Staff, "Two Degrees of Separation: The Controversy Over Modi's Educational Qualifications Explained," *The Wire*, 30 April 2016, thewire.in/politics/controversy-over-modis-educational-qualifications-an-explainer.

39. For details of the controversy in JNU, see Ajay Gudavarthy, "Nationalism Demands a Dialogue," *Indian Express*, updated 19 February 2016, accessed 21 June 2019, indianexpress.com/article/opinion/columns/nationalism-demands-a-dialogue/.

40. De Sousa, Ronald and Adam Morton, "Emotional Truth," *Aristotelian Society Supplementary Volume*, Vol. 76, No.1 (1 July 2002): 247-263.

41. Bharat versus India: Shard Joshi explained his formulation of Bharat versus India as "'India' is that notional entity, largely Anglicised and relatively better-off, that had obtained the succession of colonial exploitation from the British; while 'Bharat' is largely rural, agricultural, poor and backward that was being subjected to colonial-like exploitation even after the end of the Raj.

    Many have erroneously interpreted the expression to denote the urban–rural divide. That was far from my mind. In fact, I made it explicitly clear, even in those early stages, that the relatively opulent segment of the rural society that derived its incomes from non-agricultural activities under state-protection were a part of 'India' while the slum dwellers and the footpath occupants of cities were, in fact, refugees from 'Bharat' to 'India' in search of livelihood." www.reddit.com/r/bharat/comments/1602ah/bharat_vs_india_sharad_joshi_who_coined_the_term/ (accessed 4 July 2019).

42. Demonetization was a monetary policy announced by Prime Minister Modi that invalidated 500 and 1,000 rupee notes as legal tender. This was promised to be a mode of fighting black money/economy by invalidating "black money" stored as cash. Arun Kumar, *Demonetization and the Black Economy* (New Delhi: Penguin Portfolio Publication, 2017), 344.

43. Prashant Jha, *How the BJP Wins: Inside India's Greatest Election Machine* (New Delhi: Juggernaut Books, 2017), 178.

44. Chantal Mouffe, "Carl Schmitt and the Paradox of Liberal Democracy," *Filosofický časopis* 55, No. 6 (2007): 899–914, doi.org/10.1215/9780822377849-008.

15

Art Contra Politics: Liberal Spectacle, Fascist Resurgence

Johan F. Hartle

Art can be political, but can it really be politics? Is artistic activism the kind of politics we should be looking for? The following is an articulation of a certain discontent with the substitution of artistic politics for politics. I will use concepts drawn from the SI (Situationist International) to make sense of such a substitution, specifically the terminology of "spectacle," signifying the mediation of social relations by images.[1] The concept of spectacle, to my mind, quite adequately characterizes the reduction of politics to cultural representations, that is, the joyous (and suggestive) free play of significations, the abundant use of self-presentation ("I am a person, who. . ."), and cultural ambiguity.

This dynamic affects the relationship between art and politics, too, leading to an overestimation of the political significance of art, on the one hand, and the artistic neutralization of politics, on the other. As I will argue, the extreme example of the SI and its reception serves as an exemplary case of a logic of cultural integration which tends to determine leftist discourse.[2]

Few radical movements in the middle ground of art and politics prove as successful a reference in contemporary artistic practice as the SI, from exhibitions in corporate museums to countless references in contemporary art criticism, including the publications of star curators.[3] Needless to say, such fame does not imply any direct continuation of the forms of political organization and activism introduced by the SI and its protagonists. If my argument holds for the SI, however, it certainly holds for less consequent and less radical artistic movements. The SI was driven by passive scepticism of, if not active contempt towards, the glamorous self-presentation of the art world, and the consolidation of privilege within it. This chapter's reference to the SI and its vocabulary is therefore ambiguous. On the one hand, it plays into an aesthetic politics which it, on the other, subjects to criticism. I regard such aesthetic politics as a part of what I call the *liberal spectacle*: the capacity of the market to both expose and integrate just about anything without touching upon the material grounds of social (re-)production, the capacity to tolerantly produce an overabundance of images and representations without touching upon the structural core of the capitalist accumulation with all the logics of expansion and marginalization, of implicit and explicit violence implied.

Without overestimating the impact of art, this spectacle-based politics is dialectically linked with contemporary forms of right-wing authoritarianism as it rises on the horizon of global politics: developments of both neofascist parties in Western democracies (and beyond) and, as the more popular forms of the movement are somewhat euphemistically called, the "alt-right" (see Chapters 3, 5 and 13), which is the cultural arm of contemporary neofascism organized via social media platforms such as 4chan, 8chan and YouTube which heavily draws upon certain avant-garde techniques (such as, e.g. the *"détournement"* of the Pepe the Frog meme – see Chapter 10). These forms of politics always draw on political alienation, classically branded as *spectacle*, leaving decision-making to charismatic leaders, and are thus based upon the mediated corporate world with all of its imagery. But they also express a genuine desire for realness, toughness and "no-bullshit" politics, a desire to break free from certain aspects of spectacle-based politics, bringing back apparently real issues underneath the layers of symbolic politics, politics of representation – issues that once belonged to the left, itself. The fascist spectacle, in other words, is the *wrong answer to a real problem*: the liberal spectacle, a mistaken understanding of emancipatory politics that remains trapped in the sphere of cultural representation and sticks to cultural elites as its preferred political agents.

The concept of spectacle was conceived in the context of the SI to characterize forms of reification that detached social agents from their agency, projecting it onto representations and materialized forms of social practice. Authoritarian forms of rule, fascism in particular, could clearly be identified with such political estrangement, obvious in the glorification of technology, strong leaders, organizational discipline and the like – "the chief icons," of which, as Debord writes, are "the family, private property, the moral order, the nation."[4]

The spectacle, however, is not only to be located on the side of fascism – it also characterizes the liberal or aesthetic left: "the uninterrupted monologue of self-praise,"[5] as Debord has it, to characterize the various ways advanced, differentiated, modern but eventually capitalist societies advertise themselves as diverse and emancipatory. Both are intertwined and keep reproducing each other as false alternatives. The implicit culturalism, romanticism and elitism of the position of certain strands of contemporary artistic politics express some of the fundamental problems of the contemporary liberal left – including the calculable backlash of rightist authoritarianism. As I will argue, the impulse of the SI to merge art and politics is not a free ticket for a leftist strategy valid in every period.

By making this point, I hope to ultimately draw attention to a general strategic unpreparedness of the contemporary liberal left to confront the fascist threat: which is to say, draw attention to a lack of political realism among the left. This lack, so I argue, stands in the way of achieving more than equal representation. It once was the case that to be on the left was to address the conditions of the production of social positions (of minority groups, of dominant and dominated) and not just their *ex-post* representation in the sphere of art, culture or discourse.

The problem of a performative contradiction is unavoidable here: although my argument is that, in some sense, *activist art* is very much a *spectacle*, it is also art theoretical. This understanding, therefore, does not lead me to advocate an aesthetic programme of "art for art's sake." Rather, I will try to defend an *activism* that presupposes a break with the configurations of artistic practice and requires its objectives to sometimes resist the very label of "art" itself.[6]

CULTURAL MARXISM, COLA, OR: THE FAILURE OF LIBERAL SUCCESS

Post-workerists, like Hardt and Negri,[7] or sociologists of "critique," like Luc Boltanski and Eve Chiapello,[8] would to some extent agree with aspects of the foregoing diagnoses of the radical right. Their analyses do confirm that the "left" has succeeded in producing a new form of capitalism tailor-made to traditional leftist politics of liberation, and that the left's rebellion against institutional disenfranchisement has succeeded to a large extent. They have allowed market observers to draw narrative arcs from the streets of 1968 to the upper echelons of big business. Also, in the history of advertising such arcs are well documented: Olivetti would have hired Che Guevara (the quintessential revolutionary marketing icon), so the advert informs us. The German jeans brand Mustang suggests a direct path from reading Karl Marx's *Das Kapital* to perusing the business journal *Capital*. Neoliberal narratives of diversity, creativity, flexibility and even humanitarianism now disclose their hidden meaning as catalysts of market expansion – as they have ever since the aftermath of 1968. The concept of the "integrated spectacle," accentuated by Guy Debord, anticipated these observations: it culminates in strategies "to eliminate an unexpected upsurge in revolutionary activity."[9] Differently put, radical change is obviated in the very hyperbolic image of itself. Or, as Raoul Vaneigem wrote: "All struggles for freedom obey a law of business expansion."[10]

The viral effects of the Pepsi ad with Kendall Jenner, including its following discussion and critique, is an excellent case in point. Here, the celebrity (a spectacle) ends up sharing a moment of spontaneous agreement, and a moment of projected intimacy, with the "movement on the street" (devoid of any contents, replete with "empty signifiers"), confronted by policemen. The very moment of unification is the act of consumption in which, as Marx argues, value realizes itself: Pepsi Cola mediates the celebrity and the masses through Pepsi. In the end, freedom and mass democracy are usurped by the desire for the double spectacle: the soft drink and the celebrity. Whatever the hidden

Figure 15.1 Still from Pepsi commercial starring Kendall Jenner, featured in the company's 2017 "Live for Now" campaign

Figure 15.2 Image from Forensic Architecture, The Grenfell Tower Fire (2017–ongoing). Video footage of the 14 June 2017 fire is mapped onto a 3D architectural model of Grenfell Tower (Image: Forensic Architecture, 2018. Reproduced by permission)

implications of the ad – there are, for example, some tellingly clear moments of classism and racism involved in the representations of the celebrity and her maid – grassroots movements and neoliberal capitalism, ultimately, are not in conflict. Rather, addressing the spirit "of the movement" (*WE ARE THE MOVEMENT*, as the music in the ad has as its refrain) has become a condition of contemporary capitalism to function and to expand. All recent examples of guerilla marketing prove this logic: much like classical movement-based politics, consumer capitalism must take the streets, must "occupy" vanguard lifestyles. The alt-right, or the so-called white "identitarian" movement, or the contemporary spectacle of fascism – that is all to say, fascism as a lifestyle brand – is the mirror image. Yet there are interesting tensions. The desire of every commodity is to be universally consumable and to circumvent any and all geographical or cultural restrictions; the logic of "deterritorialization," of transgressing any kind of specific context to appeal to larger audiences of consumers. If the commodity in this new capitalist order could speak, as according to Marx's ventriloquism in *Das Kapital*, it would say: "I am a liberal universalist" – and, accordingly, its global expansion relies on a secret or perhaps not-so-secret militarism, climate change denial, the hatred of all popular classes and racism.

The recent cola debate in the German federal state of Thuringia (a secret centre of German neofascism) provides interesting testimony to the fact that liberalism coincides with a certain logic of "deterritorializing" progressivism. After Adbusters had *détourned* a Coca-Cola ad for the dismissal of the right-wing populist AfD (Alternative für Deutschland), Coca-Cola surprisingly identified with the ad, and made it public through its own channels.[11] The local National Socialist celebrity Björn Höcke then advertised the local cola brand Vita Cola (obviously without *consciously* knowing that they had used a gay couple in their advertising), which used the opportunity to also declare allegiance to the idea of liberal capitalism and distanced itself from the AfD.[12]

Of course, the Kiez-based Hamburg cola brand Fritz Cola, famous for its allusions to the leftist scene ("Nur Wasserwerfer erfrischen besser" ["Only water cannons refresh better"]), "Nieder mit dem Kaffeetalismus"

Figure 15.3   Photo from Twitter user @Matth_Borowski, posted on 3 December 2018

Figure 15.4 Advertisement by Fritz-Kola, posted on the company's Twitter account on 21 December 2017

["Down with coffeetalism"], "Barista, barista, antifascista!") used such opportunities to emphasize again its opposition to right-wing populism.[13] No cola for right-wing populists! When the commodity speaks, it says: "no to the AfD!" maybe even with the inflection of the spirit of 1968. Today, such a spirit amounts to the fact that the major companies of the American arms industries are now led by women; one of the generals of the Israeli Defense Forces is vegan. *We are the movement!*

Therefore, we might say that the left has succeeded and that its success is its very *failure*. Which left, however, succeeded and why is this success a failure, too? Such clarification is critical for anyone wishing to argue convincingly against the contemporary fascists, who are quick to maintain that contemporary society is marked by the hegemony of the left, that our current misery is its product and so forth. The most obvious success of the left is, to my mind, the success of its "cultural revolution," which succeeded in inscribing itself into contemporary culture as a profoundly normative discourse with multiple rules of correct moral conduct: manners of speaking about marginalized groups (in ways representatives of these groups often would not use for themselves), the avoidance of physical closeness as an attempt to keep sexualized violence under control, etc. But have the socioeconomic conditions of minority groups really improved through more thoughtful denominations ("Native Americans", "African Americans")?[14] And can sexual violence really be countered by extending the realm of taboo? The repressed might return in even more openly aggressive forms. The tragic dialectics of failed revolutions, that is the violent backlash they engender, has oftentimes suggested this. The municipal socialist project of Red Vienna successfully set a new cultural and ideological tone in the Austrian capital – in the moment of civil war, however, in February 1934, the unresolved political conflicts came back to the fore, ending the all-too-glorious and all-too-weak socialist project. Similarly, the Chilean revolution from 1970 to 1973, supported by singers and poets like Victor Jara and Pablo Neruda, had the cultural momentum on its side. In the end, the hard-edged questions of economic supply and military support decided the country's fate.

The success of the left's revolution was that, ultimately, dimensions of formal equality have been reinforced in forms of institutional self-policing. If anything, liberalism is the political paradigm that keeps investing in symbolic, formal, judicial struggles to fight social inequalities while leaving the economic order (property relations, market forces etc.) and also the material conditions of the production of subjectivity (the social position in the spheres of (re-)production) fundamentally untouched (see also Chapter 8). More concretely: the use of a symbolic politics of formal equality in order to avoid the structural conflicts pre-shaped by socioeconomic inequality (*political correctness*) is the textbook liberal practice. The question is: who wants to constantly feel guilty for structures one feels one cannot change (certainly not by acts of guilt, symbolic gestures etc.)?[15]

This self-policing sees the most egregious offence as the disrespect of anyone on the basis of the identity he or she has claimed in the social realm. This helps in establishing spaces free of violence and fear that offer protection to minority groups in at least some areas of society – so-called "safe spaces." Yet such rules of conduct do nothing to transform the *material* reproduction of disrespect and physical degradation of certain social groups: class and race specifically.[16]

Progressive liberalism thus tends to coincide with the friendly dialects of commodity language. Eventually, however, the commodity is not only the progressive liberal (Bernie Sanders, Elizabeth Warren, Alexandria Ocasio-Cortez). In fact, it cannot do without imperial warfare and punishing wage policies; *Breitbart* and Fox News – from the other side of the battlefield – tirelessly remind us of this fact. Primitive accumulation keeps re-appearing in and through the peaceful surface of polite and friendly market relations.

RADICAL EQUALITY AND DISTINCTION, OR:
THE SITUATIONIST TICKET

Clearly, and logically, such politics with all their contradictions are also palpable in the artistic field, which is to say, in the institutional sphere of culture. Here, the integration of "leftist" positions, in the broad and vague sense, into the institutional reality of modern capitalism, takes place with some necessity. This is partly due to the same logic that leads to the slight and vague progressivism inherent in commodity liberalism, as described above. But one also has to address the specific logic of the field of cultural production and its historical genesis to understand the importance of the link between "leftism" and the cultural sphere. In the sphere of representation and cultural politics, formal equality – or at least taking a stand for it – does not require paying a high price. On the contrary, a certain understanding of "formal equality" is inscribed into the logic of the field and thus boosts reputations rather than damages them.

The logic of the fields of cultural production has historically emerged out of struggles to constitute and maintain their own kinds of recognition, or more sociologically speaking: their own specific forms of *capital*. Pierre Bourdieu has analysed the cultural struggles and the symbolic revolutions that eventually led to the constitution of relatively autonomous fields of cultural production, the fine arts and literature, in some detail (with specific focus on Manet and Flaubert respectively).[17] According to Bourdieu, such relative autonomy also required references to universal normative standards, on the one hand, and ostentatious acts of distinction to set the boundaries in distinction to other social fields (religious, economic, political), or as Bourdieu termed it, the "field of power," on the other. The field of cultural production was thus erected performatively on the idea of a symbolic currency (cultural capital) of its own kind. The suggested universality was a condition for the field's general acceptance – not least by the market and wealthy collectors who were to expect more than just economic equivalents for their investments – although a material return on investment always remains on the horizon. "Symbolic capital," as Bourdieu has it, "is a kind of 'economic' capital denied but recognized, and hence legitimate – a veritable credit, and capable of assuring, under certain conditions and in the long term, 'economic' profits."[18]

Such inherent universalism of cultural capital is politically ambiguous. There could not have been any general legitimacy of cultural production without reference to universally accepted normative resources such as the universality of art, its general legitimacy as a source of social representation. Only through this detour could art maintain itself economically, because only as a universal good could it provide elites with the glamour and prestige that no other profane commodity could guarantee. At the same time, the inherent legitimation of the field of cultural practice played a crucial role in establishing the field of cultural production within which the autonomous treatment of aesthetic form (constitutive of the very idea of aesthetic autonomy, the autonomy of the field) alluded to the formal equality of social agents and in some cases helped to articulate their specific perspectives.

In such a way, the field of cultural production thus mirrored and repeated the normative promises of the bourgeois revolutions: it came into existence with the same burden of formal equality that modern bourgeois societies were built upon. Unlike modern capitalism, however, which can do pretty well without any sense of universal norms other than the universality of self-valorizing value, *capital itself*, the cultural field existentially depended on this promise. The constant anticipation of better worlds to come, to cosmic orders beyond, to regulative ideas of the *sensus communis aestheticus* in aesthetic theory and practice addressed this very issue. It remained an existential one for the idea of modern culture if only to be distinguished from merely particular local cultures and ideologies.

The fact that this field is built upon slightly progressive principles (of formal equality and universality) is at least twofold. It constituted a horizon of critical intellectuality (which could always be brought into play against the field of power). But the inherent structure of artistic agency is bound to the accumulation of symbolic capital. In such strife, following the argument of Bourdieu's analysis, "distinction" appeared as a key principle. Distinction means that the critique of one's own conditions of practice is a logical inevitability of establishing oneself on a higher level within that very same regime. As Bourdieu writes in *Distinction*:

> It should not be thought that the relationship of distinction (which may or may not imply the conscious intention of distinguishing oneself from common people) is only an incidental component in the aesthetic disposition. The pure gaze implies a break with the ordinary attitude towards the world which, as such, is a social break.[19]

The fate of the historical avant-garde – to see their anti-institutional intuitions integrated into newly arising and successively differentiated commercial and semi-commercial art institutions – is the most obvious example of this logic. From the point of view of such a critical sociology of "fields of power," vaguely leftist positions (critical of the predominance of economic capital and attempting to install other symbolic currencies) are therefore naturally situated in the realm of culture.[20] In fact, Bourdieu is explicit about the symbolic dimension of class that finds its expression in the symbolic economies of art. Distinction is thus also the cultural marker of class. It has certainly been widespread in the discussions around the SI.[21] The emphasis on the politically avant-gardist role of the artist makes perfect sense in a world that emphasizes formal and cultural equality, yet whose cultural politics are separated from radical economic and material transformation.

With the historical achievement of relative autonomy, the field of cultural production also accepted a certain level of neutrality or political ineffectiveness. A symbolic space for the critical and formal reflection of equality, with some distance from the field of power, the aspiration for universality became historically possible only under conditions of a social division of labour that also left the fundamental logics of capitalist society intact. As Adorno famously writes in Aesthetic Theory: "autonomous art makes itself a vehicle of ideology: The society at which it shudders is left in the distance, undisturbed."[22] No matter how one precisely spells out the relationship between the relatively autonomous field of cultural production, on the one hand, and the field of power, the manifest material structure of society, on the other – for example as compensational, parallel, superstructural etc. – one thing is clear: *cultural leftism in the former leaves the organization of the latter unscathed*. Since such autonomy is inscribed into the constitution of the field, one should also not overestimate the internal political struggles about the logics of the field itself.[23] Such struggles operate, in other words, within rigid limits.

Of course, any access to strategies of generalization and justification can also produce its own type of symbolic capital. It constitutes symbolic change. This is a lot; but it is never everything: Terry Eagleton's analysis of the ideology of the aesthetic described the inherent logic of aesthetic discourse as a compensation for lack of real social transformation. His argument holds for artistic practice, too. The SI was clear about this. Their remaining faithful to the concepts of "immanent critique," "realization" and "*Aufhebung*" (both cancelling and preserving) meant the abolition of art on one level and its continuation on another.[24] But this position and legacy remains ambiguous. For the question is: what is the value in absenting oneself from aesthetic discourse or abolishing art in order to, ultimately, realize further potentials of both? And in this scenario, which aspects of art (authorship, representational, *as if* practice etc.) does one maintain to succeed at the transition from the reproduction of its discourse to its abolition?

As exemplified above, contemporary capitalism successfully integrates numerous forms of revolt into new business models – for example Google and other Silicon Valley tech companies integrating "work" and "play" in their office design. This is all the more true for art. One of the biggest retrospective shows on the SI took place in the Museum Tinguely, a museum donated to the city of Basel by Hoffman-La Roche, the third biggest pharmaceutical company in the world.[25] Even the most radical movements, including the SI, have been used to revive, if not global business in general, then at least the machineries of a global art world. Paradigmatically, the French star curator Nicolas Bourriaud enthusiastically refers to the avant-gardist spirit of the SI in his programmatic considerations on relational aesthetics (Bourriaud's own curatorial practice is a vastly affirmative one, turning art into a decorative design of quotidian processes of communication of in-groups).[26] Relational aesthetics, so Bourriaud states optimistically, "updates Situationism and reconciles it ... with the art world."[27]

Innumerable successful artists regard the Situationist legacy as their own. No doubt, radical gestures sell well in the sphere of institutionalized provocation. The universalizing discourse of leftist policy, of emancipation, of the critique of power can easily end up as a form of legitimation for (in the end) purely cultural or aesthetic types of careers without any further political valence or impact. The more radical the gesture, the more powerfully it improves one's reputation within the regime of symbolic capital accumulation. The spectacle of self-organization, participation and collaboration – hallmarks of the Situationist practice – seems to fuel the machines of art more powerfully and persistently than any other. For any curator or artist drawing on the legacy of the SI, Situationism-as-career-strategy allows him or her to claim political authenticity, thus proving the loyalty to the universal currency of equal cultural representation. According to the dialectical logic of integration that grasps the fate of the avant-garde itself, today the Situationist ticket ensures one entry into the very heart of the artistic field. Criticizing or sublating the institutional landscape of art has always been harder than it had, at first, seemed.

INESCAPABLY ART, OR: POLITICS, FOR (A) CHANGE

In fact, there is something tragic, if not farcical, about radical politics in the arts. When the German conceptual artist Charlotte Posenenske decided to "quit" being a conceptual artist and become a union organizer, she drew attention to what seems to be the either/or consequence of this dilemma (that "being an artist" and "abolishing art" are mutually exclusive strategies), ending her career with the following words: "It is difficult for me to come to terms with the fact that art can contribute nothing to solving urgent social problems."[28] With these parting words, she refutes the programmatic concern for artistic reputation and draws the bitter, realist conclusion that her political commitment cannot be fulfilled through political art (and that political art, by "contribut[ing] nothing," can even sabotage the cause)[29] – which, in her case, was a highly intellectually evolved form of minimal sculpture. Posenenske decided to do politics-proper without reducing it to a model case for artistic discourse. She studied sociology and worked as a trade union organizer. Contemporary curators, ironically, honour her work and her political

Figure 15.5   Advertisement by Mustang, published in *Der Spiegel*, Nr. 15/1978

gesture by exhibiting the artworks that she produced before making that decision – a perfect example of the machinic relentlessness of the art world, which can only process radical political gestures as symbolically beneficial for the artist-as-author. Recently, the Dia:Beacon Art Centre in New York honoured her work – not least for its radical edginess, its critical reflection of (not) being an artist.[30] There's no way of escaping the clutches of the valorization cycle of art in a cultural economy that is built upon symbolic exchange. As Michael Corleone says in *The God-father Part III* (a trilogy that delivers an unparalleled account of primitive accumulation), "Just when I thought I was out, they *pull* me back in."[31]

This, in turn, contributes to the monopolization of politics by cultural elites. Given the social distribution of cultural capital (and its contribution to the reproduction of class structures) such a monopoly is anything but democratic. This is the very point at which the limits of artistic politics and the newly established artistic genre of artistic activism appears. For what distinguishes *cultural leftism* (or, as contemporary fascists both rightly and wrongly say: *cultural Marxism*) from leftism-proper (or *Marxism*) is its restriction of politics to representation and formal equality in discourse and cultural politics. It is within this culturalist scenario of politics that *we are all liberals now*. It is at this level that we are ill prepared to confront the fascist threat, which applauds itself for its realism, its contempt for liberal privilege in the cultural field and thus its critique of hypocrisy.

One must not simply lodge a moral complaint about the failure of the success of leftist politics in the field of cultural production. Each field has its own logics, its own specific competition for capital. But one must also not overestimate artistic politics, either. Following Debord's definition, "culture is the power to generalize, existing apart, as an intellectual division of labor and as the intellectual labor of division."[32] Artistic practice turns politics into a spectacle when it reduces the political to an element of art, artists to privileged players in the political realm. Because, first of all, transgressing the artistic field is difficult. However hard contemporary artists might attempt to turn into social organizers, social workers or the like, they eventually end up contributing to an expansion of a certain type of ersatz politics, to the colonization of politics through symbolic representation.

In this respect, interesting things happened in England under New Labour and what it called, echoing the country's imperialist history, "Cool Britannia," flanked by Oasis, Blur and the Spice Girls. The government invited socially engaged artists to clean up the mess that their new budget cuts had made in various neighbourhoods throughout the United Kingdom. This exemplifies how ready even politicians are to use participatory art to replace social programmes and policy grounded in good political economy. It is the staging of a distraction, a spectacle of participation that leaves the material and institutional social-economic realities untouched. As a kind of cultural trickle-down effect, the masses participate only in the appearance as opposed to the material reality of the very wealth their labour power produces.[33] And while this might sometimes seem to be politically radical, the projects are ultimately only successful in improving the politician's image and the artist's résumé.

Whatever this might mean for artists' biographies, it changes a lot for the place of politics in society. At contemporary biennials many things take place that art has taken over from other segments of the public sphere:[34] artistic practices reach from responsible journalism all the way through to forensics documenting human rights violations. The work of Forensic Architecture, gathering critical evidence of major human rights abuses and neglected forms of (sometimes structural) violence, is a particularly challenging example. Its work is noble, valid and aesthetically challenging. Often enough, however, the work of Forensic

Figure 15.6 Charlotte Posenenske, Relief Series B, 1967–2015, Basel 2018, Take Ninagawa Sculpture, Aluminum, convexly curved, sprayed standard RAL matte black, 100 × 50 × 14 cm © Estate of Charlotte Posenenske Dr. B. Brun

Architecture has been accused of merely being art, of not being trust-worthy in a strictly juridical context. And one might wonder why and how artists have ended up doing the work that we would expect from properly funded and trustworthy juridical and political institutions.

Of course, why should the work of collectives like Forensic Architecture not be art? The artistic field is one of competing forces and there-fore a field of struggle. This means, of course, that promoting politically progressive or radical positions in the artistic field is indirectly linked to overarching hegemonic struggles. Also, politics necessarily involves forms of aesthetic reconfiguration and vice versa.[35] The articulation of alternative visions and marginalized political positions corresponds with different aesthetic regimes, different regimes of the visible and the sayable.[36] The takeaway cannot be that one should give in to conserva-tives and depoliticize aesthetic practice. Certainly not in times in which alt-right movements are reaching out to artistic institutions, too (often by integrating avant-garde practices of *détournement*, like in the produc-tion of memes).[37] Rather, the point is to reclaim the political realm and to expand the reach of emancipatory strategies from the realm of culture.

Nothing is *necessarily* wrong with the specific structure of the aesthetic politics we find in the strategies mentioned above. And yet, like well-intentioned but misguided charity, its potential to do good despite itself is outweighed by the damage it does by side-stepping the actual problems. Well-intentioned, self-professed "political art" need not theo-retically do anyone any harm, as long as the left does not mistake these programmes of aesthetic politics for politics *as such*. It also means not mistaking the artsy few for in any sense privileged agents in the political struggle. Unfortunately, this tendency to refer to the sphere of culture as the locus, and cultural producers as the key protagonists of political struggle certainly was already not alien to the SI. Some programmatic formulations of the SI remain at least ambiguous in this respect, such as Debord's referring to the SI as an "international association of situa-tionists [who] can be seen as a union of workers in an advanced sector of culture."[38] Why would it really be *their* politics that is supposed to free the world?

One of the main theoretical predecessors of the Situationists, certainly of the theory of spectacle, Georg Lukács, addressed this dilemma quite explicitly with the critique of his own youthful "romantic anti-capitalism."[39] Rather than laying claim to power in a way that might actually make a difference in the world, romantic anti-capitalists express their discontent in art and literature, but without ever leaving in any substantial way the symbolic realm of cultural representation: a comfortable place for social criticism. The romanticist paradigm of art being prior to politics, however apocalyptic and apparently critical it might present itself, eventually allows for a depoliticizing and elitist self-enjoyment of artistic reputation. Such ways of mistaking art for politics displaces politics into the realm of the aesthetic. It can also distort the intentions by which it is driven: the opportunistic striving for fame in the sphere of privilege and separation hidden in emancipatory pretence. Also, it relies on liberal elites holding prestigious positions within a specific sphere of social practice. Hopes for political change brought forward by players within the artistic field could turn out to be exaggerated – especially because their "critical stance" becomes a reputation booster within a symbolic economy that rewards being critical, diluting it into merely a successful strategy for success and cultural distinction. In the process, the *substantial* distinction of leftism – a critical involvement in a history of dirty struggles about economic ownership, state monopoly and violence – is sapped of its strength as it becomes another strategic identity among many, useful to maintain privileged positions within liberal institutions. But praxis, Adorno suggests in his lectures on moral philosophy, begins only where it starts to hurt.[40] Political praxis might put you in a position of "merely" a union organizer or a party member rather than an artist with an apparently privileged perspective on political articulation. It might be the only way, though, of preventing the worst and of regaining a sense of political realism.

No one is ever to blame for fascism except fascists. But the fascist (and in principle Nietzschean) critique that politics of equality are fundamentally hypocritical is not unambivalent. Of course, the politics of equality is not *necessarily* hypocritical. Hypocrisy literally signifies an overload of abstract theory out of step with concrete praxis. Political discourse in contemporary capitalism has become highly sensitive to inequality in discourse and cultural and institutional representation without, however, managing to even slightly ameliorate the material reality of economic exploitation and expansionism accordingly. The SI's communist understanding of politics, the emphasis on seizing the means of production by acts of radical, council democracy, was perhaps excessively utopian, but in some sense more politically *realist* than their aesthetic successors. It was meant to confront the real preconditions of symbolic practices in the realm of socioeconomic power. It is precisely here that the SI ceases to be a movement of mere artistic activism and enters the *field of politics proper*. It is thus also this red line at which the legacy of the SI does or does not represent a form of activism that, as it is concerned with artistic production alone, is destined to fail.

NOTES

Unless otherwise stated, URLs were last accessed on 31 July 2019.

1. See Guy Debord, *Society of the Spectacle*, trans. Donald Nicholson-Smith (New York: Zone Books, 1994), 12f.
2. The reference to the SI is also due to the emergence of this paper, a first version of which was given at the Spectacle of Fascism conference at SFU Vancouver in April 2017.
3. See for instance, Daniel Birnbaum and Kim West, eds., *Life on Sirius: The Situationist International and the Exhibition After Art* (Berlin: Sternberg Press, 2016); Stefan Zweifel and Hans Ulrich Obrist, eds., *The Situationist International 1957–1972* (Zurich: JRP Ringier, 2007); and, as discussed later in the text: Nicolas Bourriaud, *Relational Aesthetics*, trans. Simon Pleasance and Fronza Woods (Paris: Les presses du réel, 2009).
4. Debord, *Spectacle*, 77.
5. Ibid., 19.
6. An optimistic (and in some way late-romanticist) example for the belief that art and artistic activists can and should be at the forefront of contemporary politics can be found in Gregory Sholette, *Delirium and Resistance: Activist Art and the Crisis of Capitalism* (London: Pluto Press, 2017).
7. Michael Hardt and Antonio Negri, *Empire* (Cambridge, MA: Harvard University Press, 2000).
8. Luc Boltanski and Eve Chiapello, *The New Spirit of Capitalism*, trans. Gregory Elliot (New York: Verso, 2005).
9. Guy Debord, *Comments on the Society of the Spectacle*, trans. Malcolm Imrie (New York: Verso, 1990), 9.
10. Raoul Vaneigem, *The Book of Pleasures*, trans. John Fullerton (Berkeley, CA: Pending Press, 1983), 28.
11. Palko Karasz, "Germany Uses Coca-Cola, and Santa Claus, to Denounce Far Right," *The New York Times*, 11 December 2018, accessed 31 July 2019, www.nytimes.com/2018/12/11/world/europe/germany-afd-coca-cola.html.
12. www.focus.de/panorama/welt/panorama-afd-rechtsaussen-hoecke-wirbt-fuer-vita-cola-doch-kannte-er-wohl-nicht-deren-werbung_id_10054142.html, accessed 31 July 2019. Thomas Laschyk, "Peinlich! AfDler will Coca Cola boykottieren und trinkt versehntlich linke 'Fritz-Cola'!" *Der Volksverpetzer*, 8 December 2018, accessed 31 July 2019, www.volksverpetzer.de/social-media/fritz-kola/.

13. www.fritz-kola.de/2018/08/31/offene-augen-statt-blinder-hass/, accessed 31 July 2019.

14. In the Canadian context, it is striking to see how progressive academics keep emphasizing their historical guilt by highlighting the act of violence that the current order has been built upon: the fact that their institutions are standing on stolen land. So far so good. But why celebrate the politics of guilt without consequences by *merely* emphasizing that land has been stolen from First Peoples, without directly mobilizing for land reform? Why not start every progressive academic get-together with a petition for economic change and land reform?

15. See the publications by Adolph Reed Jr. and Walter Benn Michaels, specifically Walter Benn Michaels, *The Trouble with Diversity: How We Learned to Love Identity and Ignore Inequality* (New York: Metropolitan Press, 2006) and Adolph Reed Jr., "Nothing Left. The Long, Slow Surrender of American Liberals," *Harper's Magazine*, March 2014.

16. See Asad Haider, *Mistaken Identity: Race and Class in the Age of Trump* (London: Verso, 2018). See also Samir Gandesha's excellent review "Insurgent Universality," *Radical Philosophy* 2, No. 4 (Spring 2019): 89–93.

17. Pierre Bourdieu, *The Rules of Art*, trans. Susan Emmanuel (Cambridge: Polity Press, 1996); Pierre Bourdieu, *Manet: A Symbolic Revolution*, trans. Peter Collier and Margaret Rigaud-Drayton (Cambridge: Polity Press, 2017).

18. Bourdieu, *Rules of Art*, 142.

19. Pierre Bourdieu, *Distinction*, trans. Richard Nice (Cambridge, MA: Harvard University Press, 1984), 31.

20. Bourdieu, *Rules of Art*, 337 f.

21. As one can read in the 1958 responses to the questionnaire published in the SI journal:
"The masses, i.e. the non-ruling classes, have no reasons to feel concerned with any aspect of a culture or an organization of social life that have not only been developed without their participation or their control, but that have in fact been deliberately designed to prevent such participation or control." "Response to a Questionnaire from the Center for Socio-Experimental Art," Bureau of Public Secrets, accessed 31 July 2019, www.bopsecrets.org/SI/9.artquestions.htm.

22. Theodor W. Adorno, *Aesthetic Theory*, trans. Robert Hullot-Kentor (London: Bloomsbury, 2013), 226.

23. Jens Kastner, "Art and Activism (Against Groys)," trans. Manuela Zechner, European Institute for Progressive Cultural Policies, December 2014, eipcp.net/policies/kastner/en/print.html.

24. See famously, the characterization of dadaism and surrealism in Debord, *Spectacle*, 136.

25. "The International Situationist: 1957–1972. In girum imus nocte et consumimur igni," [Press release], accessed 31 July 2019, www.tinguely.ch/de/ausstellungen/ausstellungen/2007/situationistische-internationale.html.

26. Bourriaud, *Relational Aesthetics*. Cf. Claire Bishop, "Antagonism and Relational Aesthetics," *October* 10 (Autumn 2004): 51–79.

27. Bourriaud, *Relational Aesthetics*, 85.

28. Quoted after Leah Pires, "Charlotte Posenenske," Art in America, 1 June 2019, www.artinamericamagazine.com/reviews/charlotte-posenenske/.

29. Charlotte Posenenske, "Statement" [Manifesto], *Art International* No. 5 (May 1968): 50.

30. "First North American Retrospective of Pioneering Minimal and Conceptual Artist Charlotte Posenenske Will Debut at Dia: Beacon March 2019" [Press release], 4 December 2018, accessed 31 July 2019, www.diaart.org/about/press/first-north-american-retrospective-of-pioneering-minimal-and-conceptual-artist-charlotte-posenenske-will-debut-at-diabeacon-march-2019/type/text.

31. Francis Ford Coppola (dir.), *The Godfather Part III* (San Francisco, CA: Paramount Pictures/Zoetrope Studios, 1991).

32. Debord, *Spectacle*, 180.

33. See my and Samir Gandesha's introduction to our co-edited volume *Spell of Capital* (Amsterdam: Amsterdam University Press, 2017), 9–19.

34. The Manifesta in Palermo was a particular example in this respect: documentary-based videos on refugees' biographies, ISIS victims, structural racism, military bases and human rights violations in the Mediterranean.

35. See my and Samir Gandesha's introduction to our co-edited volume *Aesthetic Marx* (London: Bloomsbury, 2017), x–xlix.

36. Such is the argument of Jacques Rancière, ever since his seminal *The Politics of Aesthetics: The Distribution of the Sensible*, trans. Gabriel Rockhill (London: Continuum Press, 2004).

37. Cf. Ana Teixeira Pinto, "Artwashing," in *Texte zur Kunst*, No. 106 (2017): 162–70.

38. Guy Debord, "Theses on the Cultural Revolution," in *Guy Debord and the Situationist International: Texts and Documents*, trans. John Shepley (Cambridge, MA: MIT Press, 2004), 62.

39. Georg Lukács, *History and Class Consciousness* (Cambridge, MA: MIT Press, 1971), x.

40. Theodor W. Adorno, *Problems of Moral Philosophy* (Stanford, CA: Stanford University Press, 2001), 9.

Notes on Contributors

Alexandru (Alec) Balasescu is an anthropologist, writer, curator and author of *Paris Chic, Tehran Thrills: Aesthetic Bodies, Political Subjects* (ZETA Books, 2007). He publishes extensively in international journals covering interdisciplinary and cross-cultural approaches to urbanism, design, material culture and the body. His research has received support from the Center for German and European Studies, UC Berkeley; the Wenner Gren Foundation for Anthropological Research; the British Library; the French Institute of Research in Iran; and the Open Society Institute. Over the past six years, he has held administrative positions and was engaged in projects of urban regeneration through arts and culture in Bucharest and Istanbul. He also taught at several universities, including The American University of Paris, RUW Bahrain, and Galatasaray University in Istanbul. He co-edited the special issue of the *Journal of Development* on urban sustainability (vol. 54.3, 2011). Dr. Balasescu obtained his LEED AP accreditation in Vancouver and is a founding member of the Moving Matters Traveling Workshop, based at UC-Riverside.

Patricia M. Barkaskas earned an MA in History, with a focus on Indigenous histories in North America, and a JD, with a Law and Social Justice Specialization, from the University of British Columbia. She is the Academic Director of the Indigenous Community Legal Clinic and an Instructor at the Peter A. Allard School of Law. Patricia has practised in the areas of child protection (as parent's counsel), criminal, family, as well as civil litigation and prison law. She has worked closely with Indigenous peoples in their encounters with the justice system and has worked for Residential school survivors as an historical legal researcher for the Indian Residential Schools Settlement Agreement. In addition, she has written Gladue reports for all levels of court in BC. Her current and future teaching and research interests include access to justice, clinical legal education, decolonizing and Indigenizing law, particularly examining the value of Indigenous pedagogies in experiential and clinical learning for legal education, and Indigenous laws. Patricia is Métis from Alberta.

Tamir Bar-On is one of the world's leading experts on the French and European New Right. He is a professor in the School of Social Sciences and Government, Tecnológico de Monterrey in Queretaro, Mexico, and a member of the Mexican National System for Researchers since 2015. Dr. Bar-On has taught at Yale University, the University of Toronto, Wilfrid Laurier University, the University of Windsor, and the Royal Military College of Canada. He has written four books, including two about the French and European New Right: *Where Have All the Fascists Gone?* (Ashgate, 2007); *Rethinking the French New Right: Alternatives to Modernity* (Routledge, 2013); *The World Through Soccer: The Cultural Impact of the Global Sport* (Rowman and Littlefield, 2014); and *Beyond Soccer: International Relations and Politics as Seen through the Beautiful Game* (Rowman and Littlefield, 2017). He is working on a new edited volume called *Old Right and New Right on Both Sides of the Atlantic* (2019). Bar-On is a member of the European Consortium for Political Research – Standing Group on Extremism and Democracy. He is also part of the Editorial Committee, *Explorations of the Far Right*, ibidem Press.

Joan Braune specializes in Frankfurt School Critical Theory and social/political philosophy. In particular, her work is an addition to the rediscovery of Erich Fromm's contribution to Critical Theory. She has published *Erich Fromm's Revolutionary Hope: Prophetic Messianism as a Critical Theory of the Future* (Sense Publishers, 2014), along with a number of chapters, articles and reviews. Her latest research explores the relationship between theory and practice, drawing again upon Critical Theory but also expanding into connected questions in Caribbean philosophy, critical pedagogy, and Catholic Social Thought.

Hilda Fernandez-Alvarez works as a Lacanian psychoanalyst in private practice and as a psychotherapist, registered with the BC Association of Clinical Counsellors, for a public institution (Vancouver Coastal Health) in Vancouver, Canada. She received an MA in Clinical Psychology from the National Autonomous University of Mexico (UNAM), an MA in Spanish Literature from the University of British Columbia (UBC), and she has more than 20 years of Lacanian training. She is engaged in a PhD programme in the Department of Geography at Simon Fraser University (SFU), where she is conducting research on discursive spaces of trauma and the provision of services, awarded with a VCHRI Team Grant.

She co-founded the Lacan Salon in 2007 and currently serves as its clinical director. She leads a clinical seminar in Vancouver since the fall of 2015 and has published a number of articles on psychotherapy and psychoanalysis. She is passionate about the transmission of psychoanalysis and community building.

Samir Gandesha is currently Associate Professor in the Department of the Humanities and the Director of the Institute for the Humanities at Simon Fraser University. He specializes in modern European thought and culture, with a particular emphasis on the nineteenth and twentieth centuries. His work has appeared in a wide range of journals including *Political Theory, New German Critique, Constellations, Logos, Kant-Studien, Philosophy and Social Criticism*, the *European Legacy*, the *European Journal of Social Theory, Discipline Filosofiche, Estudios Politicos, Zeitschrift für kritische Theorie, Radical Philosophy* and *Constelaciones: Revista de Teoria Critica*. He is co-editor with Lars Rensmann of *Arendt and Adorno: Political and Philosophical Investigations* (Stanford, 2012), and co-editor with Johan Hartle of *Spell of Capital: Reification and Spectacle* (University of Amsterdam Press, 2017) and *Aesthetic Marx* (Bloomsbury Press, 2017). In the spring of 2017, he was the Liu Boming Visiting Scholar in Philosophy at the University of Nanjing and Visiting Lecturer at Suzhou University of Science and Technology in China. He was Visiting Fellow at the Hochschule für Gestaltung in Karlsruhe was Visiting Lecturer at Faculdade de Filosofia, Letras e Ciências Humanas – FFLCH-USP (Universidade de São Paulo).

Gary Genosko is Professor of Sociology at Lakehead University, Canada, and held a Canada Research Chair in Technoculture Studies from 2002 to 2012. His first book, *Baudrillard and Signs* (Routledge, 1994), established his position as a critical semiotic theorist, and his 2016 book, *Critical Semiotics: Theory, from Information to Affect* (Bloomsbury), asks the question of whether semiotics can make an affective turn. His book *McLuhan and Baudrillard: The Masters of Implosion* (Routledge, 1999) situated the two thinkers in the then burgeoning cyberculture. Recently, two volumes – *When Technocultures Collide* (Wilfred Laurier, 2013) and *Remodelling Communication* (University of Toronto Press, 2012) – have been forged in the crucible of communication and cultural studies. Dr. Genosko collaborated with Jay Hetrick on *Machinic Eros: Félix Guattari's Writings on Japan* (Univocal, 2015) and with Nick Thoburn

264 · SPECTRES OF FASCISM

and Franco Bifo Berardi on *After the Future* (AK Press, 2011). Together with Scott Thompson, he published a groundbreaking study of governmental administrative surveillance in Ontario, *Punched Drunk: Alcohol, Surveillance and the LCBO 1927–75* (Fernwood, 2009). Current projects involve the lives of journals, in *Back Issues: Periodicals and the Formation of Critical and Cultural Theory in Canada*, and a collection of his key writings on Guattari, *The Reinvention of the Social: Writings on Félix Guattari*, as well as a monograph on the Canadian painter, designer and collaborator with Marshall McLuhan, *Harley Parker: The Making of Epigrammatic Man*.

Ajay Gudavarthy is Associate Professor at the Centre for Political Studies, Jawaharlal Nehru University (JNU), and his areas of interest include political theory, contemporary political movements, civil society and democracy, and post-colonial theory. Prior to teaching at JNU, he also taught at the National Law School, Bangalore from 2003 to 2006. His most recent book, *Cultural Politics in Modern India*, was published by Aakar Delhi in 2015, the same year he was a Visiting Fellow at the Centre for Modern South Asian Studies, Tübingen University, Germany. He is currently working on *Democracy and Revolutionary Violence*, which will be published by Sage, writes regularly for various news dailies including *The Hindu, Indian Express, Himal South Asian* and *Deccan Herald*, and is a regular commenter on national television.

Vijay Gudavarthy is currently Assistant Professor at the School of Economics, University of Hyderabad, where he has worked since 2006. He is a member of Workers Solidarity Network (WSN). He has also worked as a Research Fellow at the Institute of Human Development (IHD), New Delhi. He has 28 research papers published in national and international journals and as chapters in books. His recent publications include: G. Vijay and Tathagata Sengupta, "The Uncivil and De-Institutionalizing Labor Relations of Accumulation Through Disuse: The Case of the Brick Kiln Industry in Telangana," in D. Narasinha Reddy and Kailash Sarap, eds., *Rural Labour Mobility in Times of Structural Transformation* (Singapore: Springer Publications, 2017), 327–45; and Tathagata Sengupta and G. Vijay, "Understanding Rural Distress and Uncivil Social Networks of Economy in Eastern India; The Case of the Odisha-Telangana Brick Kiln Labour Circular Migration Stream," in Rajani X. Desai, ed., *India's Working Class and Its Prospects: Studies,*

Reports, Notes (Mumbai: Subarnashree Prakashini; Balasore for Research Unit in Political Economy (RUPE), 2019).

Johan F. Hartle, DPhil, is Rector at the Academy of Fine Arts, Vienna and Adjunct Professor for Philosophy and Art Theory at the School of Intermedia Art (SIMA) at the China Academy of Art (CAA) in Hangzhou, China. After finishing his dissertation at the University of Münster in 2005, he has been Visiting Research Scholar at the Hebrew University, Jerusalem, and the Università Roma Tre, Rome. His general field of research is legacy of Marxism in contemporary aesthetic and cultural theories and institutional theories of art. His book publications include: *Der geöffnete Raum. Zur Politik der ästhetischen Form* (Fink, 2006); *Beate Geissler & Oliver Sann: Personal Kill* (Moderne Kunst, 2010); Rainer Ganahl and Johan Frederik Hartle, eds., *Dadalenin* (Edition Taube, 2013); Johan Frederik Hartle and Thijs Lijster, eds., *De Kunst van kritiek. Adorno in Context* (Octavo, 2015); Samir Gandesha and Johan Frederik Hartle, eds., *Spell of Capital: Reification and Spectacle* (Amsterdam, 2017); and *Aesthetic Marx* (Bloomsbury, 2017). He is currently finishing a book on the visual culture of Red Vienna (*Die Sichtbarkeit des Proletariats*).

Am Johal is Director of Community Engagement at Simon Fraser University's Vancity Office of Community Engagement, within the SFU Woodward's Cultural Unit. Previously, Johal worked on the Vancouver Agreement, a collective effort to address urban economic and social development. He was a co-founder of the University of British Columbia's Humanities 101 programme and Chair of the Impact on Communities Coalition. He has also been an advisor to two provincial cabinet ministers (Transportation and Highways; Community Development, Cooperatives and Volunteers). Johal holds undergraduate degrees in Human Kinetics (UBC) and Commerce (Royal Roads University), an MA in International Economic Relations from the Institute for Social and European Studies (Hungary), and a PhD in Communication and Media Philosophy from the European Graduate School (Switzerland).

Jaleh Mansoor is a historian of modern and contemporary cultural production, specializing in twentieth-century European art, Marxism, Marxist feminism and critical theory. She received her PhD from Columbia University in 2007 and has taught at the State University of New York Purchase, Barnard College, Columbia University and Ohio

University. Having worked as a critic for *Artforum*, and a frequent contributor to *October*, *Texte zur Kunst* and *The Journal of Aesthetics and Protest*, among others, Mansoor has written monographic studies on the work of Piero Manzoni, Ed Ruscha, Agnes Martin, Blinky Palermo, Gerhard Richter and Mona Hatoum. She has co-edited an anthology of essays addressing Jacques Rancière's articulation of aesthetics' bond to politics, entitled *Communities of Sense: Rethinking Aesthetics and Politics* (Duke University Press, 2010). Her first book is *Marshall Plan Modernism: Italian Postwar Abstraction and the Beginnings of Autonomia* (Duke University Press, 2016). She is currently working on a book, tentatively entitled *Concrete Abstraction: The Work of Art in the Age of Mechanical Labour*, on the entwinement of labour, value and "bare life" in the work of Santiago Sierra and Claire Fontaine, among other contemporary practices that examine the limits of the human.

Laura U. Marks works on media art and philosophy with an intercultural focus. Her most recent books are *Hanan al-Cinema: Affections for the Moving Image* (MIT, 2015) and *Enfoldment and Infinity: An Islamic Genealogy of New Media Art* (MIT, 2010). She programmes experimental media for venues around the world. As Grant Strate Professor, she teaches in the School for the Contemporary Arts at Simon Fraser University in Vancouver, Canada, on unceded Coast Salish territory.

Vladimir Safatle is Professor at Universidade de São Paulo, Department of Philosophy. He has been Visiting Professor at Paris VII, Paris VII, Toulouse, Louvain, Stellenboch and Essex and Visiting Scholar at University of California at Berkeley. He is the author of *Grand Hotel Abyss: Desire, Recognition and the Restoration of the Subject* (Leuven, 2016) and *La passion du ne'gatif: Lacan et la dialectique* (Georg Olms, 2010), amongst others.

Ingo Schmidt is an economist and Assistant Professor of Labour Studies Program at Athabasca University. He earned his PhD from the University of Göttingen and wrote a doctoral thesis on trade unions and Keynesianism. Dr. Schmidt has taught at different universities in Germany and Canada in the past and was a staff economist with the metal workers union, IG Metall, in Germany. He has co-authored and edited a number of books, most recently *The Three Worlds of Social Democracy – A Global View* (Pluto, 2016) and, with Carlo Fanelli, *Reading "Capital" Today*

(Pluto, 2017). His articles have appeared in a number of German- and English-language journals, including *Historical Materialism*, *Labour/ Le Travail*, *Monthly Review*, *International Critical Thought* and *Working USA*. Dr. Schmidt is also the economics columnist of the monthly paper *Sozialistische Zeitung*.

Index